ISO 9000 ALMANAC

1994–95 Edition

Timeplace, Inc.

Edited by
Eric D. Peters

IRWIN
Professional Publishing
Burr Ridge, Illinois
New York, New York

IRWIN
Concerned About Our Environment

In recognition of the fact that our company is a large end-user of fragile yet replenishable resources, we at IRWIN can assure you that every effort is made to meet or exceed Environmental Protection Agency (EPA) recommendations and requirements for a "greener" workplace.

To preserve these natural assets, a number of environmental policies, both companywide and department-specific, have been implemented. From the use of 50% recycled paper in our textbooks to the printing of promotional materials with recycled stock and soy inks to our office paper recycling program, we are committed to reducing waste and replacing environmentally unsafe products with safer alternatives.

This publication is designed to provide accurate and authoritative information in regard to the subject matter covered. It is sold with the understanding that neither the author nor the publisher is engaged in rendering legal, accounting, or other professional service. If legal advice or other expert assistance is required, the services of a competent professional person should be sought.

From a Declaration of Principles jointly adopted by a Committee of the American Bar Association and a Committee of Publishers.

Editor-in-chief: Jeffrey A. Krames
Project editor: Susan Trentacosti
Production manager: Bob Lange
Cover designer: Tim Kaage
Printer: The Maple-Vail Book Manufacturing Group

ISBN: 0-7863-0243-7

Printed in the United States of America

1 2 3 4 5 6 7 8 9 0 MP 1 0 9 8 7 6 5 4

The field of ISO 9000 is growing rapidly. Its standards have changed the way the world is doing business. The ISO 9000 standards cover every topic in every business. The main focus of ISO 9000 is documentation. The documentation of the quality system is essential for making quality products.

This ISO 9000 Almanac has been compiles to assist organizations in their attempt at setting up or continuing a quality ISO 9000 system. The almanac is a compilation of previous sourcebook in conjunction with over hundreds of new entries.

The Almanac is intended to be used as an all encompassing guide to ISO 9000 materials for the first time user as well as the quality veteran. The sourcebook brings together the resources needed to help you find quality materials on virtually any subject.

The listings will include:

- Consultants
- Registrars
- Seminars
- Books
- Videos
- Software

To help search for organizations or topics of interest, use the indexes listed in the back of the Almanac.

These include the:

- Title
- Registrar
- Consultant
- Consultant Geographical
- Subject Index
- Source Index

Every title, author and listing is cross-referenced with these indexes in order to facilitate your information search.

ISO 9000 has become an integral part in the way organizations are doing business in the U.S. and around the world. Consumers expect nothing less than the best quality product. By developing or improving a quality program your company will keep its competitive edge.

We have intended this book to be easy to use and comprehend. We certainly hope we have covered all bases in putting the book together. However, for any mistakes, inadvertent omissions or inaccuracies, this editor accepts the blame and extends sincere apologies and the promise to correct in future editions.

The ISO 9000 Almanac has been compiled for our customers in an attempt to keep organizations, large and small, informed of the latest quality and ISO 9000 training materials in the field of ISO 9000. Organizations must keep up with its competition. Hopefully, this sourcebook can help.

The following persons have made a contribution to the Almanac.

Chairman of the Board
Avak Avakian

President:
Mark Dane

Vice President:
Charles Jutkiewicz

Special Assistants:
Rocco Cimino
Tiffany Suzewits

Research staff:
Jim Brovelli
Marie Lemont
Brad Lingham

The programming staff:
Alex Landsman
Ralph Osborne

Data Entry Department:

Data Entry Manager
Pia Castelline

Data Entry Staff:
Rocco Cimino
Tadas Dilba
Barbara Hinckley-Alcorn
Corinne Mahoney
Jean McInnes
Tiffany Suzewits
Carol Tuttle
Steven Mc Mahon
Rob Gagnon

CONTENTS

SECTIONS

INDEXES

CONSULTANT SECTION

ABS INDUSTRIAL VERIFICATION, INC.
16855 NORTHCASE DRIVE
HOUSTON, TX 77060
Phone: 713-873-5200
FAX: 713-874-9553

ABS Industrial Verification, Inc. (ABS IV) is a worldwide company specializing in the full service verification process. ABS Industrial Verification, Inc. is the new name of ABS Worldwide Technical Services, Inc. (ABSTECH) which has been providing services to industry and government since 1971.

ABS IV's objective is to provide quality services to insure compliance with standards and specifications designated by the client.

ABS Industrial Verification is an independent global organization offering distinct advantages to clients.

ABS IV's Field Representatives, many of whom are multilingual, are employed in the inspection to recognized standards and specifications of a wide range of industries including:

- *Power*
- *Process Industries (including refining, petrochemical, oil/gas)*
- *Ports (including cranes, material handling and vapor control systems)*
- *Land-based Transportation*
- *General Industries*

Their experience includes inspection of materials, electrical and mechanical equipment, boilers, pressure vessels, piping systems, steel structures, diesel engines, cranes, transportation equipment, control systems and related equipment.

Because ABS IV is an independent global organization, it offers distinct advantages to clients. Its personnel can implement programs or be instrumental in assisting management in resolving individual technical problems. ABS IV provides experienced technical personnel who are practical, common sense thinkers and doers-people whose inspiration and roots are founded in the tradition of industrial self-regulation, impartiality, and confidentiality that have been the hallmark of the parent organization for more than a century and a quarter.

How Can ABS Industrial Verification Help You With ISO 9000 Registration?

- ABS IV can assist you in selecting the correct ISO 9000 Standard to be registered to and establishing a system for compliance
- ABS IV can perform a status assessment to establish your current quality systems position compared to the requirement
- A matrix identifying the necessary manual revisions, procedures, and work instructions for your application can be prepared
- ABS IV can provide expert assistance in the development and writing of manuals, procedures, and work instructions
- ISO 9000 management overviews and detailed training programs on ISO requirements are available

SUMMARY OF BASIC SERVICES AVAILABLE FROM ABS INDUSTRIAL VERIFICATION

Worldwide Inspection:

ABS Industrial Verification, Inc. (ABS IV) through its worldwide network of offices provides inspection, certification and quality assurance services in over 250 offices in 92 countries on six continents.

Source Inspection - ABS IV's highly skilled inspection staff can provide inspection services in accordance with internationally accepted standards and your specifications during the manufacture of materials and equipment for the power, oil, petrochemical, transportation and other land-based industries.
Site Inspection - ABS IV can assemble a team of specialists who will provide inspection and technical assistance during the new construction of power plants, refineries, etc. as well as provide qualified staff to augment your own inspection or engineering staff during scheduled maintenance periods.

In-service inspection - ABS IV engineers can assist you in implementing plants/systems or in-service inspection in accordance with accepted/recognized inspection programs. This work may be conducted in conjunction with ABS IV's engineering staff to assist in the establishment of an applicable in-service inspection program including proper acceptance/rejection criteria.

ABS IV inspectors can be your eyes and ears on your own or a supplier's assembly line. The firm inspects raw materials, production procedures, quality control measures, performance testing and packaging to ensure that all meet your specifications.

Quality Consulting:

ABS IV Quality Engineers will be able to assist you with the development of Quality Systems for your particular process, regardless of whether you operate in a manufacturing or a service environment.

ABS Industrial Verification provides expert assistance in such varied disciplines as structural, mechanical, metallurgical and electrical engineering. It offers quick, effective solutions to your problems and can provide extra manpower and expertise to keep your project on schedule.

Technical/Engineering Services:

The ABS Industrial Verification specialized engineering staff can verify your design specification, drawings and design calculations to ensure that they meet project and regulatory requirements. Additionally, the staff can assist in justifying/verifying your component/system design specification through specialized computer modeling and engineering analyses.

Whether your plans and specifications are produced by a vendor or by your own staff, ABS IV engineers can verify project requirements and conformance to industry standards.

Certification:

ABS Industrial Verification's highly qualified engineering and field staff provides certification services for various products and systems ranging from containers, pressure vessels and cranes through vapor control systems. ABS Industrial Verification is recognized as a Certificate of Completion Agency. The firm certifies that a project has been finished and that it performs to capacity.

Other Consulting Services:

The experienced ABS Industrial Verification staff can provide additional manpower and expertise to keep your project in compliance with the various applicable specifications and regulatory requirements.

The staff can assist with the preparation of operating instructions, quality assurance manuals, or other technical documents for the most complex industrial procedures.

Vendor Qualification:

With experienced personnel spanning the globe, ABS Industrial Verification can assess the capabilities of your potential suppliers in accordance with the specific requirements of your purchase order. They can assist in qualifying vendors per your requirements.

Surveys:

On-hire/Off-hire surveys - ABS IV local staff will carry out on-hire/off-hire surveys of leased machinery, such as earth moving equipment, mobile cranes, containers, etc.

Damage Surveys - ABS IV specialists can carry out damage surveys after your equipment has suffered an accident and provide recommendations for temporary or permanent repairs.

Condition surveys - Prior to committing yourself to the purchase of a major piece of equipment, the local staff will provide a comprehensive condition survey allowing you to make a better decision.

Whether you need to know if a potential supplier has the capability to handle your order, the extent of damage to a facility on the other side of the world or how many people are needed to staff a project, ABS IV can gather the necessary data and prepare a comprehensive report.

ABS GROUP WORLDWIDE

All ABS Group offices are linked by a communication network which provides timely technical information and management assistance to representatives even in remote areas.

ABS offices are located in the following cities:

Chicago, IL	Abu Dhabi	Singapore
Houston, TX	London Taipei	Yokohama
Paramus, NJ	Mexico City	
Portland, OR	Rio de Janeiro	

Affiliated Companies:

- ABS Quality Evaluations, Inc. (ABS QE)
- ABS Boiler Marine Insurance Co. (ABS BMIC)
- AMTECH Worldwide Industrial Services, Inc. (AMTECH)

ADVANTAGE MANAGEMENT SYSTEMS
P.O. Box 915290
LONGWOOD, FL 32791-5290
Phone: 407-699-8756
FAX: 407-774-3234

Advantage Management Systems has learned, after working with over 200 organizations in the last 10 years, that the average company operates at approximately 2/3 of its true potential. Management often doesn't know what these problems are, where they are or how to mobilize employees to eliminate these performance losses and prevent new ones from occurring.

Advantage Management Systems specialize in helping companies become more competitive: operating better, faster and cheaper. They guarantee their client's success. They have specialists that help companies with ISO certification, but believe that an organization must first have the necessary improvement systems in place to ensure customer requirements are clearly defined and processes are capable of producing the desired outcome consistently before ISO activities begin. Naturally, management commitment is an integral part of making this process a success.

Advantage Management Systems, Inc. helps medium and smaller organizations improve their performance, profitability and quality by providing a variety of services that:

- *establish and financially quantify performance improvement opportunities,*
- *develop the strategy, structure, tools and skills to positively change company culture,*
- *educate management and employees in methods that transform an organization into a world class competitor, able to meet global standards,*
- *supports the company's efforts to produce successful results, guaranteed!*

As much as one-third of what gets done in organizations is wasted. Even the best-managed companies have a "cost of waste" that exceeds their net income: an exciting opportunity to improve resource utilization, reduce cycle times and get more done for less. Success is achieved through identification of improvement targets and a work force empowered with the knowledge, skills and will to improve.

The more the world changes, the greater the need to get back to basics. Tomorrow's leaders will focus their entire organization on maximizing the effectiveness of operations: going beyond the limits of existing Quality, Productivity and Customer Service programs with concepts, systems and strategies for achieving Peak Performance. Six fundamental principles can show how it's done:

1. Transactions

The things organizations "do" everyday to satisfy customers and support their employees are transactions. Every worker must understand the four different transaction types and know their role in assuring customer service/satisfaction.

2. Processes

Successful transactions depend on the design, development and improvement of work processes which guide and support performance of daily activities. Every manager and supervisor needs to know the six factors which assure process capability and consistency.

3. People

To get the best return on their "human resource" investment, today's organizations are re-examining and re-establishing basic beliefs about why people do what they do and how to help people do things right routinely.

4. Communications

"Doing the right things right" requires a clear, continuous flow of information throughout the organization. This new level of communications effectiveness can be achieved through knowledge of:

- The communication process (networks/flows)
- "Barriers and tribes" and how to eliminate them
- Communications pitfalls and five ways to avoid them

5. Problems

One of the secrets of continuous improvement lies in finding and eradicating the real causes of transaction problems. How to go beyond treating symptoms and the "fire fighting trap"? The basics of transactions, processes and people show how to concentrate your organization's energies on prioritized performance improvement and reduction of the "cost of waste."

6. Strategy

Successful navigation through the 1990s requires a clear, strategic vision and coordinated business planning to support its accomplishment. These six powerful fundamentals create the foundation for your own vision/mission, and provide the principles to guide employees in achieving it.

The Advantage Management System strategy helps business leaders gather information and assess their present situation before taking on the challenge of moving ahead. Several choices are available, depending on needs:

Introduction/Needs Analysis

- Introduction and Self-Assessment Workshops - Sessions designed to guide decision-makers in discovering areas of opportunity and identifying applications of the Peak Performance principles to current business needs.

- Basic Business Assessments - Formal surveys of operations which identify and quantify priority needs. Examination can include "cost of waste" evaluation, customer satisfaction survey and analysis of employee attitudes.

Senior Management Orientation

- Peak Performance Overview/Planning Sessions - Workshops which familiarize groups of business leaders with Peak Performance principles and develop a recommended strategy/"Road map" for total organizational involvement.

- Managing for Peak Performance Seminars - In-depth, intensive, learning experiences for executives and senior managers who will lead in implementing their organization's strategic "Road map." Seminars are designed for mixed group/conference facility format, or can be conducted on-location, dedicated to a specific organizations' management teams.

Individual Employee Education

- Train-Your-Trainers Courses - Advanced courses which prepare selected management team members for teaching Peak Performance principles to the rest of the work force. Content includes tools, skills, project selection and application guidelines, as well as instructor/classroom skills training.

- Peak Performance Training for Employees - High-value, easy-to-teach employee education packages which support in-house trainers during delivery and application of performance improvement concepts in the work place.

Application and Results

Onsite consulting. Experienced consulting professionals assist with local implementation to produce early application of principles, practical successes and high-impact results.

AFFILIATED CONSULTING GROUP, INC. (ACG)
P.O. Box 923
Marietta, OH 45750
Phone: 800-552-2510
Fax: 614-374-3409

Affiliated Consulting Group (ACG) is a nationwide organization of consulting firms specializing in performance improvement services in operations, human resources, marketing and sales.

ACG offers consulting services to plan, implement, audit and document ISO 9000 requirements for technology developers and end users. All consulting is custom-fitted to your company's needs.

ACG conducts onsite training and consulting in:

- ISO 9000 basics
- Elements of the Standards
- How to plan and implement
- Developing a Quality Manual
- Written Procedures
- Internal Auditing
- Corrective Action
- Third Party management

Also, Quality Management Systems Training to technology developers and end users is offered.

AMERICAN INSTITUTE FOR QUALITY & RELIABILITY

P.O. Box 41163
San Jose, CA 95160
Phone: 408-275-9300
Fax: 408-275-9399

The American Institute for Quality & Reliability (AIQR) has been providing onsite training to industry for over 15 years. They've continued to lead the nation in technical training partly due to their careful and routine monitoring of industry dynamics and trends which has kept them at the forefront of technological needs; partly due to the depth and selection of courses and the knowledge of their instructors; and, partly because of the importance specialized training has become to organizations.

The Institutes founder and president, Al Chamitoff, worked in industry for over 20 years. This is where he first recognized the tremendous role that corporate-wide training played in the success of Northern Telecom, Four Phase Systems, and Atari, three companies where he was actively involved in the training process in addition to holding positions as manager, director, and vice president, respectively. It was these experiences that prompted Mr. Chamitoff to start a full-fledged training and consulting organization, now known worldwide as AIQR, Inc.

AIQR ONSITE TRAINING PROGRAM

"Training" is basically all that AIQR does - it's no wonder that they take every aspect very, very seriously. They know they must be able to address all types of training needs quickly and efficiently; they must have only top-notch instructors available; and, they must be able to coordinate all requirements of the training, from the planning stage through the training itself, with efficiency and detail. Their success with the aforementioned may be, in fact, the main reasons why they have continued to grow since it's inception in 1978.

Guidance and Assistance

Instigating onsite training begins within your organization. In what area(s) of your organization is training required? What are your needs and objectives? What methods or technologies will solve your unique problems or concerns? The actual process may begin with an engineer who takes the initiative to address what the needs are and presents them to his superior or upper management. AIQR can do an evaluation of what your needs and objectives are based on information provided by you, and put them in a presentable form (usually through a proposal packet). Any special requirements that are unique to an organization can be tailored and included to assist in a presentation.

Course Selection/Course Tailoring

Determining exactly which courses will effectively meet your training needs is a vital step and should be looked at closely. AIQR works with you to determine the most suitable course to meet your specific training needs for optimizing the training value. Once the appropriate course has been determined, AIQR works together to tailor the overall program to include or implement any special requirements that are unique to your organization.

Planning

Once your training has been approved, planning the workshop is the next step. Through their experience, AIQR has encountered all types of possible pitfalls that may arise. This works to your advantage, especially if the contact within your company is unfamiliar with this type of planning. They work closely with you to ensure that all details are accounted for and training comes off without a hitch. What special needs or requirements exist? Will the training be held at your plant or at an outside training center? How many days of training are required? What areas should be emphasized? etc., are all things to consider. They provide you a complete checklist including an instructor's classroom layout, equipment needs, and any other considerations.

Drawing Review

In special situations, it may be necessary for the instructor to review a few select drawings to become familiar with your product or product design. Whether your product is a fuel injection system or a metal storage cabinet, a brief review of the product drawings may aid the instructor in his attempt to focus the training to your objectives.

Instruction

Each AIQR instructor has been thoroughly interviewed, evaluated, and has demonstrated his or her abilities through traceable references that span many years of hands-on and industry experience. Each instructor also remains current through certified continuing education. Discussions take place between AIQR and your organization prior to instructor selection for better matching of skills to your training needs; and they provide you with an instructor biography for your review. Maintaining a select group of industry leaders is one of the greatest advantages that a firm specializing in training fulfillment can provide.

Flexibility

Onsite training provides endless flexibility. For example: Are the students able to be away from their jobs for three straight days or would it be better to train on consecutive Mondays over a three week period? Is the first part of the week best or the last part? What month is best? Should the training be held onsite at the organization or at a nearby hotel or training center where distractions are held to a minimum? Should the class be split into two groups run back-to-back to minimize the length of time personnel are away from their jobs?, Etc. AIQR works with you to determine which options are best for optimum results.

Follow Up and Evaluation

Once your training workshop(s) has been completed, an AIQR representative will follow-up to evaluate the results and solicit questions and/or other responses that may exist. Each student is given an evaluation form at the end of the workshop which AIQR reviews and make notes and/or recommendations. Special follow up programs can be designed to meet your organizations specific needs.

Pre-Testing - Post-Testing

Pre- and Post-testing is also available to measure student comprehension. Each student is given a test on the subject matter prior to the training and then again at the end.

Guarantee: AIQR backs up all their workshops with a full satisfaction guarantee, something other training organizations don't offer.

AIQR Courses Available for Onsite Training

Listed below are the most requested courses provided by AIQR:

- Geometric Dimensioning and Tolerancing
- Graphic Inspection Techniques
- Just-In-Time Manufacturing
- Failure Mode and Effects Analysis
- Design of Experiments - Taguchi
- Functional Gaging and Inspection
- Statistical Methods for Decision Makers
- Statistical Process Control
- Quality Control Techniques
- Design of Low-Cost Jigs and Fixtures
- Interpreting Design Drawings
- Tolerance Stack-Up Analysis

- Practical Reliability Techniques
- Geometric Dimensioning and Tolerancing - The ISO-Way
- ISO 9000 - Level's 1 and 2
- How to Become A Qualified Supplier
- Quality Function Deployment
- Qualification Testing

- Industrial/Manufacturing Management
- Quality Cost Reduction
- Technical Products Marketing
- Process Engineering
- Total Quality Management
- Metric Engineering Design

AMERICAN QUALITY CORPORATION
A UNION OF COMM-OMNI AND FGH CONSULTING
BOX 473
200 INDUSTRIAL PARKWAY #10
CHAGRIN FALLS, OH 44022
Phone: 216-247-7030
Phone: 800-543-8790
FAX: 216-247-6199

After eight years of association, COMM-OMNI and FGH Consulting have joined forces in a joint venture as American Quality Corporation. AQC has the exclusive rights to quality assurance software programs developed by FGH. AQC was formed to combine the management and marketing expertise of COMM-OMNI with the hands-on experience of FGH.

Over the past eight years, FGH has implemented quality systems for 35 companies throughout the U.S. and Canada. These systems have mct requirement for a range of quality requirements such as ISO 9000, Ford Q1, MIL-Q-9, etc. In support of these systems, FGH has developed a line of software that enables their consultants to implement a total quality system in two to three weeks at a considerable cost savings to clients.

American Quality Corporation offers the same services and guarantees the systems they install to meet any customer requirement. The philosophy of AQC is that a common sense approach to quality is easily understood by employees and customers alike. All quality systems are developed around a company's existing procedures. This reduces the time required for full implementation and assures better acceptance by company employees.

During each step of the design of a system, the consultant works directly with company personnel responsible for implementation. When the quality manual is completed, the company has a staff of trained employees ready to begin implementation. AQC believes that employee training should consist of hands on application with limited involvement in theory.

For an AQC consultant , the development of a quality system is a matter of revising the basic manual to meet the needs of individual clients. The result is that each client has a uniquely designed quality system documented in a manual in a short period of time.

AMERICAN SUPPLIER INSTITUTE
15041 COMMERCE DRIVE SOUTH
SUITE 401
DEARBORN, MI 48120-1238
Phone: 313-271-4200
Phone: 800-462-4500
FAX: 313-336-3187

The American Supplier Institute, Inc. (ASI) is a nonprofit company whose mission is to help organizations throughout the world improve their ability to meet the needs of their customers. ASI is a recognized leader in providing training and consultation on quality technology and management methods.

ASI offers the following services regarding ISO 9000:

- Executive briefing. This covers the political and international trade implications of ISO 9000, its general contents and comparisons with other quality standards and awards, the process, time and cost of becoming registered (certified) to one of the ISO 9000 series standards, and why your company should or should not become registered. These briefings are normally presented at the customer's location.

- Customized, in-house training and assistance to prepare for ISO 9000 registration. Individualized consultation and assistance is provided to identify and meet any needs the customer may have to assure successful ISO 9000 registration. Typically, this service begins with an assessment of the company's position relative to ISO 9000 requirements, performed by certified, experienced auditors. Appropriate assistance can also be provided to prepare for the registration process.

All of the above training and consultation services are performed by certified auditors who possess years of practical experience in various manufacturing and service industries. ASI staff members have also served on the Board of Examiners of the Malcolm Baldrige National Quality Award.

In addition to training and consultation on ISO 9000, ASI also offers public seminars and in-house facilitation and training on SPC, Quality Function Deployment (QFD), Taguchi Methods, Total Quality Management (TQM), Simultaneous Engineering, and other supportive technologies.

ASI offers an open-enrollment seminar:

- Auditor Training Course
- Lead Auditor Training Course
- Understanding & Applying Course
- Internal Auditor Training Course
- Assessment & Implementation Consulting Services

APPLIED QUALITY SYSTEMS, INC.
2845 HAMLINE AVENUE NORTH
ST. PAUL, MN 55113
Phone: 612-663-7902
FAX: 612-633-7903

Applied Quality Systems (AQS) offers consulting and training to clients in the manufacturing sector. Headquartered in Minneapolis/St. Paul, the professional staff is able to provide services to clients from coast to coast.

Applied Quality Systems is committed to tailoring its services to meet the unique needs of an organization. From planning and basic training to successful implementation, AQS is committed to its clients' success. AQS' Total Company approach to Quality focuses on activities that insure long-term, company-wide, results.

AQS quality offerings include:

- *Full service ISO 9000 implementation and training*
- *ISO 9000 /TQM integration*
- *TQM implementation*
- *Basic concepts of Quality*
- *Basic and Advanced Leadership Training*
- *Team Building*
- *Problem solving*
- *Strategic Planning*
- *Strategic Benchmarking*

AQS bases its full service offerings on the blending and tailoring of Quality principals outlined by the acknowledged leaders in the field. This includes the teachings of Dr. W. Edwards Deming, Dr. Joseph Juran, Dr. Armand Fiegenbaum, Tom Peters and Philip Crosby.

Mark Ames, General Manager and Senior Consultant has a Masters Degree in Manufacturing Systems Engineering. He has been developing and implementing effective educational programs for industry since 1978.

AQS SERVICES

Consulting:

AQS can help you create and optimize a system that will help you successfully implement ISO 9000 in your organization. The firm's implementation program is based on six simple principles:

- The ISO 9000 system you create must benefit your organization's internal operation. Improved productivity and quality must be natural by-products.
- Your ISO 9000 system must satisfy the needs of your customers. Whether driven by regulatory requirements or preference, ISO 9000 compliance will become a must for companies that want to remain competitive in tomorrow's global marketplace.
- Your company will need its own system. A system that is "purchased" will not match the needs of your organization. It will not be effective for your organization month after month, year after year.
- Your employees will need to "own" the system you create. They need to feel it works for them and reflects in true measure the way they do business on a daily basis. In order for this to happen your employees must create the system that works for you and for them.

- Your system must pass the rigorous verification process conducted by an independent auditor that will lead to ISO 9000 certification of compliance.
- Your system must be self-sustaining. It must be supported by effective management review and internal audit system.

ISO 9000 and Total Quality Management:

Total Quality Management and ISO 9000 are complementary systems. If your are already involved in Total Quality Management, Applied Quality Systems will help you use these tools to speed your ISO 9000 project. If you are planning Total Quality Management in the future, Applied Quality Systems will help you ensure that TQM is the natural follow-on to your ISO 9000 project.

Applied Quality Systems offers a comprehensive approach that focuses on the unique needs of your organization. The AQS training and implementation program will help you to:

- Gain the support and involvement of your management team and employees
- Develop a plan that will effectively kick off your ISO 9000 project with minimum up-front disruption and delay
- Insure that ISO 9000 meets your organizational needs and goals in a timely manner with minimum cost
- Identify key players throughout your organization and insure they are aware of their roles and responsibilities in your implementation plan
- Help you anticipate any barriers that may arise to ISO 9000 implementation and develop plans that will overcome them
- Insure complete compatibility with existing or follow-on TQM initiatives

ISO 9000 CERTIFICATION PACKAGE

Corporate Training and Implementation Planning:

Senior Management training and implementation planning is critical to the success of any project. Applied Quality Systems insures your management team becomes familiar with ISO 9000 and its implications for your organization. AQS will help you create a road map for implementation that focuses on effective communication and insures team ownership. At the end of this phase, your management team will have a complete framework for the documentation you will need to come into compliance with ISO 9000.

Department Training and Implementation:

Department implementation teams will be critical to your success. Departments need to identify and create the documentation, records and controls necessary to comply with ISO 9000. This is best accomplished by identifying and reinforcing existing linkages between what departments are currently doing and what the standard requires. At the end of this phase, department teams not only understand the implications of the standard for their work area but have working documents that will be used to effectively operate your quality system and pass the rigorous scrutiny of an external audit.

Ongoing support:

As your Quality System takes shape, AQS will provide the support that will allow you to identify opportunities for improvement in productivity that naturally accompany an effectively implemented ISO 9000 system.

ARCH ASSOCIATES
15770 ROBINWOOD DRIVE
NORTHVILLE, MI 48167-2041
Phone: 313-420-0122
FAX: 313-420-0122

Arch Associates provides a full scope of customized client support services through its network of midcareer multi-disciplinary associates. Arch focuses on cost effective development of existing client resources to satisfy needs.

Support level ranges from singular third party audits against various guidelines or training of quality standards, traditional/contemporary quality tools to full service development, documentation, work area implementation and on-going monitoring of Total Quality Systems complying to ISO 9000 Series and other appropriate quality requirements, standards or practices. Arch has incorporated ISO 9000 Series compliance into client quality plans and has implemented these systems since 1989.

Consulting Activities:

In addition to expected TQM and quality standards support, Arch Associates currently is providing complete project management support for a European client initiating a North American "green field" manufacturing operation, supporting new facility completion and startup for a North American manufacturer and developing a European distribution system for an American manufacturer.

ISO 9000 Seminar:

Significant demand has been experienced for Arch's comprehensive two day course "Quality Standards - ISO 9000 Series PLUS" which debuted in early 1991. This course addresses the underpinnings of various movements for quality standards, international public and quasi-public organizations, ISO 9000 - ANSI/ASQC Q90 Series Standards, Product Regulations, Technical Standards, ISO registration process and resources. Arch believes this broad perspective is necessary for cost effective incorporation of ISO Standards into the overall business / TQM plan. The course is taught by associates holding ASQC CQE, CRE and CQA certifications and have successfully completed the BSI Lead Assessor Course and Examination.

Services Available:

Audits
- Process, product, system
- Simulated ISO 9000
- Simulated Baldrige

Evaluations
- Gage Capability
- Machine Qualification
- Process Potential

Planning
- Customer Identification
- Total Requirements Definition
- Process Development

Training
- Total Quality Awareness
- Applied SPC, QFD
- Quality Standards (ISO, etc.)

Client Representation During Customer Audits

Total Quality System Development, Documentation and Deployment

ARGYLE ASSOCIATES, INC.
49 LOCUST AVENUE
NEW CANAAN, CT 06840
Phone: 203-966-7015

Argyle Associates, Inc. is a management consulting firm specializing in quality technology, product assurance, and process improvement through total quality management. Argyle provides clients with a broad range of specialized consulting and management support services designed to positively influence serious quality-related issues.

Since Argyle's formation in 1981, the firm has successfully facilitated quality enhancement processes for more than 150 companies by assisting them in achieving their quality objectives and customer satisfaction goals.

The principal businesses served include manufacturing companies, process industries, and service organizations. Additionally, Argyle has served numerous professional societies, trade associations, and educational institutions.

Clients include over fifty "Fortune 500" corporations, and more than 100 medium-sized and smaller companies in the United States, Canada, Europe, the Caribbean, South America, and Japan.

Primary Areas of Practice:

- Quality System Assessment
- Quality Improvement
    - Total Quality Management
    - Process Analysis
    - Process Re-engineering
    - The Management Process
    - Performance Measurement
- Statistical Process Control
- Malcolm Baldrige National Quality Award
- Education and Training

QUALITY SYSTEM ASSESSMENT

An independent and objective viewpoint enables Argyle consultants to be extremely effective in performing a variety of quality system audits, assessments, and reviews in commercial, government-regulated, and defense industries. Clients retain Argyle to perform "simulated reviews" in preparation for their anticipated customer or regulatory agency assessments. These simulated reviews include briefings and formal feedback reports to assist client organizations in improving their quality system. Argyle clients have earned meritorious recognition for excellence, as well as outstanding quality awards and preferred quality ratings, from their customers.

Typical Assessment Performed:

Defense/Aviation
- DOD: QSR/SSR
- FAA: QASAR

Food and Drug
- FDA: GMP

Automotive
- Ford: Q-101/Q-1/TQE
- GM: "Targets""

International
- ISO 9000 Standards

EDUCATION AND TRAINING

Argyle offers comprehensive education and training programs to support the quality improvement process. A series of "core modules" has been developed by Argyle specialists. They are presented to clients primarily as in-house seminars specifically tailored to current client process situations.

Argyle is frequently called upon to assist clients in developing their internal education and training curriculums. This enables the organization to sustain state-of-the-art capabilities in quality management and technology. Argyle believes it is essential for everyone involved in an organization to understand the concept and fundamentals of the quality enhancement process.

Argyle educational and training programs are customized to meet specific client objectives and unique training needs. Courses and seminars are given either at client facilities or at appropriate off-site locations.

ADDITIONAL SERVICES

Legal Support:

Argyle has been frequently called upon to provide expert testimony concerning serious quality issues. Services have included product liability investigations, quality system analyses, quality standards development, and corrective action assessments. Domestic and international clients include law firms and the general counsel of major corporations.

Procurement:

Argyle recognizes the complexities involved with procured material quality. The firm assists clients with development of procurement systems, vendor/vendee relations, and supplier partnerships - including procurement specifications, purchase order provisions, supplier evaluation procedures, rating systems, source inspection, vendor surveillance, and auditing.

Quality Engineering:

Argyle also assists companies in strengthening their quality engineering function. The firm serves clients in the areas of design reviews, inspection and quality planning, quality cost and data analysis, management information flow, problem-solving, and the introduction of corrective measures for improving product quality and productivity.

Quality Information Systems:

Argyle assists clients in developing and integrating quality information systems into their management system to produce timely and meaningful performance indicators, linked to critical processes to drive important business priorities. Argyle also assists with development of complete procedural sets - including policies, operating procedures, and work instructions - for both commercial and government-regulated industries.

ASSOCIATED BUSINESS CONSULTANTS, INC.
201 EAST KENNEDY BOULEVARD
SUITE 715
TAMPA, FL 33602
Phone: 813-223-3008
FAX: 813-223-5406

Associated Business Consultants (ABC), Limited, is listed by the British Department of Trade and Industry as qualified to perform ISO 9000 consulting for those companies receiving financial assistance from the government. ABC, Ltd with six offices in the UK is the third largest ISO 9000 consulting firm in the UK. The expertise that gained them the DTI listing has been provided to the American ABC Registered Lead Assessors via a system of understudy to the British Registered Lead Assessors.

ABC has 50 plus consultants on staff in the UK and the U.S. who provide consulting in ISO 9000 preparation, quality auditing, procedures development, and quality systems. ABC uses only Registered Lead Assessors for ISO 9000 consulting in order to provide qualified personnel. In addition to being qualified as Registered Lead Assessors, most of ABC's consultants are qualified in the various ISO standards; BS 7750 for environmental issues, ISO 9000-3 for the "TickIT" software program, etc.

ABC provides seminars on a variety of topics:

- Introduction to ISO 9000
- Implementing ISO 9000
- Internal Auditor Training
- Documentation
- Statistical Process Control
- Total Quality Management.

ABC also provides seminars and lectures in conjunction with the Chamber of Commerce and the local chapter of the American Society for Quality Control.

ASSOCIATION FOR QUALITY AND PARTICIPATION
801-B WEST 8TH STREET
CINCINNATI, OH 45203-1607
Phone: 513-381-1959
FAX: 513-381-0070

The Association for Quality and Participation (AQP) is a renowned worldwide resource dedicated to the continuous improvement of quality through participation, human growth, and organizational effectiveness. Founded in 1977 to help companies implement quality circles, AQP has expanded its scope of services to encompass virtually every aspect of the exploding quality and participation movement.

AQP is a not-for-profit professional association dedicated to the principles and practices of employee involvement, quality improvement and full participation of the entire workforce. AQP does not promote one specific philosophy, but blends the best of all techniques throughout courses and education sessions.

Managers consult AQP on everything from union management and project teams to management task forces. AQP offers courses explaining socio-technical analysis. Through conferences, courses and publications, they can also assist companies in creating gainsharing and incentive programs.

As the scope of the movement has grown, so has their organization. Today, they have over 8,700 members and 80 local chapters, with a projected membership of 15,000 by 1995. And as they grow, they continue to develop new programs to meet the changing needs of customers.

Education

Never before has the field of participative management been so exciting. And never have there been so many educational opportunities. AQP is proud to be the leader in education for Employee Involvement professionals. They were the first to offer facilitator training for team leaders. Their basic courses are still the most popular in the marketplace. And they continue to address the cutting edge of new issues, such as the impact of Employee Involvement on bargaining units, and the implementation of the ISO 9000 series of standards.

Resources

AQP offers the largest listing of books, tapes and materials for the EI professional. They continually review new works, which saves members the time of investigating everything on the market.

AQP negotiates with publishers to get the lowest possible prices for members. In addition, every member automatically receives two AQP periodicals. The highly-respected Journal for Quality and Participation features discussions of today's critical issues concerning integration of Employee Involvement, quality, and leadership. The AQP Report a bi-monthly newsletter, regularly reports the activities and interests of members and their chapters and keeps them in touch with each other.

To broaden their scope, AQP is continually reaching out to quality professionals and executives from a variety of backgrounds. For example, they are now developing materials and courses for senior executives in the fields of health care, Employee Stock Ownership Plans (ESOP), utilities and government.

For fast and timely information, members can take advantage of the AQP Information Center. It provides immediate access to over 1000 AQP articles and presentations on Employee Involvement. The Information Center's lending library houses hard-to-get literature and documents including research findings, government reports, and sample forms, as well as national, regional and local periodicals. The AQP Information Center is dedicated to providing answers and solutions to participation and quality concerns.

Conferences

Every year over 5,000 people attend AQP conferences. At the annual Spring Conference and Resource Mart, the largest conference of its kind devoted to Employee Involvement, all members are encouraged to come and enhance their skills, view presentations by the best teams in the country, and share the success of the Excellence Award recipients. Conference attendees also have the opportunity to meet with dozens of consultants and vendors about the latest supplies and services.

The annual Fall Forum presents advanced workshops and seminars on timely topics. At Employee Involvement as a Business Strategy (EIBS), which is limited to 150 CEO's, the field's foremost authorities come together for three days to lead, educate and challenge participants like never before. Lastly, at the Symposium on Work Redesign, those responsible for organizational design discuss how to redesign work units, departments and entire organizations.

Research

To make sure they are delivering the products and services that truly match their members' goals, AQP is engaged in a number of research projects.

It started in 1989, when they established a grant program to fund research in the areas of Employee Involvement, quality, and organizational effectiveness. Since then, they have provided funds for a comprehensive study on Employee Involvement in downsizing. They are conducting knowledge skills analysis of all types of quality professionals. With the help of the Hay Group, they are exploring the bottom-line results of Total Quality Management (TQM) processes. And, they recently began working with Gallup to further understand the concerns and interests of members.

Membership

AQP is a resource for achieving goals in quality improvement, human resource development, and customer service. Members have access to the nation's largest, most comprehensive and most useful body of knowledge pertaining to Employee Involvement.

AQP membership includes professionals from some of the most noted organizations in the world. Prestigious corporate and educational leaders sit on the board of directors. The Academy is comprised of an elite and distinguished advisory group of professionals.

Members receive substantial discounts on AQP conferences, courses, training and resource materials. In addition, they receive The Journal for Quality and Participation and The AQP Report free of charge.

AT&T GLOBAL MANUFACTURING & ENGINEERING

6063 FRANZ ROAD
SUITE 104
DUBLIN, OH 43017
Phone: 614-792-8485
FAX: 614-792-8606

AT&T, long regarded as one of the world's leaders in telecommunications, provides ISO 9000 Preparation services through its Quality Management and Engineering Division. The consultants on staff are all IQA-approved Lead Auditors.

Management Overview Training:

This session will provide the management staff with the information necessary to make informed decisions concerning ISO deployment. The management session will analyze the ISO issues from a planning perspective.

Baseline Audits:

This audit will address the same areas as an actual ISO registration audit. The baseline audit will provide you with an independent review of the strengths and weaknesses of your quality system. A desk audit of your Quality Manual will also be conducted.

Awareness Training:

This session will introduce your employees to ISO 9000. The familiarity gained during this session will enable the participants to "speak the same language" during the registration process. This session is best suited for people who have the need to interact on ISO related issues.

Implementation Program:

The first part of the Implementation Program is a one-day "mini-audit" of your facility. This "mini-audit" will establish a preliminary baseline for the facility and enable the ISO consultant to become familiar with your quality system.

Two to three weeks later, the Implementation Workshop is conducted. In this session, the requirements of the standard will be reviewed and action plans will be developed. The outcome of this session will be a fully documented action plan for implementation of the ISO requirements.

A follow-up session will take place 75 days after the workshop. This session may include the assessment of progress, discussion of roadblocks with team members, question and answer, etc.

Implementation Support and Ongoing Assistance:

On-site services often take place after the formal training and action plan development: These services include documentation development, deployment team facilitation or resident ISO coordinator status. AT&T consultants are prepared to provide as much on-site support as you require.

Pre-Registration Audits:

Similar to a baseline audit, this audit would be conducted just before the registration audit to make a final confirmation of conformance to the standard.

Final Audit Preparation:

Services include training of audit tour guides, assistance during the actual registration audit, etc.

ATEK
332A COOLEY STREET
SUITE 287
SPRINGFIELD, MA 01128
Phone: 413-525-0149
FAX: 413 525 0395

Atek recommends compliance to ISO 9000 without the expense of registration for those companies that are not required by their customers to be registered.

Quality services offered by Atek:

- Quality System Implementation
- ISO 9000, MIL-Q-9858
- Cost of Quality Identification and Analysis
- Source Inspection, Surveillance and Quality System Audits
- Quality Policy and Procedure Manual Revisions

Engineering services offered by Atek:

- Trouble-Shooting and Problem Identification
- Design for Manufacture
- Production Engineering and Technical Support
- Cost Reduction Implementation and Process Analysis

Atek has Certified Quality Engineers through the American Society of Quality Control (ASQC) and Registered Assessors for ISO 9000 through the Registrar Accreditation Board (RAB) and the Institute of Quality Assurance (IQA). Atek is qualified to assess and implement all items necessary to demonstrate compliance to an ISO 9000 Quality Management System.

BECKWITH & ASSOCIATES, INC.
CUSTOM COMMUNICATIONS CO.
5108 DARROW ROAD
PO BOX 696
HUDSON, OH 44236
PHONE: 216-653-8700
FAX: 216-650-2774

Whether your need is for a large scale training program or purely personal, you'll find Beckwith's courses to be just what you're looking for.

Self-instructional in-Plant Training Programs:

- Basic Shop Orientation and Basic Machining
- Intermediate Shop
- Math and Engineering Drawings
- Numerical Control
- Updated Geometric Tolerancing Series
- Basic Welding
- Electronic Assembly and Soldering

BENCHMARK TECHNOLOGIES CORPORATION

1995 TREMAINSVILLE ROAD
TOLEDO, OH 43613
Phone: 800-637-9536
Phone: 419-474-6609
FAX: 419-474-8655

Benchmark Technologies Corporation is an engineering-based management services firm that specializes in quality improvement and operations management.

Founded in 1980, the company has established a strong track record of successful development and implementation of Total Quality Management and Continuous Quality Improvement programs within the manufacturing industry in particular.

Substantial Mechanical, Industrial and Quality engineering expertise is supported internally by strong organizational, financial and general business management skills that enable the company to offer a full range of manufacturing support services specifically tailored to each individual client's situation.

Benchmark has extensive experience within the context of numerous performance standards and operating criteria:

- *MIL-Q*
- *TFE*
- *Q-1*

- *ISO 9000*
- *TQM*

Representative services include:

Business Management
- Business Planning
- Organization Development
- Management Information Systems
- Financial Analysis
- Market Research/Studies
- Property Management/Maintenance

Quality Program Management
- Corporate Quality Assurance and Procedures Manuals
- Advanced Quality Planning
- Cost of Quality
- Preparation for Customer Audits
- Supplier Quality Audits
- Inspection and Gauging Systems
- Data Collection and Analysis
- Statistical Process Control
- Failure Mode and Effect Analysis
- Process Capability Studies
- Quality Improvement Teams
- Non-Destructive Testing/Systems
- Design of Experiments

Manufacturing Management
- Mechanical and Industrial Engineering
- Equipment Acceptance Criteria and Evaluation
- Process Control Systems
- Welding Specifications/Certifications/Inspection
- Dimensional Layout
- Simultaneous Engineering/Modeling

Training
- Training personnel from operators to managers in statistical process control, problem-solving, team-building, Failure Mode and Effects Analysis, Design of Experiments, metrology and associated quality sciences, and computer applications.

Contract Personnel
- Temporary personnel for technical specialty and management functions

BENSLEY CONSULTING
P.O. Box 301
Westfield, IL 62474-0301
Phone: 217-967-5465

Frank Bensley, consultant, assists client organizations in achieving certification and in implementing a Quality Management System certifiable to ISO 9000 series standards.

Skills and Competencies:

- ASQC Certified Quality Engineer
- ASQC Certified Quality Auditor
- Certificate of Competence Lead Assessor Traceable to Registration Board IQA
- Member of Industrial Advisory Council, School of Technology at Eastern Illinois University
- Consultant to Industry on the Management of Quality & Productivity
- Strong and Varied Manufacturing Experience

Available Services:

Seminars for Business and Industry:
- Executive Overview Seminar
- Implementing an ISO 9000 System in Your Company Seminar
- Documenting your Quality System Consulting
- Internal Auditing Training

ISO 9000 Primer - A Comprehensive ISO Handbook

BQS, INC. IMPLEMENTATION & FACILITATION SERVICES

110 SUMMIT AVENUE
MONTVALE, NJ 07645
Phone: 201-307-0212
Phone: 800-624-5892
FAX: 201-307-1778

BQS is a leading company in the field of quality support and improvement services. BQS is dedicated to providing comprehensive, cost effective, support services to the quality industry throughout North and South America, Europe, and Asia.

SERVICE ELEMENTS

BQS Quality Improvement Services:

BQS provides hands-on support consulting services for companies seeking assistance in such areas as standards implementation, quality systems design and development, and facilitation for program integration. Specific support expertise includes:

- European Standards Facilitation Services - ISO 9000 Certification
- Supplier Certification Program Development and Support
- Quality Systems Implementation

BQS Auditing and Evaluation Services:

The BQS Audit and Evaluation Service is committed to satisfying industries' requirement to adequately evaluate and monitor the capability of quality systems, manufacturing processes, and special production requirements. BQS, with each audit activity, provides a complete detailing of audit requirements, consistent audit formats, and comprehensive audit reports. Each step in the BQS Audit Plan is monitored to ensure that the detail and depth of the final evaluation exceeds customer expectations. Elements of the BQS Audit Services include technical review, field management and audit scheduling. The current scope of the audit program includes:

- Quality Systems Auditing
- Process Audits and Capability Studies
- Facility and Equipment Evaluations

BQS Resources - Inspection:

BQS Resources provides inspection support services for customers requiring source inspection, test witnessing, first article capability reports, in-plant inspection, and expediting. These services differ from the "consulting" level activities, (audit and systems implementation), in that BQS field representatives act directly under the control of a customer's quality engineering group. BQS supports the specification of inspection requirements, indoctrination of field employees to these requirements, and ongoing periodic review of job performance by the BQS Technical Support Group.

BQS Seminars:

- ISO 9000 Documentation
- ISO 9000 Internal Quality Auditor

BREWER & ASSOCIATES, INC.
2505 LOCKSLEY DRIVE
GRAND PRAIRIE, TX 75050
Phone: 214-641-8020
FAX: 214-641-1327

Brewer & Associates, Inc. is a full service consulting firm providing quality systems engineering services since 1986. The consulting programs include a blending of organizational procedures with an in-depth review of imposed quality standards. In addition to ISO 9000/ASQC Q90 series, the firm has the experience to address specific requirements of MIL-Q-9858, API-Q1, Z-299, FAR 121/45, GMP and other standards.

Clyde Brewer, Principal, is a Registered Professional Engineer and an ASQC Certified Quality Auditor. He is advisor for ASQC inputs for the ISO Quality Specification for Service Industries. He is Vice President of Quality Systems Registrars, Inc., the first U.S. company accredited to certify quality systems to the ISO 9000 (ANSI/ASQC Q90) standards.

Mr. Brewer has over thirty five years experience in quality management with over 25 of these years in aerospace quality. As Director of Quality for an oil field equipment manufacturing and service company, he was responsible for instituting programs for regulated products and quality improvement.

Training Services:

Brewer & Associates, Inc. offers training through its affiliate company, B-K Education Services. The courses taught by B-K Education are both in-house and public seminars. The titles of these courses, listed in Volume 1, Seminars & Events Section, include:

- Effective Quality Auditing Workshop: How To Perform Effective Quality System Audits
- Refresher Course for ASQC Certified Quality Auditor Examination
- ISO 9000 Quality Management System Design: How to Prepare for the ISO 9000 Series Quality System Registration
- ISO 10011-2 Lead Auditor Training for Worldwide Auditor Qualification

Consulting Services:

- Quality Systems Analysis, Design, Implementation
- Complete Engineering Services
- Market Evaluations
- Expert Witness Service
- Training Plans
- Management and Technical Presentations
- Procedures/Work Instructions
- Technical Representation
- Supplier Evaluations
- Strategic Planning
- Marketing Plans
- Technical Evaluations
- Seminar Design
- Technical Writing
- Productivity Evaluations
- Management Reviews, Audits, Surveys, Measurement

BUREAU VERITAS GLOBAL SYSTEMS
129 MAIN STREET
BINGHAMTON, NY 13905-0006
Phone: 607-773-8471
Phone: 800-248-5832
FAX: 607-773-8474

Global Systems Associates was formed to support and advise business management as a full service company specializing in the application of current quality techniques, training, and management to increase productivity and create improvement in both manufacturing and service business sectors. Global Systems Associates is able to draw upon a base of professionals that is well qualified in product background, process background, education, and quality, business, and management methods.

Services:

- Audits, Evaluations, Surveys - supplier quality assurance
- Total Quality Systems - development and implementation
- Expert Witness - litigation support
- Technical Course Development - training and education
- ISO 9000 Seminars - overview, detail, lead assessor course
- Quality Tools - statistics, SPC, and related quality techniques

Global Systems Associates provides open-enrollment training courses which can be customized to fit any unique situations within the broad topic the firm offers.

ISO 9000 seminars include:

- Management Overview of ISO 9000 and Quality System Registration
- ISO 9000 Quality System, Quality System Assessment Workshop
- Quality Registration Advisory Service
- Needs Analysis
- Documentation Review
- Quality System - ISO 9000 Implementation
- ISO 9000 Compliant Documents Workshop
- Quality System and Manual Development
- Periodic Progress Review
- Pre-Assessment
- Internal Auditor Workshop
- Team Facilitation Coaching Skills Workshop
- Lead Assessor Training

C.L. CARTER, JR. AND ASSOCIATES, INC.

811 SO. CENTRAL EXPRESSWAY
SUITE 434
RICHARDSON, TX 75080
Phone: 214-234-3296

C.L. Carter, Jr. & Associates, founded by Dr. Carter in 1964, has been serving business, industry, government and individuals on an international basis through a professional team of nationwide associates. With 40 years of experience and knowledge, Dr. Carter directs and is able to deliver quality assurance, quality control, inspection, reliability, safety, training, auditing, ISO 9000, and QA management systems that are productive, profitable, people oriented, and cost-effective for small, medium and large organizations of all types.

Dr. Carter, the author of nine published books, one film, and many training seminar work books. He also consults, counsels, speaks, trains and prepares people to perform and produce quality products and services, on time, at the lowest total cost. Chuck Carter is a Lead Auditor with an accredited ISO registrar. He is a P.E., CQE, CRE, CQA, CMFLE, and a certified management consultant.

Scope of Services:

Quality, reliability, safety & training by Chuck Carter and his associates provides you with quality assurance management systems that are tailored to your needs for short and long-term growth and development as based on your projected goals and objectives. Quality systems by Carter will meet or exceed commercial, industrial, business, medical, military and ISO 9000 requirements.

The QA Management systems are geared to your organization and are based on ISO 9000 standards.

Dr. Carter will personally audit your entire operation and provide a verbal and written report to executive management. The firm is prevention-oriented and favor detailed design reviews, vendor quality assurance programs, configuration control and closed-loop corrective action internally and externally to the customer. Carter and Associates will consult with your organization and assist in training all personnel in all ISO 9000 requirements, including auditing.

Commitment by Client Management

Quality Systems by Dr. Carter and his associates require client management commitment on a long-term basis. Long-range planning is required along with management involvement, dedication, understanding, willingness and perseverance in concert with the 'central theme' of all Carter systems: "Quality, reliability, safety, training and people pay great dividends to those organizations who follow the plan and management system of prevention, control, assurance, assistance and auditing." Dr. Carter stresses simplicity, basics, clarity and understanding in all of the quality, reliability, safety and training programs.

Capabilities:

- Document QA manual per ISO 9000/ANSI-ASQC Q91, 92, 93
- Establish company quality goals and objectives
- Implement QA policies, procedures and total QA system on full or part-time basis (contract)
- Conduct study of career development/staffing needs
- Develop QA workmanship standards manual
- Develop quality cost program
- Develop productivity and continuous quality improvement program.
- Develop cost reduction and configuration control programs
- Audit product and people safety

- Establish supplier QA program
- Develop internal and external QA audit procedures
- Conduct customer satisfaction surveys and audits
- Provide direct assistance with ISO/Q90 registration, pre-assessment audits, executive training

Training & Development:

- Organize and provide quality education, training courses and seminars as appropriate to needs
- Write employee job descriptions
- Motivate management and employees through training
- Develop employee/management involvement programs
- Change attitudes and develop a positive quality culture
- In-plant seminars and courses on quality and TQM subjects of interest
- Training, qualification and certification of production operators and QA auditors/inspectors

Benefits:

- ISO 9000/Q90 QA manual conformance and registration
- Documented and functioning Quality System
- Employee involvement in total quality improvement
- Prevention of problems via participation and training
- Efficient control of processes and products
- Implementation assistance on full or part-time basis
- Prioritized goals for planned growth
- Reduced scrap, repairs and rework costs
- Reduced quality costs
- Improved communication, coordination and cooperation, internal and external
- Assistance with ISO/Q90 registration process and related costs
- Customer satisfaction surveys and audits
- Total quality management system startup
- Concise, clear reporting system and records
- Trained, qualified, motivated goal oriented people
- Product liability risk reduction
- Improved productivity and profitability
- Long-term career development of human resources
- Identification and retention of talented people
- Satisfied customers and new business potential on a local, nationwide and worldwide basis

CENTER FOR QUALITY & PRODUCTIVITY
ROUTE 252 & MEDIA LINE ROAD
MEDIA, PA 19063-1094
Phone: 215-359-5367

DCCC has broadened their range of services to include full TQM implementation consulting. Through their many years in practicing and providing training in TQM, they've gained solid experience in what makes a Quality system work. Now, they've translated that experience into a structured implementation model that includes everything from executive leadership to trainer certification. DCCC's goal is to help you adapt this model to your organization and provide the training needed to become autonomous.

For the past six years, Delaware County Community College has been at the forefront of Total Quality Improvement both as a practitioner of Total Quality principles and in training business and industry, government and educational institutions. Now, on the leading edge of ISO 9000, their consultants are among the first in this country to have met the education requirements established by the UK's Institute of Quality Assurance.

DCCC is an approved Office of Personnel Management (OPM) vendor for Total Quality training and is included in the "Authorized Federal Supply Schedule Catalog."

ISO 9000 CONSULTING SERVICES

- Pre-Assessment Audits
    - Assessment of current quality system in relation to the appropriate ISO 9000 standard
- ISO Workshop
    - In-depth examination of ISO 9000 standards
- Internal Audit Systems
    - Internal audits where needed, review of current internal audit systems or assistance in establishing a system to comply with ISO 9000 standard requirements
- Quality Manual Review
    - Point by point review to ensure conformance to ISO 9000 standard
- Preparation for Registration
    - Includes self-assessment, documentation, implementation and pre-assessment

Currently, the College has two ISO courses:

- "International Standards for Quality" is an introduction to ISO 9000 that is designed to prepare participants for implementation of the standards. It is open to all members of an organization and they strongly encourage those who will be working with ISO 9000 to attend.

- The "Internal Auditor Workshop" covers more advanced material and is intended to provide participants the specific knowledge and skills they need to perform the ISO 9000 internal audit. This course is designed for persons who will be conducting the internal audits required under ISO 9000 certification.

COLUMBIA QUALITY MANAGEMENT INTERNATIONAL
P.O. Box 506
Orefield, PA 18069
Phone: 215-391-9496
Fax: 215-391-9497

Columbia Quality Management International (CQMI) is a partnership between Columbia Quality, Inc. (USA) and Quality Management International, Ltd. (UK). CQM offers an extensive range of training programs and services aimed at assisting with quality education, development, and implementation.

CQMI is committed to the belief that successful Quality Management depends on the simultaneous development of people, processes, and systems. Understanding that there is no packaged formula to make this happen, CQMI's consultants deliver advice designed to further develop the organization's knowledge base and make more efficient use of resources.

The three primary services offered by Columbia Quality are consulting, independent assessments for improving performance, and training.

Consulting Services:

CQMI offers consulting services for implementation of ISO 9000 quality management systems. With CQMI consulting services your organization will be able to: reduce the time for implementation, optimize the use of internal resources, avoid false starts and find out what works best (and what doesn't work). The consulting services are fully integrated with the training and auditing services to provide a complete package for implementation. These services include: audit and ISO training, model selection, providing a detailed "game plan," facilitating and coordinating the implementation plan, and providing direction for the preparation of documents.

Auditing Services:

CQMI offers clients assistance in the area of quality system auditing. Through CQMI's international network of companies, RAB Certified Lead Auditors/Auditors and IQA Registered Lead Assessors/Assessors are available throughout the world.

CQMI audit services include:

- Internal Quality Audits
- Pre-Certification Evaluations
- Third Party Certification Staff Support
- Beyond ISO 9000 Contractual Standards - Quality Management Benchmark Assessments

Training:

CQMI courses and seminars are designed to develop awareness of quality principles, and teach the techniques involved in managing quality and improving the performance of an organization.

CQMI offers a range of standard courses. All courses can be tailored to the requirements of your organization and presented in-house. Training Services include:

- Executive Briefing
- Quality Systems and ISO Standards
- Managing Quality
- Quality Awareness

- From Process to Procedure
- Leading International Auditor/Lead Auditor Training
- Internal Quality Audit Course

Columbia Quality Management International Office Locations:

EUROPE

QMI
Quality Court, The Precinct
Egham, Surrey
UK TW20 9HN
Phone: 011-44784 472424
Fax: 011-44784 471799

QMI - North Sea Ltd.
Bridge House
1 Riverside Drive
Aberdeen
UK ABN1 2LH
Phone: 011-44224 212750
Fax: 011-44224 587777

QMI
Craigie Hall
6, Rowan Road
Glasgow
UK G41 5BS
Phone: 011-44-41-4276884
Fax: 011-44-41-4273534

PACIFIC RIM

QMI - Quest Sdn Bhd
The Penthouse, Wisma Muisan
300, Jalan Raja Laut
50350, Kuala Lumpur, Malaysia
Phone: 010 603 292 1779
Fax: 010 603 292 1297

COMPLIANCE AUTOMATION, INC.
17629 El Camino Real
Suite 207
Houston, TX 77058
Phone: 713-486-7817
Fax: 713-486-0115

Compliance Automation, Inc. is a spin-off of Bruce G. Jackson & Associates, Inc. devoted to the development, maintenance, sales, training, and support of the Document Director tools.

Compliance Automation, Inc., will continue to develop increased functionality and portability to support the government/contractor requirements market. It will expand the application of the Document Director tools into the commercial sector for ISO 9000 compliance and for proposal preparation.

Compliance Automation, Inc. will continue to provide training in Requirements Definition and Management, and is developing more detailed classes to help clients write and maintain better requirements.

CONTEMPORARY CONSULTANTS CO.

15668 IRENE STREET
SOUTHGATE, MI 48195
Phone: 313-281-9182
Phone: 313-284-3119
FAX: 313-281-4023

Contemporary Consultants is a full consulting firm dedicated to the advancement - through teaching, coaching, directing, counseling and consulting - of scientific knowledge in the fields of Quality, Management Training, and Organizational Development.

Founded in 1984, Contemporary Consultants has provided direction and has gained experience in the areas of Manufacturing, Service, Health-Service, Defense, Chemical and other sectors of the economy.

The objective is to reduce an organization's overall cost, improve profits and provide an organization with an efficient and effective operation to compete in today's competitive world market. To do that, Contemporary Consultants focus on the need assessment (survey or audit). In the audit these major areas are reviewed:

- *Company goals/plans*
- *Management - Administration - Finance - Quality - Quality Manual/Planning*
- *Cost - Accounting/Value Analysis*
- *Delivery - Material Handling*
- *Technology - Engineering*

Contemporary Consultants' goal is to stimulate your personnel to meet the goals of increased productivity and quality by assisting in the above areas.

Consulting:

Contemporary Consultants work with client management and with the current culture at a client's site in improving quality management and quality systems. Consulting is offered as follows:

- ISO 9000
- Employee Motivation
- Basic/Advanced SPC
- Basic/Advanced DOE
- Taguchi Methods
- Quality Function Deployment (QFD)
- Audits
- FMEA
- Cost of Quality

Training:

- A course to cover the concept, the essence and the requirements of an ISO Standard. The participant learns how the standard came about, why it is necessary, how it can help your organization, and how you can go about implementing the new standards.

- A course to cover all the above material plus the actual mechanics of an audit, the group dynamics involved, the preparation, the actual audit, the findings, the presentation of the results, and the follow-up.

The CCC approach is to help clients understand the concept of ISO 9000 standards and to prepare them for the certification.

CONTINENTAL DESIGN AND MANAGEMENT GROUP

ONE GATEWAY CENTER - FIFTH FLOOR
PITTSBURGH, PA 15222
Phone: 412-553-6700
FAX: 412-553-5609

LISTING OF SERVICES

ISO Consulting Support:

- Total Quality management
- ISO 9000 Implementation
- ISO 9000 Documentation Development
- ISO 9000 Lead Assessor Training
- ISO 9000 Training
- ISO 9000 Pre-Assessments
- ISO 9000 Consulting

Quality Services Support:

- Subcontractor Assessment
- Internal Auditing
- Internal Training
- Quality Evaluations
- Feasibility Studies
- Quality Cost Studies

COOPERS & LYBRAND
1100 LOUISIANA
SUITE 4100
HOUSTON, TX 77002
Phone: 713-757-5200
FAX: 713-757-5249

In addition to Coopers & Lybrand's more traditional financial services, C&L provides an array of business related services through its Management Consulting Services (MCS) practice. In the manufacturing consulting area, it is ranked as the largest consulting practice in the world.

In the Quality area, Coopers & Lybrand is one of the leading suppliers of consulting services for both the private and public sectors. With a primary emphasis on implementation of continuous improvement methodologies and techniques, Coopers & Lybrand's knowledgeable professionals have been extremely successful in helping clients achieve strategic objectives as well as improve bottom line results. With significant experience an ISO 9000 implementation in both Europe and the United States, Coopers & Lybrand is well positioned to assist throughout the world.

Coopers & Lybrand ISO 9000 Services:

Coopers & Lybrand's ISO 9000 services are designed to assist clients with all phases of preparation for ISO 9000 registration. While each assignment is tailored to the needs of the individual client, services typically fall into the following categories:

- Management Education and Awareness
- Status Assessments
- Implementation Planning
- Implementation Support
- Staff Training
- Simulated Audits

The Approach:

Coopers & Lybrand's approach is based on our proven methodologies and structures for helping clients address quality related strategic and operational issues. The highlights to this approach include:

- Structured methodology for ISO 9000 implementation
- Client-driven approach that not only assists clients with preparing for initial certification but also for required periodic certifications
- Twin-Track TQM methodology for continuous improvement
- Cultural and economic assessment for management of change

The Benefits:

Manufacturers are finding that there are many benefits to ISO 9000 compliance in addition to simply meeting their customers' requirements for compliance. Some of these benefits include:

- Improved quality and productivity
- Enhanced market image
- Increased firm value
- Access to European and other global markets
- Reduced efforts required for customer audits

Executive Briefing:

This is an executive briefing to provide a description of the background, certification process, and business implications related to ISO 9000.

CUSTOM COMMUNICATIONS CO.

5108 Darrow Road
P. O. Box 696
Hudson, OH 44236
Phone: 216-653-8700
Fax: 216-650-2774

Whether your need is for a large scale training program or purely personal, you'll find Beckwith's courses to be just what you're looking for.

Self-instructional in-Plant Training Programs:

- Basic Shop Orientation and Basic Machining
- Intermediate Shop
- Math and Engineering Drawings
- Numerical Control
- Updated Geometric Tolerancing Series
- Basic Welding
- Electronic Assembly and Soldering

DELAWARE COUNTY COMMUNITY COLLEGE
DU PONT QUALITY MANAGEMENT & TECHNOLOGY CENTER
LOUVIERS 33W44
P.O. BOX 6090
NEWARK, DE 19714-6090
Phone: 302-366-2100
Phone: 800-441-8040
FAX: 302-366-3366

The key to business success is to provide customers with the best value through quality leadership and continuous improvement in all products and services. Du Pont's staff feels so strongly about this that Du Pont has adopted this principle as the corporate quality policy.

Du Pont's quality improvement processes are under the stewardship of the Quality Management & Technology Center. Its 80-plus professionals have trained over 25,000 persons in quality management and counseled senior managers on quality improvement at over 200 Du Pont sites worldwide and more than 50 outside companies.

The Center's services are used by both external and internal clients. Du Pont's broad-based experience eliminates trial and error and capitalizes on field-tested techniques and proven results.

All services are built around a proven philosophy. This philosophy encompasses quality leadership, anticipating customers' needs, providing results-oriented skills and creating employee involvement.

Consulting:

Services are provided by professionals with years of experience in quality management and technology. Du Pont's quality management consultants can help you to evaluate your improvement needs, implement continuous improvement processes, or design special training. The firm's quality technology consultants will help you implement quality systems based on core methodologies such as statistical process control and experimental design.

Specialized services in ISO 9000 consulting are focused on each of the key phases in the process that takes you to registration of your quality system.

Du Pont's experienced consultants offer you support in strategic planning, team and organizational development, writing the required procedures and quality manual, and developing an internal audit system to meet the standards of third party ISO 9000 registrars.

Whether you are upgrading your processes as part of your business strategy, preparing for a supplier audit, or earning international quality standards registration, Du Pont's wide variety of seminars and services can help you. The Du Pont staff will work with you to select the particular combination of training and consulting that best fits your needs.

Strategic ISO 9000 Quality System Planning:

A qualified consultant with experience and knowledge of ISO 9000 will lead the management group through a strategic planning process to decide if they will pursue ISO 9000, what resources are required, where their system currently stands versus ISO 9000, and how to get started.

Quality Manual Review:

A consultant with knowledge of ISO 9000 requirements and quality system auditing experience will review the organization's Quality Manual for compliance with ISO 9000, at any stage from first draft through pre-assessment.

Quality System Audit:

A team of qualified and experienced quality system auditors will conduct an on-site pre-assessment of an organization to determine if their quality system complies with ISO 9000 and is fully functional. The team may include a qualified and experienced auditor from the client's organization. Another option is to have a qualified auditor lead the organization's own audit team through initial internal audits.

Other Du Pont Consulting:

Many other Du Pont Quality Management & Technology consulting and training offerings may be helpful to sites working toward ISO 9000 registration and implementing a quality system. Du Pont has extensive experience in all aspects of quality management and technology, including statistical methods, continuous improvement, and problem-solving.

Seminars and Video:

- Product Quality Management - proven and practical statistics seminars which help you learn how to focus on prevention processes and methods for both building quality into products during development as well as ensuring quality of conformance to requirements during production. These seminars cover topics such as experimental design, process control, and problem solving methods.

- Quality Standards Seminars - a series of seminars that take you from understanding international standards through the development of a world class quality system to registration of that system within the framework of ISO 9000.

ISO 9000 is rapidly becoming the necessary entryway to preferred supplier status and continued export growth. Du Pont's second generation seminars reflect experience in registering both internal and external clients. Du Pont alone has certified more than 50 quality systems worldwide.

The Du Pont Quality Management & Technology Center offers public seminars and a video on ISO 9000. Open-enrollment seminars include:

- Implementing the ISO 9000 Standards
- Understanding the ISO 9000 Standards Overview
- How to Prepare a Quality Manual for ISO 9002
- Quality System Auditor Training
- Quality System Lead Assessor Training

Video:

- ISO 9000: The First Step to the Future - This is a two-module videotape training package on ISO 9000.

ECKERSBERG & ASSOCIATES CONSULTANTS
819 BOWLING GREEN ROAD
HOMEWOOD, IL 60430
Phone: 312-799-6880

Robert A. Eckersberg is principal of Eckersberg and Associates, has over 30 years of technical and management experience in manufacturing and service industries small business to multinational corporations, providing automotive, aerospace and electronic products, utilizing a diversity of manufacturing processes and materials, produced by high-volume, job-shop and continuous flow production methods.

He has presented seminars to all levels of management, industrial associations and has taught at the graduate and undergraduate levels at a variety of colleges and universities.

He holds a B.S. degree in business/science, a B.A., M.A. in product design/development and education. Currently he holds 35 design/engineering patent assignments in the U.S., Canada, Europe and Japan.

Mr. Eckersberg is a member of ASQC and has worked with top management on implementing total quality control concepts tailored to satisfy the stringent requirements outlined for Q-1, 6-Sigma, ISO 9000 and the Malcolm Baldrige certification.

EDWARD A. REYNOLDS QUALITY ASSURANCE CONSULTING
BOX 1074
MATTITUCK, LONG ISLAND, NY 11952
Phone: 516-298-4090

Edward A. Reynolds is a consultant with many years in Quality Control and Quality and Productivity Improvement as an inspector, engineer, manager, corporate director, associate professor and independent consultant.

Mr. Reynolds is a Certified Quality and Reliability Engineer, Fellow of ASQC and British IQA, and a member of ASNT, ASTM and ISA.

Consulting Activities:

Mr. Reynolds has worked with over 400 organizations in the U.S. and abroad on almost every type of consumer, industrial and military product - from atomic submarines to zippers and potato chips to penicillin.

Mr. Reynolds has been active in QA/QC/SPC Training since the 1940s; produced training films and videos; planned and conducted university graduate and undergraduate courses, inspection apprentice programs, and engineering and management seminars for universities, corporations and technical associations; and written handbook chapters and many papers on Quality Training.

As a consultant, he does all assignments personally. His recent work is largely in assistance for specific problem solving, objective surveys and audits to recommend methods for improvement and temporary, on-job leadership to establish or improve Quality programs. This has included serving as Acting Quality Head for a variety of major U.S. corporations for periods of two to twelve months, and, on a part-time basis, for many smaller companies.

Mr. Reynolds is currently working with a major corporation to aid in having their operations in full compliance with ISO 9000.

EIL INSTRUMENTS, INC.
307 U WEST TREMONT AVENUE
CHARLOTTE, NC 28203
Phone: 704-376-2237
FAX: 704-332-5494

EIL Instruments, Inc. is the largest nationwide measurement and control instrumentation sales and service company in the US. Several of the 28 EIL Sales/Service Centers in North America have been successfully audited against ISO 9002/ANSI/ASQC Q92. The scope specified in the registrations is FOR| "Repair, calibration, customization and distribution of test, measurement and control instrumentation." Services are provided in-house and on-site at the customer's facility.

EIL. provides a variety of compliance services to meet the ISO 9000 Series requirements for the "Control of Measuring and Test Equipment (Inspection, Measuring, and Test Equipment)." These comprehensive requirements range from the Adequacy of Calibration Equipment to the Acceptance of Newly Purchased Test and Measurement. Services also include Documentation, Corrective Action, Traceability, Calibration Records, Intervals, and Recall System.

Compliance Assistance Program:

- Official US Guideline Documentation Package
- List of elements required for Metrology program (includes examples and recommendations); ISO 9001, 9002, 9003 - Section 4; ISO 9004 - Section 13

Additional Services include audit assistance, calibration services, equipment inspections, training, quality assurance manuals, and all necessary elements to satisfy section 4 or 13 for the "Control of Measurement and Test Equipment (Inspection, Measuring, and Test Equipment)"

Custom Tailored Service Plans:

- ISO 9000 Compliance Services - Provides documentation for audits, assets, and records in addition to calibrations and repairs traceable to NIST.
- Full Maintenance Contracts - Scheduled calibrations including material and labor to ensure the instrument's performance is according to manufacturer's specifications.
- Calibration Contracts - Scheduled calibration with maximum cost savings.
- Blanket Purchase Agreement - If you do not know what your service requirements are going to be, you can still take advantage of customized service at a discount.
- Extended Warranty - This is the service side of EIL's test and measurement instrument distribution business.

Sales and Service Capabilities Include:

- Test Equipment Distribution - EIL is a nationwide stocking distributor for some of the largest test equipment manufacturers in the U.S., including Beckman, Fluke, Huntron, Leader, and Hewlett-Packard.
- Power/Utility - EIL sells and services a broad range of power instruments, including clamp-on meters, insulation and high pot testers, recorders, CT's and PT's, power analyzers, and ground resistance testers.

- Measurement & Control Instruments - EIL sells and services a variety of measurement and control instruments, including analog and digital panel meters, switchboard meters, meter relays, signal conditioners, counter and timers, and controllers. EIL also offers value-added meter services such as special ranges and scales, mirror scales, meter suppression, peak hold and adjustable span.
- Repair & Calibration Service - Onsite or at one of over 20 facilities, for general purpose test equipment, microwave, telecommunications, biomedical equipment, and industrial/process instruments.

EXCEL PARTNERSHIP, INC.
75 GLEN ROAD
SANDY HOOK, CT 06482
Phone: 203-426-3281
FAX: 203-426-7811

EXCEL is an International Quality Management Consultancy and Training organization with offices in both the UK and the U.S. Quality management professionals established EXCEL Partnership in response to the need for individual companies to gain ownership of their quality systems, especially ISO 9000.

EXCEL can integrate a "quality philosophy" by developing Quality Management Systems to ISO 9000 in the manufacturing, process and service industries. Because every company is viewed as unique, Excel provides as much or as little support as necessary to achieve a quality implementation program suitable for client companies.

EXCEL offers:

- *Training - A variety of "tailor-made" management development courses, and regular training courses which cover all aspects of Quality Management.*
- *Consultancy - Support is designed to complement the training courses, with emphasis placed on a pragmatic "hands-on" approach.*

EXCEL personnel have delivered consultancy support and training in the Far East, Middle East, Japan, India, Europe and throughout the U.S. covering:

- *Laying the foundation for good management systems through the implementation of Quality Systems to ISO 9000*
- *Developing the culture of a company-wide Quality Improvement process through the adoption of Total Quality Management*

QUALITY STRATEGY

Strategy:

- The implementation of an effective Quality System is a necessary part of an overall Quality Strategy.
- To implement an effective Quality Management System, a company needs to consider the various regulatory and commercial requirements placed upon it including:

- ISO 9000
- DoD requirements
- GMP's
- Malcolm Baldrige criteria

Implementation:

Through a combination of training and consultancy, EXCEL will help you implement a Quality System for your business.

- EXCEL Partnership works closely with you to help understand the relationship of these differing approaches to Quality Management.
- EXCEL helps support the development of an integrated approach to Quality Management.

QUALITY SYSTEMS SURVEY

EXCEL can assess the Quality Systems within a company against the requirements of ISO 9000.

From this initial survey, Excel can:

- Identify areas requiring improvement or development within the Quality System
- Prepare, in conjunction with the company, an action plan to address those areas - including the identification of training needs
- Provide assistance and advice on the development and implementation of systems - including assistance in the preparation of a Quality Manual and associated procedures and documentation
- Assist in the presentation of system requirements to involved management and staff
- Conduct a pre-assessment audit to ensure the effective implementation of the Quality System prior to the final audit by a registration body

THE EXCEL PARTNERSHIP

There are three key elements to achieving total quality and they apply equally to Excel.

Systems:

With its combined experience in the application of quality management systems, both as assessors for certification bodies and as practicing Quality Managers and Commercial Business Managers, EXCEL is uniquely aware of the practical aspects of quality management. For a quality management system to work, it must be worked.

Processes:

EXCEL's experience within a wide variety of industries means that staff have the expertise to deal with specific quality problems in practically every technological area. With EXCEL's assistance, companies in fields completely new to formal quality assurance schemes have achieved registration to ISO 9000 by a national certification body, thus becoming the "first in their field" to achieve such recognition.

EXCEL treats every client individually and will give you as much or as little support as is needed to achieve your objectives. As soon as you are in control, involvement will decrease to the point where EXCEL will simply monitor progress and provide any necessary advice to keep the project on course and on time.

People:

The strength of any organization lies in its people. Communication and training are therefore key tasks to help those people become more effective. The EXCEL Partnership includes staff who have worked at the forefront of management development and Quality Auditor training in the UK for over a decade. They are fully experienced in implementing total quality programs and developing team skills with organizations of every size. EXCEL has played a key role in setting up several well known certification schemes, both in the UK and overseas.

In addition to tailor-made management development courses, EXCEL also runs regular training courses for Lead Assessors, for internal auditors and a general introduction to Total Quality Management.

THE EXCEL TRAINING COURSES - ISO 9000

EXCEL offers a series of training packages to support your organization's registration process to ISO 9000.

Consultancy support is designed to complement these EXCEL training courses - with emphasis placed on a pragmatic "hands-on" approach to implementing quality systems.

The following courses can be run either in-house or as open enrollment courses:

Practical Communication and Development Seminar

This seminar is designed to provide an overview of the requirements of ISO 9000. It is an ideal starting point for gaining involvement in the Quality Improvement process. It combines tutor presentations, course handouts and discussion sessions.

This seminar is of most value when run in-company as part of the overall implementation process of ISO 9000. It can be structured to your needs - either one-half or a full day as necessary.

Although an initial session is targeted to Senior Management, all levels of personnel within an organization will eventually benefit from attendance. This seminar has been attended by thousands of people in a wide variety of manufacturing and service industries.

How to Implement ISO 9000 Series

EXCEL's partners have presented this course since the introduction of Quality Standards in the 1970s. Attendees will gain a thorough understanding of the standard - both its value and limitations.

The background and essential content of the ISO 9000 series of standards is presented. Certain sections of the standard are dealt with in great detail. The interpretation and application by the major Accredited Registration Bodies is also discussed.

Through lectures, workshops and case studies, attendees gain a thorough understanding of the ISO 9000 Series. This course has been run worldwide in various industry sectors. It usually covers two days and attendees receive a course manual.

All levels of personnel within an organization benefit from attendance, especially those directly involved in the implementation of ISO 9000. This seminar has been attended by thousands of people in a wide variety of manufacturing and service industries.

Preparing Quality Manuals and Procedures

Emphasis is placed on overcoming the problems faced by those whose task it is to prepare quality manuals and procedures.

The following areas are addressed:

- Background on documenting a system
- Consideration of all the elements
- Understanding the written task
- Support base necessary
- Controls on procedures
- Getting everyone involved
- Content of procedures
- Examples and hints
- Confidentiality, detail, structure, etc.

Through lectures, case studies, teamwork and presentations attendees gain an understanding of the preparation of manuals and procedures. This course has been run for various industries within Europe including those involved in manufacturing, process and service. It can be structured for either one or two days and attendees receive a course manual.

Quality Assurance personnel, line managers and supervisors who are required to document their quality systems and practices into manuals and procedures to comply with ISO 9001/2 benefit from attendance.

ISO 9000 Auditor Training

Auditing is a powerful management tool in establishing how effective a company is in controlling the quality variable. In addition to developing the techniques of internal auditing, an introduction to product audits and supplier assessment is provided.

The objective of an audit is not to find fault , but rather identifying opportunities for improvement.

The following areas are addressed in detail:

- How to undertake an effective Quality Management System Audit against ISO 9000
- How to construct an audit program and develop checklists
- How to evaluate the significance of audit findings
- How to improve communication skills in the presentation of audit reports
- How to implement Quality Improvement through the progression of corrective action programs

Theoretical background is developed by the use of practical, interactive workshops on auditing systems and techniques, thus providing attendees the opportunity to practice their skills during simulated audits. This practical emphasis along with a tutor to delegate contact hours allows a substantial degree of individual guidance and tuition. It is usually a two- or three-day course.

In addition to those wishing to undertake internal audits, this course is useful to managers whose departments will be subject to these audits.

FRED A. HOFFMAN & ASSOCIATES
602 APOLLO PARKWAY
WESTFIELD, IN 46074
Phone: 317-896-3072
FAX: 317-896-3072

Fred A. Hoffman & Associates is dedicated to providing the most results oriented, cost effective, tried and proven programs to assist clients with ISO 9000 certification, total quality management and continuous improvement programs. All Hoffman programs maximize the return on investment in the shortest time frame possible. The firm's goal is to earn the right to be seen as a valuable resource to client companies now and in the months to come.

Fred A. Hoffman & Associates will show you how to get started and make recommendations for quickly dispelling the barriers that may impede the ISO 9000 certification process. The Needs Assessments and Pre-Assessments services are cost effective and result in many tangible and intangible rewards not otherwise realized. As a result of these assessments, your organization will find out what it will cost and how long it may take to become certified to the ISO standards.

Other ISO 9000 services include complete in-house facilitation, training auditors, training staff, training on how to write effective manuals and procedures, programs for "improving employee and organizational effectiveness", complete technical and documentation support and other associated training programs.

ISO 9000 Services available:

- Executive Overview/Training
- Complete program implementation, consulting and facilitation
- Needs assessments - Projecting time and costs for certification
- Pre-Assessments - Projecting you readiness for certification
- Programs for cultural change, removing barriers and accelerating your journey to ISO certification
- Internal auditor training
- Team member training
- Critically critique quality manuals, workmanship standards and procedures
- Quality attitude survey
- Complete/efficient technical secretarial services
- Help in identifying and selecting your registrar

GILBERT/COMMONWEALTH, INC.

P.O. Box 1498
READING, PA 19603-1498
Phone: 215-775-2600
FAX: 215-775-2670

Gilbert/Commonwealth, Inc. offers ISO 9000 training and consulting in partnership with its London subsidiary, Gilbert Associates (Europe), Limited (GA(E)L). The firm's consultants are ASQC Certified Quality Auditors and have outstanding experience in the nuclear industry. The firm also offers ANSI N45.2.23/NQA-1 Lead Auditor Certification training and consulting and a Nuclear Codes and Standards program.

Consulting:

Gilbert/Commonwealth provides consulting services in the following areas:

- Quality System Audits and Assessments
- Program Development
- Quality Inspection Services

These services can be provided on an as-needed basis at your facility to assist you with quality program.

Training:

Gilbert/Commonwealth offers a range of Auditor Training and Standards-related public seminars, as well as custom on-site training programs.

The following courses and seminars are offered for presentation on-site and can be tailored to fit your specific needs:

- ISO 9000 Series Overview for Manufacturers
- ISO 9000 Series Overview for the Nuclear Industry
- ISO 9000 Series Auditing, Including Optional Facility Assessment
- ISO 9000 Series Management Overview
- ISO 9000 Systems Lead Auditor Training
- Quality Program Development and Implementation
- Commercial Grade Surveys and Source Verifications
- Auditing for Non Auditors: What to Expect When the Auditors Knock on Your Door (A Management Overview: How to Get the Most Out of Your Audits)

HARRY E. WILLIAMS & ASSOCIATES
15111 BUSHARD STREET
SUITE 93
WESTMINSTER, CA 92683
Phone: 714-531-7103

Harry E. Williams, Ph.D., MBA, BSE, PE, has thirty years of quality management in the electronics, electrical and electromechanical industries which he draws upon in serving clients. As a management consultant, Mr. Williams provides services to client companies to: upgrade quality system; manage supplier rating and improvement; and facilitate supervisor and manager training seminars in ISO 9000, TQM, SPC, and zero defects.

QUALITY ASSURANCE CONSULTING ELEMENTS

Quality System:

Implementation or upgrade of a Quality System to the requirements of:

- MIL-I-45208
- MIL-Q-9858
- MIL-Q-9858A
- MIL-STD-1535
- ISO 9000
- Best Commercial Practice
- Product Liability Protection
- Special/Contractual

Supplier Quality Assurance:

- Supplier Rating Systems
- Supplier Improvement Programs
- Supplier Surveys/Source Inspection Policy
- Effective Communication Systems
- Receiving Inspection/Purchasing Support

Personnel Development:

- Supervisor/Manager Training Programs
- Inspector/Inspection Training
- SPC/TQM/Calibration/Records
- Cost Effectiveness of Inspection
- Seminars: MRB, Correction Action, Zero Defects, etc.
- Safety Analysis and Reporting
- Recruiting, Interviewing and Orientation of New Employees

Additional Options:

- Personnel Utilization Analysis
- Audits, Surveys or Employee Evaluations
- Job Descriptions and Job Specifications
- Cost Effective Organizational Structures
- Shop Scrap and Yield Analysis
- Tooling/Methods and Operations Evaluations

- Customer Returns/Field Failure Analysis
- Cost of Quality and Trend Reporting
- Product Development and Improvement
- Cost Reduction and Productivity Programs
- Work Environment Evaluations
- Design Review Techniques

Additional task assignments unique to the client's needs or goals are negotiable.

HAZELWOOD PRIDDY & ASSOCIATES, INC.

600 COMMERCE DRIVE
SUITE 608
CORAOPOLIS, PA 15108-3173
Phone: 412-262-5040
FAX: 412-269-0396

Hazelwood Priddy & Associates, Inc. was established in 1986 not only to provide training for management and hourly personnel in TQM, ISO 9000, SPC and other quality issues, but to implement these programs on the shop floor or in the office. Hazelwood Priddy & Associates, Inc. has provided simplified approaches to complex quality requirements based on the Deming continuous improvement philosophy, while creating as little disturbance to the present system as possible. The firm's TQM program has produced excellent audit results and quality ratings for its clients. Increased income, decreased quality costs, employee participation and compliance to automotive, military and international quality standards ISO 9000 are the benefits of these programs.

Services and Areas of Expertise:

Hazelwood Priddy has worked in the primary metals, chemical processes, refractories, building materials, plastics, foundries, plating, slitting, shearing, rolling, heat treating, forging, machine shop services and support services such as sales, engineering, purchasing, accounting, customer service, and QA.

HUNTINGTON QUALITY ASSOCIATES

P.O. Box 905
HUNTINGTON, IN 46750
Phone: 219-356-6006
FAX: 219-356-5044

Frequently, the hardest part of manual writing is visualizing the end product and overcoming inertia to get started. Huntington Quality Associates has addressed these obstacles with the HQA sample Quality System Manual and a copy on disk.

The manual follows the ISO 9001: 1987 (Q91) standard

Each of the twenty sections of the manual correspond with the twenty sections of the standard. The wording has been carefully chosen to comply with the standard and help you picture the minimum expected by the standard. HQA explains the approach that may be used to modify or tailor the contents of the manual to fit your own quality system.

Common pitfalls associated with writing a quality system manual may include:

- Spending too much money and time,
- Devoting more time to the quality manual than to the procedures and system implementation, including too much or too little in the manual,
- Misinterpreting paragraphs of the ISO 9001 standard.

INFORMATION MAPPING, INC.

300 THIRD AVENUE
WALTHAM, MA 02154
Phone: 617-890-7003
FAX: 617-890-1339

Information Mapping, Inc. is a major seminars and service company. Information Mapping works with Fortune 1000 businesses and government agencies worldwide - helping them attain measurable improvements in the communication of information. The company's methodology has special relevance for companies seeking ISO 9000 certification.

The Information Mapping Method

The Information Mapping method is a proprietary, research-based methodology for analyzing, organizing, and presenting information. Easily understood by writers and non-writers alike, the method presents skills that are directly relevant and immediately applicable to any ISO 9000 certification effort.

Creating Documentation That Meets ISO 9000 Standards

Through close collaboration with Information Mapping experts, you'll receive help to:

- Develop a realistic master plan for ISO 9000 documentation development - based on your time frame and resources
- Create working models of ISO 9000 documentation that all writers can follow - quickly, confidently
- Use ISO 9000 documentation to effectively communicate job performance and product quality standards to employees, managers, and knowledge workers
- Work with subject matter experts to eliminate gaps in your quality systems, documents, and records
- Ensure that your ISO 9000 documentation is complete, accurate, up-to-date, accessible.

Establishing an ISO 9000 Document Control System

Receive help to establish a logically structured document control system that will:

- Identify those individuals - whether employees, customers, or suppliers - authorized to ensure that your ISO 9000 documentation is current and effective through periodic review
- Establish ongoing management reviews of your quality system's suitability and effectiveness, including any necessary, corrective action
- Set up trails between ISO 9000 documents and related information
- Install a document reference index - accessible to all personnel and indicating the most current version of each ISO 9000 document
- Establish clear, consistent standards for job performance and product quality - standards against which ISO 9000 auditors can measure compliance.

Implementing Quality Management Systems

This service offering focuses on performance improvement - helping you link individual job performance to organizational goals. You'll receive help to:

- Spearhead an organization-wide commitment to quality by communicating management priorities
- Assign quality responsibility and accountability across the organization
- Ensure quality output and efficient work behavior
- Achieve measurable improvements in day-to-day product and service quality

INTEGRATED MANAGEMENT RESOURCES

119 ADAMS DRIVE
STOW, MA 01775
508-897-7064

Founded in 1989, Integrated Management Resources is comprised of former senior executives with international business backgrounds and perspectives. These IMR principals each have over 15 years of business experience, specialize in one or more business disciplines and provide consulting, interim management, training and seminar services.

In June 1991, IMR became a member of the Affiliated Consulting Group, a national organization of results oriented consulting firms headquartered in Marietta, Ohio.

IMR has a slightly different view of ISO 9000 than most consulting organizations. While IMR certainly understands and provides services in manufacturing processes and quality control, IMR realizes that ISO compliance also includes computer software design and development and manufacturing and software documentation standards.

Business Charter:

IMR strives to assist clients in increasing sales, expanding markets, reducing costs and improving efficiency. Emphasis is on implementation and interim management to guide companies in transition and crisis, provide objective business and market analysis and effect change leading to competitive advantage and growth.

Professional Services:

IMR works with manufacturing, distribution, and for-profit service companies. The principals have extensive experience in the fields of high technology, computers, telecommunications, defense, aerospace, medical instrumentation, and industrial products.

More specifically, the IMR principals are experienced in: general management, marketing, international business, engineering, manufacturing, quality, customer service, training, accounting, market research, change management, business development, strategic planning, and information systems.

Client Profile:

Clients range from Fortune 100 to startup and emerging companies.

ISO 9000 Consulting Services:

- Leading ISO 9000 manufacturing compliance projects
- Analyzing current manufacturing and quality control processes
- Reviewing product engineering design and documentation
- Leading software compliance projects
- Reviewing software engineering design documentation

Seminars/Speaking Topics/Training:

Seminars and training are customized to specific client requirements.

- ISO 9000 and Being Internationally Competitive
- What is ISO 9000?

- ISO 9000 and Product Design
- ISO 9000's Role in Manufacturing and Quality Control
- ISO 9000 and the Software Development Process
- Preparing for the Registration Audit
- Compliance with Engineering and User Documentation Standards

INTERNATIONAL INSTITUTE FOR LEARNING, INC.
110 EAST 59TH STREET, SIXTH FLOOR
NEW YORK, NY 10022-1380
Phone: 212-909-0557
FAX: 212-909-0558

The International Institute for Learning and Excel Partnership offers an effective and efficient resource for organizations seeking outside assistance with the knowledge, experience and reputation to help them prepare for ISO 9000 registration. The trainers have delivered consultancy support and training courses for European and U.S. certification bodies, as well as firms around the world.

International Institute for Learning's on-site training and consultancy includes:

ISO 9000 Planning/Assessment

- Reviewing the existing Total Quality Initiative and creating/integrating the ISO 9000 implementation strategy.

A Quality Systems Survey

- Assess the Quality Systems with a company against the requirements of ISO 9000. From this survey IIL can:
    - Identify areas requiring improvement or development
    - Help prepare an action plan to address those areas, including the identification of training needs
    - Provide assistance and advice on the development and implementation of systems, including assistance in the preparation of a Quality Manual and associated procedures and documentation
    - Assist in the presentation of system requirements to involved management staff
    - Conduct a pre-assessment audit to ensure the effective implementation of the quality system prior to the final audit by a registration body

Customized ISO 9000 training courses include:

- The Executive Briefing on ISO 9000
- ISO 9000 Awareness Training
- How to Implement ISO 9000
- Preparing Quality Manuals and Procedures
- ISO Internal Auditor Training
- How to Implement ISO 9000 in the Service Industries
- ISO 9000 for Government Contractors
- Software QA and ISO 9000-3

INTERTEK TECHNICAL SERVICES, INC.

9900 MAIN STREET
SUITE 500
FAIRFAX, VA 22031
Phone: 703-591-1320 ext. 3025
FAX: 703-273-4124

INTERTEK Technical Services, Inc., is a full service company providing contract Quality and Procurement Services to most of the Fortune 500 companies in over 400 worldwide locations. It is a company of the UK-based Inchcape Testing Services.

INTERTEK's services include inspections and test support, audits and surveys, ISO 9000 preparation services, MIL-STD certification, regional supplier management, supplier quality assurance, and quality program training.

INTERTEK originated the quality contract services industry two decades ago. Today, quality professionals use INTERTEK's full services to complement their staffs for improved:

- *Quality and Delivery*
- *Budget Control*
- *Management Efficiency*

INTERTEK Technical Services

INTERTEK Technical Services makes helping companies prepare for ISO 9000 System Certification its business. INTERTEK does this by providing professionals that meet rigorous INTERTEK qualification standards, and offer in-depth, hands-on experience with the ISO Standards. INTERTEK's people provide Consulting and Preparation Services to assist in the critical "get-ready" stage of pursuing ISO 9000 System Certification.

INTERTEK Technical Services has developed a full range of Consulting Services to prepare its customers for a successful assessment the first time around.

INTERTEK has designed its Consulting and Preparation Services to be flexible and straightforward to use. One, or any combination of these services may be used to achieve an objective. INTERTEK's Regional Business Managers and Assessors assist in selecting the right combination of services in accordance with customer's needs. The following is an overview of the services the firm offers:

System Evaluation and Program Planning

INTERTEK Technical Services performs a review of the documented Quality Management System against the selected ISO Standard; evaluates how well the documented system is implemented through interviews with personnel, and examines the objective evidence.

Plan Implementation Management

INTERTEK Technical Services acts as a management representative to coordinate and direct the preparation team and system implementation activity. INTERTEK also provides steering team support and reports of progress against schedule.

System Development Support

INTERTEK Technical Services determines and documents practices and business processes by interviewing and flow-charting. The company writes procedures; trains and orients operational personnel in system use; and assists in implementation of the documented system and/or enhancements.

Post Implementation System Assessment

INTERTEK Technical Services performs a preliminary assessment to ensure complete and effective implementation of the system. Any non-compliances are identified, as are areas that need further development and/or documentation.

Certification Assessment Support

On-site representation is provided during the assessment for certification. In this mode of operation, INTERTEK can assist in the adjudication of any non-compliances identified during the assessment for certification activity performed by the certification body or registrar.

Seminars include:

- Orientation to ISO 9000
- Overview of Practical Auditing
- Training Class: Practical Auditing Course
- Training Class: Lead Assessor Training Course

INTERNATIONAL QUALITY RESOURCES CORPORATION, INC. (IQRC)
P.O. BOX 232
COLLEGE POINT, NY 11356
PHONE: 718-463-6939
FAX: 718-463-6939

International Quality Resources Corporation, Inc. (IQRC) provides worldwide service on a range of quality, reliability and maintainability, and certification areas. Michael Itzkevitch, president of IQRC, draws upon the experience and expertise of associates throughout the world for consulting and training in software reliability analyses, logistics support analyses, total quality management, audits and surveys, inspection, test witnessing, and materials expediting.

ISO 9000 Services and Training Offered:

- Seminar for top management to learn benefits of implementation of ISO 9000 Quality Systems and to provide guidelines for development of corporate quality policies (4 hours)
- Quality Systems Assessment - a UK-registered training course for Lead Assessors (5 days including exam)
- ISO 9000 Documentation Preparation (in-house consulting)
- ISO 9000 Quality Systems Deployment (in-house consulting)

ISO-NOW CORPORATION

ONE APPLE HILL
SUITE 316
LOEHMANN'S PLAZA, ROUTE 9E
NATICK, MA 01760
Phone: 508-651-0996
FAX: 508-655-4066

The ISO-NOW Corporation was founded to assist companies in all phases of ISO 9000 implementation. The firm's professional staff has technical expertise reducing quality assurance programs to practice. As a result, ISO-NOW can expedite the compliance process and guide client companies efficiently and rapidly through the maze of regulations in the ISO 9000 system.

Consulting Expertise:

The ISO-NOW Corporation staff consists of senior technical managers, quality engineers and trainers. They have led quality control departments for major corporations. They have experience in plants passing the rigorous ISO 9000 registration standards.

The staff's technical background includes chemical, mechanical, process engineering and IC manufacturing. They have expertise specific to your industry and your particular functional needs. They are experienced in supporting project management, teaching and factory training programs.

The staff teaches ASQC courses and has authored SPC texts. The principals are ISO 9000 certified lead assessors. They are experts in reducing TQM training and internal auditing to practice. They are specialists in adapting statistical QC and design experiments to specific applications.

When you work with ISO-NOW Corporation, you are working with specially chosen experts who:

- Work with your management team to develop an overall ISO 9000 program strategy
- Assess your current status vs. the standards
- Identify areas requiring improvement - documentation, process, purchasing, traceability, inspection and test
- Coach your functional managers on how to implement the ISO 9000 program
- Perform a final, full pre-registration audit to catch oversights and speed certification

In House Facilitation Programs:

- Initial site visit and program evaluation
- Internal audit training (to ISO 10011 standard)
- Document review (Quality Manual compliance check)
- Site audit (written assessment of the operating QMS)
- Subsystem implementation modules
  - Document control
  - Process control
  - Design control
  - Contract review
  - Management review
  - Vendor certification
  - Traceability

Seminars include:

- Qualifying for ISO 9000 certification

JAMES LAMPRECHT, ISO 9000 CERTIFIED CONSULTANCY AND TRAINING

1420 N.W. GILMAN BOULEVARD
SUITE 2576
ISSAQUAH, WA 98027-7001
Phone: 206-644-9504
FAX: 206-557-8905

Dr. Lamprecht has over twenty years of experience as a consultant, lecturer and researcher in the fields of industrial statistics, economic development and total quality management. As an independent consultant, Dr. Lamprecht spent two years consulting in Europe (UK, France, Norway, N. Ireland, Spain and Germany), on issues relating to ISO 9000 implementation and registration, Statistical Process Control, Design of Experiments, supplier audits, team facilitating, company surveys, quality system implementation, problem-solving techniques and other related activities.

Highlights of Dr. Lamprecht's experience include:

- Leading over two dozen ISO 9000 public seminars conducted throughout the U.S. and France
- Conducting half a dozen in-house ISO 9000 seminars
- Assisting several companies implement an ISO 9000 quality system
- Reviewing and editing quality manuals for a variety of industries
- Internal auditor training for a subsidiary of a U.S. multinational
- Helping design and implement a quality management system for a Norwegian aluminum plant
- Designing an experiment which helped save tens of thousands of dollars on a aluminum coating process in Wales, UK
- Performing ISO 9000 pre-audits for half a dozen European firms
- Conducting European seminars on supplier evaluation for a major multinational
- Developing a quality system for three major subsidiaries of an American firm
- Presenting seminars in the U.S. and Europe, on ISO 9000 implementation strategy, Statistical Process Control, Total Quality Management, Acceptance Sampling, and SPC for non-manufacturing applications
- Training and leading Quality Circle teams in problem-solving activities

Services:

- ISO pre-assessment audit is designed to:
  - Evaluate, compare and contrast current quality assurance system with the ISO 9000 series requirements
  - Determine how much resources will be required to achieve registration
- In house implementation seminars on the ISO 9000 series. The seminar focuses who will need to do what by when (2-3 days)
- Half-day executive seminar presenting an overview of ISO 9000: What it is? Who should consider registration? How much does it cost?
- Consultancy, review and editing on all aspects of ISO documentation requirements and suggested formats including quality manuals
- Internal audit seminars/workshop (2-4 days)
- Pre-assessments
- Certification Audits

Professional Affiliation:

American Society for Quality Control: ISO 9000 Assessor Certified: IQA (London) and AFAQ (France)

Other Related Activities:

Certificate of completion for the following courses:

- Team Facilitator Training for Continuous Improvement. Tennessee Associates
- Managing for Consistency. Tennessee Associates
- Executive Course in Managing for Consistency. Tennessee Associates
- An explanation of Taguchi's Contributions to Quality Improvement. College of Engineering. University of Wisconsin.
- Simulation Modeling for Decision Making. The Institute for Professional Education
- ISO 9000 Lead Assessor Training Course. Passed course approved by the Assessor Registration Board (UK) (1991)

Papers and Publications Relating to Quality:

- "Demystifying the ISO 9000 Series Standards," published in Volume IV, no. 2 issue of Quality Engineering (1992)
- "The Significance of the International Standards Organization ISO 9000 Series for the Drilling and Production Related Businesses," Oil and Gas Journal May 6, 1991 issue
- "How to Become ISO 9000 Certified," Oil and Gas Journal, May 6, 1991 issue
- "The ISO 9000 Certification Process: Some Important Issues to Consider" in the August, 1991 issue of Quality Digest
- "ISO 9000: Strategies for the 1990s" in the November, 1991 issue of Quality
- Book: ISO 9000: Preparing for Registration. Published by Marcel Dekker, April 1992.
- Implementing the ISO 9000 Series - Marcel Dekker, March 1993
- Qualite a la Francaise, Quality Progress, June 1993

JSJ GROUP, LTD.

P.O. Box 18235
ROCHESTER, NY 14618-0235
Phone: 716-247-8900
FAX: 716-426-2164

Since The JSJ Group commenced operations in 1981, it has served many clients in the area of review of chemical reactions, pharmaceutical reactions, polymerization processes, pollution processes, and minerals processes through lecturing, training and specific consultation on reaction kinetic problems.

This includes both the process for production of chemicals and for treatment of hazardous and toxic materials. The reaction kinetic problems are similar for the two areas.

The experience has encompassed pollution control including review of the biological processes for secondary waste treatment.

The services provided by The JSJ Group, Ltd. include expert witness testimony as well as a broad range of other technical support.

Pilot Plant Assistance

For new processes, particularly those involving agitation or gas liquid mass transfer, the appropriate pilot procedure can be developed to allow generation of the correct data for scale up within reasonable limits of operating parameters. Specific analysis of results has been provided to determine reaction rate control versus mass transfer control steps so that an accurate breakdown of the separate steps can be made for scale up purposes. Scale up calculations will be made and process specifications written for the full-scale installation.

Process Trouble-Shooting

Often, after installation, process or formulation changes may affect the results of the entire production run. On occasion, equipment may not live up to its warranty rating, causing the problems. It is often difficult to trouble-shoot the process to determine what the point of the problem is. The JSJ Group provides services in this area for many operations, including mixing of liquids, oxidation reactions, hydrogenation syntheses, biological reactions, dry powders and solids, and pastes and viscous materials.

Equipment Testing

The JSJ Group, Ltd. can provide specific test procedures for checking performance warranties on equipment, and is prepared to supervise such test work in conjunction with the supplier and the purchaser.

Testimony

The JSJ Group, Ltd. has provided assistance in legal matters doing research on the process for attorneys to prepare the case, direct consultation with attorneys and clients in preparing the case, and testimony, where required.

Basil Michel, the principal of The JSJ Group, Ltd. is a registered Professional Engineer in New York State and has excellent credentials as the author of many technical articles impacting the process of materials for production of chemicals as well as for pollution abatement.

The JSJ Group has a unique capability of technical and commercial experience to bring to bear on equipment and process performance in a wide variety of industries. Its president, Basil J. Michel, has over

20 years of experience within the corporate structure where he has held increasingly responsible positions in technical areas. His credentials include significant experience in the research and development area at Mixing Equipment Company, the manufacturers of Lightning Mixers, where he was the author of over 50 research reports, and ultimately had the responsibility for all research and development at the vice presidential level.

He has been a guest lecturer at technical society meetings and seminars on a variety of subjects covering many industries throughout the United States and Europe. As a member of the American Institute of Chemical Engineers, he has contributed by speaking at their meetings. He is currently on the speaking staff of Chemical Process Magazine Seminars and was a contributor at the American Institute of Engineers Diamond Jubilee meeting in Washington DC in 1983.

BUSINESS DEVELOPMENT SERVICES

There is a broad mix of companies supplying equipment and instrumentation to the chemical process, biomedical (pharmaceutical), minerals processing, water treatment and pollution control industries. Some companies need new products to supplement mature lines. Others are in the start-up phases, needing marketing and technical assistance to commercialize their products. Some want to make the transition from good products suppliers to technology oriented products influencing process results.

The JSJ Group, Ltd., through its internal resources and a network of consultants provides strong business, marketing and technical leadership for all of these companies. Since 1981, The JSJ Group, Ltd. has handled over 50 projects in various areas for companies ranging in size from start-up companies of a few hundred thousand dollars a year to established firms of over $100 million. The range of problems from start-up companies to companies in transition to companies with mature product lines has been served by The JSJ Group in one capacity or another. The scope of projects includes:

New product introduction and marketing

Working with inventors and researchers, The JSJ Group has prepared audiovisual presentations, sales force training guides, technical sales manuals, and has assisted in setting appropriate advertising programs.

Technology transfer

Through new product searches for already established products in other parts of the world which can be directly licensed into existing manufacturing facilities, or technical developments and inventions which are ready for the applications of strong mechanical and process development efforts on the part of the U.S. company have been handled successfully by The JSJ Group. Through a network of foreign consultants, projects are screened and brought directly to executives, saving time, travel and energy while companies still pursue the new product avenues of interest to them.

Business planning

Running the gamut from full strategic planning to reviews of procedures from a sales standpoint, forecasting for production scheduling and inventory control, review of the competitor's status in the marketplace, including financial, product and marketing, have been handled on a regular basis for clients on a retainer basis and on a spot basis for other companies.

KASTLE CONSULTING GROUP
P.O. Box 207
Englewood, OH 45322
Phone: 513-890-6416

Kastle Consulting Group is a full service manufacturing/quality assurance management consulting firm. They offer management consulting services that help companies become successful in producing high quality products and services. They strive to promote development of Quality Management Standards for the express purpose of improving operating efficiency, productivity, and product quality, while reducing costs.

KCG also provides a wide variety of easy to use software application programs. Training programs for individuals and groups on the ISO 9000 series standards are available. In addition, the firm is actively engaged in providing complete consulting services to firms seeking ISO 9000 certification. KCG is committed to helping companies gain that winning edge.

ISO 9000 CONSULTING SERVICES

Strategic ISO 9000 Quality System Planning

KCG will lead the management group through a strategic process to decide which ISO 9000 standard to pursue, what resources are required, where your system currently stands versus ISO 9000, prepare a project budget and schedule, and in general help you to get started.

Review Quality Manual

A KCG consultant with knowledge of ISO 9000 requirements and quality system auditing experience will review the organization's Quality Manual for compliance with ISO 9000, at any stage from first draft through pre-registration audit.

Quality System Audits

An onsite pre-assessment audit of the organization will be conducted to determine if your quality system complies with ISO 9000 and is fully functional. The KCG team may include a qualified and experienced auditor from your organization.

Other KCG Consulting

Many other KCG Quality Management and Manufacturing Management consulting and training offerings are available to sites working toward ISO 9000 certification and implementing a quality system. KCG has extensive experience in all aspects of Quality and Manufacturing Management Systems, including statistical methods, corrective action systems, vendor performance improvement programs, continuous improvement, and problem-solving.

QUALITY CONSULTING SERVICES

- Total Quality Management
  - Assessment, training, implementation
- ISO 9000 Series Standards
  - Pre-certification assessments, quality audits,
  - Quality manual preparation, implementation
- Military Standards (MIL-Q-9858 & MIL-I-45208)
  - Assessment, conformance, implementation

- Statistical Process Control
- Subcontractor Management Systems Analysis
- Corrective Action Systems Evaluation
    - Internal and external
- Cost of Quality
    - Measurement techniques, cost reduction
- Malcolm Baldrige Award Criteria

MANUFACTURING CONSULTING

- Master Schedule and Planning
- Capacity/Capability Assessment and Planning
- Make-Or-Buy Assessment and Planning
- Subcontract Management
- Design/Producibility/Concurrent Engineering
- Critical Processes/Materials
- Manufacturing Planning and Cost Analysis
- Production Control
- Work Measurement/Learning Curves

KEVIN DRAYTON ASSOCIATES

190 Fox Road
Dalton, MA 01226
Phone: 413-684-4648

Kevin Drayton Associates helps companies and organizations prepare for the process of registration to ISO 9000 series specifications. Emphasis is placed on education and corrective actions. Kevin Drayton is himself a Certified Lead Assessor, educated by British Standards Industries personnel and certified through Rochester Institute of Technology.

In-House Consulting:

When hired as on-site consultants, Drayton Associates undertakes the process of evaluating present systems and processes in relation to anticipated registration level. Drayton Associates duplicates the process of assessment that is followed by auditors from registration bodies. This assessment furnishes the data necessary to devise corrective actions and formulate strategies of system implementation and maintenance. The firm's goal is to provide counsel and guidance that, when enacted, positions companies strategically for registration. Drayton Associates can be available at the time of the actual registration assessment to aid with the process and provide needed information.

Kevin Drayton Associates' in-house service consists of the following:

- Review of quality plans and documentation
- Data collection via audit
- Development of corrective actions

This systematic approach provides detailed information as to systems readiness and involves key personnel at every step. All findings are constantly provided for management review to insure that sound decisions are made for the particular business.

Workshops:

The firm has devised workshops that focus on training personnel in the requirements of the ISO 9000 series. The workshops are intense educational experiences, and participants gain a working knowledge of what the specifications mean, how they are interpreted, and how they can benefit their particular organization in preparing for registration.

Workshops teach participants how to:

- Define registration to meet customer needs
- Measure and monitor progress in preparing for registration
- Prepare for external audits
- Structure an effective Quality Manual
- Effectively maintain registration
- Qualify for ISO 9000 Registration

Supplier Certification/Validation:

Kevin Drayton Associates provides services in the area of third party certification and validation of suppliers. The firm ensures that the suppliers you have chosen or are in the process of selecting have the capabilities and capacities necessary to make your relationship a success. The firm's personnel also perform inspections of product, audits of supplier facilities, and can take on program/project management tasks on-site in your behalf. Because the firm's entire business has TQM as its core, the personnel who represent you through Kevin Drayton Associates have as their goal not only the assurance that quality product is shipped, but that the teaming relationship which is a vital part of TQM is nurtured. They take the time to determine quality requirements and specifications as well as those process items which are critical to the particular application. Items released from a supplier's facility by inspection staff will not be subject to the tedious return-after-inspection loop.

Internal/External Audits:

Kevin Drayton Associates also provides expertise in preparing and implementing audit plans. It is a well-known fact that unless systems are constantly measured against some known criteria, they tend to decline in effectiveness. They disintegrate. The firm provides audit capabilities both at your facility and that of suppliers. Whether your needs are for audits to specs such as MIL-I-45208, MIL-Q-9858, or specially tailored plans of your own design, the firm can ensure quality performance. Drayton Associates provides guidance in preparing your company for corporate or government audits, such as Product Configuration Audits and Configured Item Verification Reviews.

The firm's process of preparing clients for registration is closely linked to TQM philosophy. By utilizing a team approach to document preparation and training, and by gathering empirical data as to the state of the present quality system, Drayton Associates ensures that knowledge of the quality system is spread throughout the organization and commitment to corrective action is attained.

The firm's background stems from many years within the General Electric Aerospace industry and a complete familiarity with specifications such as MIL-I-45208 and MIL-Q-9858. The staff's experience covers a wide range, from metal fabrication to electronic test and assembly, including service organizations. That knowledge is invaluable in assessing the needs of diverse industries preparing for registration.

Certification by British Standards Institute as Lead Assessors for ISO 9000 gives Kevin Drayton Associates the ability to focus on known areas of deficiency and gather data using the same techniques employed by the registrars themselves.

LLOYD'S REGISTER TECHNICAL SERVICES, INC.
ONE CORPORATE PLAZA
2525 BAY AREA BOULEVARD
SUITE 690
HOUSTON, TX 77058
Phone: 713-480-5008
FAX: 713-480-5313

Lloyd's Register is the world's oldest and largest ship classification society; it has also been long established in the industrial and offshore inspection fields. With more than 1500 surveyors located at over 240 offices and operating in more than 100 countries, LR offers more widespread and intensive international coverage than any similar organization. Wherever in the world Quality Assurance is required, there is an office locally.

The world's leading ship classification society has ensured the highest standards of materials and workmanship in ship construction for over 230 years. Fifty years ago, the experience and reputation gained with ships led to a demand for LR inspection in many other fields of industrial construction and manufacture. Today, Quality Assurance has come to the fore in industry and, once again, Lloyd's Register is a leader in the field.

QUESTIONS AND ANSWERS ABOUT LLOYD'S REGISTER TECHNICAL SERVICES, INC.

What can LR offer the high volume producer?

Engineering integrity. This is essential in modern industrial products, to ensure safety and reliability in service; LR believes this is best achieved by the implementation of comprehensive quality assurance systems. The firm's long experience in establishing such systems is available worldwide.

And for the smaller operator?

The same integrity. The needs may differ; overall the aim is the same - to provide an efficient, safe product at a competitive price.

What range of consultancy can LR provide?

Lloyd's Register offers services for supplier assessment, national and customer standards, assistance in developing quality manuals and the assessment of quality management systems once established. Whatever your QA problems, LR can provide help. Extensive laboratory facilities enable the firm to verify product quality as part of the overall consideration of a client's manufacturing system.

But what if I don't manufacture anything?

Quality Assurance is just as important, and LR understands there are often instances when the need for Quality Assurance goes unrecognized in service industries. The firm's experience in these areas puts Lloyd's Register in an unrivaled position to help.

Is the development of a QA system cost-effective?

Without doubt. Many companies testify to this. Technical journals regularly publish papers quoting significant reductions both in scrapped and defective products and in quality appraisal costs (inspection, tests, trouble-shooting, etc.) resulting from the fact that quality is built in at every stage. Such cost reductions far outweigh the additional costs of operating an effective quality assurance system.

Indeed, many companies report that their QA systems have resulted in additional sales - and increased profits.

Will LR assist in preparing for a formal QA assessment under the UK Government scheme?

Yes. Assistance can be provided on a direct basis or through the agency of the UK DTI Enterprise Initiative. Since the UK Government's Strategy for Quality was published in 1982, many companies have received financial assistance to commission a QA consultant help them prepare for a formal QA assessment by a third party certification body. In many instances the QA consultant has been LR. Even if you do not qualify for this scheme LR can still help you on a consultancy basis.

How does a company proceed from here?

You will almost certainly find that you can benefit from professional advice on setting up or improving your quality systems. LR tailors its services to meet your needs, so the firm recommends you ask about your specific requirements. Advice is available without obligation.

Assessing quality management systems on a consultancy basis:

Having already assessed some of the most complex and successful quality management systems in the world in both shipyards and manufacturing industry, LR is well placed to advise any client on a consultancy basis. At whatever state of development a quality management system stands, LR can help further its progress. As a firm's order book moves up-market, so its customers' quality assurance demands become more and more exacting; formal assessment to achieve and maintain higher quality standards will be imposed. LR consultancy can help ensure these new requirements are achieved as assessments become more demanding, so it becomes vital that quality-related activities fully reflect the system documented in your Quality Manual.

WHAT LLOYD'S REGISTER'S QUALITY ASSURANCE SERVICE MEANS TO YOU

As a manufacturer...

- The benefits of a half century of experience in manufacturing industry
- Third party advice on the development of your quality management systems to any national or international quality assurance standard nominated
- Expert assistance in the creation or improvement of a quality manual and associated documentation
- Independent assessment of your quality management systems, with recommendations for essential corrective action. LR can carry out these assessments to any national or international quality assurance standard nominated
- Specialist help in preparing for a quality audit or a third party assessment

As a client...

- The benefits of LR's worldwide experience in Quality Assurance
- The skilled services of well qualified, experienced QA consultants
- Expert assistance with applying QA standards
- Your supplier assessed to any QA standard

AFFILIATE COMPANY SERVICES

An affiliate company, Lloyds Register Quality Assurance, Ltd. is listed separately as a third party registration organization.

LOWE & ASSOCIATES
P.O. Box 130
Middlebury, CT 06762-0130
Phone: 203-754-8633

Lowe & Associates helps clients to manage for quality. James A. Lowe, Jr., Principal, offers consulting, implementing and training services. Lowe & Associates works with clients on all elements of a Total Quality Management (TQM) system. As well, Lowe and Associates aids clients and their staff in preparing for registration to the ISO 9000 series of standards.

System Audit:

An evaluation of the internal quality systems and procedures as detailed in the ANSI/ASQC Q90 and ISO 9000 series standards for Quality Systems Elements.

System Documentation:

Assisting clients with documenting their Quality Management System

System Implementation:

Educating Clients' employees to follow and improve on the company's quality management system

ISO 9000 Registration Process

Guiding clients' staff through the steps of ISO 9000 registration

Quality Systems Implementation & Training:

Assistance in developing:
- Quality plans
- Quality objectives
- Milepost
- Cost of quality program
- Customer focus requirements: Internal and External
- Supplier audits
- Statistical process control applications and techniques
- Group problem solving techniques
- Measuring and analyzing work processes
- Team leadership
- Self-directed work groups

MANAGEMENT SYSTEMS ANALYSIS, INC.

P.O. Box 136
ROYERSFORD, PA 19468
Phone: 215-948-8387

Management Systems Analysis, Inc. is managed by James Highlands, who has over 20 years experience in the field of quality. This includes his consulting work with Management Systems Analysis and previous positions with Bechtel Corporation, where he provided auditing and consulting services to many of the major projects throughout North America.

These positions and his consulting work with Management Systems Analysis have included extensive experience in Quality and Management System, systems development and evaluation. Clients include well-known companies which range from multinationals to small and medium-size enterprises.

The company currently provides consulting services in system development, auditing and evaluation for the nuclear, defense and commercial industries; including consulting in the ISO 9000 Standards, the ASME Code, ANSI/ASME NQA-1, and the Military Standards.

SERVICES AVAILABLE INCLUDE:

Consulting Services:

MSA offers experienced consultants to assist your company in the following areas:

- Quality Systems Evaluation - development and implementation of quality systems and procedures
- Technical Support - evaluation of quality and technical requirements necessary to meet customer, industry or government requirements - prudency reviews
- Internal Analysis/Audit of organizational effectiveness including recommendation of corrective action necessary.

Audits and Surveys:

MSA's certified personnel can perform vendor or supplier audits or surveys using a company's approved forms or those of MSA. MSA will document all deficiencies for evaluation and corrective action or, by request, will perform the follow-up activities. Personnel are qualified to ANSI N45.2.23-78, ASME NQA-1, and ISO 10011.

Manual Preparation:

MSA can update or completely rewrite Quality Assurance Manual and procedures to comply with industry standards or government regulations. All manuals are customized to the facility and based upon the established system wherever possible.

Seminars:

MSA can conduct training seminars in the areas of quality systems and standards, and auditing, at the client's facility, stressing practical applications of applicable standards, auditing and surveying techniques.

MAUCH & ASSOCIATES

2460 WISCONSIN AVENUE
DOWNERS GROVE, IL 60515
Phone: 708-352-4301

Mauch & Associates provides services in three separate areas. First, consulting is provided in Total Quality Management (TQM) and ISO 9000 quality systems. Second, the firm conducts supplier audits to the ISO 9000 standards, serving as pre-assessment audits to ISO registration. Third, the firm offers training courses in Quality Control Management, inspection management principles, Statistical Process Control (SPC), quality cost accounting, and quality engineering techniques. Clients also receive administrative assistance with preparing quality manuals, procedures and forms development.

Mauch & Associates has worked with over 60 businesses developing quality systems based upon the ISO 9000 requirements since 1987. The firm works exclusively in the United States implementing ANSI/ASQC Q90 Quality Systems.

Mauch & Associates offers its clients:

- Management Overview
- QC Training
- Pre-Assessment Audits
- Quality System Critiques
- Documentation Critiques
- Policy Critique
- Compliance Pre-Audit
- ASQC Certified Quality Auditors
- ASQC Certified Quality Engineers
- ASQC Certified Reliability Engineers

Consulting Services:

In addition to Total Quality Management, Mauch & Associates offers services which specialize in developing individual elements in a Quality program. These elements may include: incoming inspection, audit, reliability, in-process inspection, design of experiments, and calibration. The firm also provides the follow administrative assistance:

- Quality Manual Preparation: With the European Economic Community ISO 9000 registration program requiring a comprehensive evaluation of your quality manual and program, your manual must meet their requirements.
- Inspection Procedure Development: Technical writing capabilities needed to insure that your inspection procedures communicate your requirements exactly.
- Test Procedure Development: Technical writing capabilities needed to insure that your test procedures communicate your requirements exactly.
- Quality Information System Development: Pull all your information together into a complete information system. Managing your quality Data base effectively will help provide your company with vital performance information when it's needed. Mauch & Associates can help you with your information systems needs.

AUDITING SERVICES

Quality Audits are a management tool used to evaluate, confirm, or verify activities related to Quality. These audits are conducted using a positive and constructive process. These audits help prevent problems in the organization being audited through the identification of activities liable to create future problems.

Type: Facility Review
Standard Applied: Internal
Application: To determine whether a potential supplier has a process capable of producing quality products or services
Elements Audited:

- Company Background
- Personnel
- Products/Services
- Plant Facilities
- Specialty Manufacturing
- External Influences
- Design Engineering

- Material Control
- Manufacturing
- Human Factors
- Capacity
- Repair
- Service Support
- Quality overview

Type: Quality Systems Analysis
Standard Applied: ANSI/ASQC Q91-1987 (ISO 9001)
Application: Design/Development, Production, Installation and Servicing
Elements Audited:

- Management Responsibility
- Quality System Principles
- Contract Review
- Documentation Control
- Purchasing
- Purchasing Supplied Product
- Product Identification and Traceability
- Process Control
- Inspection and Testing
- Inspection, Measuring, and Test Equipment

- Inspection and Test Status
- Control of Non-conforming Product
- Corrective Action
- Handling, Storage, Packaging, and Delivery
- Quality Records
- Internal Audits
- Training
- Servicing
- Statistical Techniques

Type: Quality Systems Analysis
Standard Applied: ANSI/ASQC Q92-1987 (ISO 9002)
Application: Production and Installation
Elements Audited:

- Management Responsibility
- Quality System Principles
- Contract Review
- Documentation Control
- Purchasing
- Purchasing Supplied Product
- Product Identification and Traceability
- Inspection and Testing
- Inspection, Measuring, and Test Equipment

- Inspection and Test Status
- Control of Non-conforming Product
- Corrective Action
- Handling, Storage, Packaging, and delivery
- Quality Records
- Internal Audits
- Training
- Statistical Techniques

Type: Quality Systems Analysis
Standard Applied: ANSI/ASQC Q93-1987 (ISO 9003)
Application: Final Inspection and Test
Elements Audited:

- Management Responsibility
- Documentation Control
- Product Identification
- Inspection and Testing
- Inspection, Measuring, and Test Equipment
- Inspection and Test Stations

- Control of Non-conforming Product
- Corrective Action
- Handling, Storage, Packaging, and delivery
- Quality Records
- Training
- Statistical Techniques

Type: Quality Systems Analysis
Standard Applied: ANSI/ASQC Q94-1987 (ISO 9004)
Application: Quality Management and System
Elements Audited:

- Management Responsibility
- Quality System Principles
- Economics (Quality Costs)
- Quality in Marketing
- Quality in Specification and Design
- Quality in Procurement
- Quality in Production
- Control of Production
- Product Verification

- Calibration System
- Non-Conformity Control
- Corrective Action System
- Handling and Post Production Functions
- Quality Documentation and Records
- Personnel
- Product Safety and Liability
- Statistical Methods

TRAINING SERVICES

Open-enrollment seminars related to ISO 9000 include:

- Quality Audit Principles
- Quality Engineering Exam Review

MOODY-TOTTRUP INTERNATIONAL, INC.

350 McKnight Plaza Building
105 Braunlich Drive
Pittsburgh, PA 15237
Phone: 412-366-5567
Fax: 412-366-5571

Moody-Tottrup International aims to service the quality requirements of all types of organizations by providing Quality Assurance Consultancy, Training and Auditing services to businesses who intend, or have started, to implement a quality assurance management system which meets the requirements of the revised ISO 9000 and ANSI/ASQC Q90, along with other recognized Quality Systems Specifications.

Moody-Tottrup International offers the following services:

I. Consultancy
- Advice and assistance to companies for development of a Quality Assurance Management System
- Implementation of a Quality Management System, TQM, and the Quality image in the company
- Development of Quality Assurance systems to enable a company to be certified in accordance with the ISO 9000 Quality Assurance standards

II. Training
- Quality Assurance training of personnel in the understanding and implementation of the ISO 9000 Standards
- Quality Assurance seminars for ISO 9000
- ISO 9000 Home Study Course
- ISO 9000 Registered Lead Assessor Certification course

III. Auditing Services
- Moody-Tottrup can provide various auditing services such as:
  - ISO 9000 adequacy and compliance audits
  - Independent third party for internal audits
  - Supplier audits for Supplier Certification
  - Pre-assessment of the Quality System for ISO 9000

ISO 9000 Quality Awareness Seminar

Moody-Tottrup offers seminars for companies requiring training for Awareness, Overview, Interpretation, and Implementation of the ISO 9000 Quality Assurance requirements. The seminar can be held at the facility of your choice.

Moody-Tottrup will provide:
- An informative, open forum seminar to provide all of your answers and details on ISO 9000
- A certificate of training for each attendee
- The relevant set of ISO 9000 Quality Standards

ISO 9000 Implementation Workshop

Moody-Tottrup offers a workshop for Implementation of ISO 9000 providing training for writing ISO 9000 QA Manuals, QA Procedures, and Work instructions for companies requiring more in-depth training for ISO 9000 Quality Assurance Requirements. The seminar can be held at the facility of your choice.

Moody-Tottrup will provide:
- An informative, hands on workshop to provide all of your answers and details of ISO 9000
- A workshop that involves and encourages participation from all attendees

- A certificate of training for each attendee
- The relevant set of ISO 9000 Quality Standards

ISO 9000 Procedures Writing Workshop

Moody-Tottrup offers a workshop for Implementation of ISO 9000 providing training for writing ISO 9000 QA Manuals, QA Procedures, and Work instructions for companies requiring more in-depth training for ISO 9000 Quality Assurance Requirements. The seminar can be held at the facility of your choice.

Moody-Tottrup will provide:
- An informative, hands-on workshop to provide all of your answers and details of ISO 9000
- A workshop that involves and encourages participation from all attendees
- A certificate of training for each attendee
- The relevant set of ISO 9000 Quality Standards
- Details for proper format for writing procedures and work instructions per ISO 9000

ISO 9000 Home Study Course

ASQC (American Society of Quality Control) has formed RAB (Registrar Accreditation Board) to ensure quality among those who certify quality systems. RAB have approved the course studies of only 32 companies internationally. One of these is BMIQA Limited, a sister company of Moody-Tottrup. This course is available through Moody-Tottrup International.

There are 12 sections in the course package which can be studied at your own convenience. After each section there is an assessment question paper which should be completed and sent to Moody-Tottrup International for grading. The question papers will be returned by mail with any problem areas noted.

This course is not designed to turn you into a highly skilled quality manager but it will, subject to your own efforts, lay the foundation for a sound knowledge of the requirements of quality management and how this is affected by the ISO 9000 and ANSI/ASQC Q90 specification requirements.

The course has been designed for virtually anyone who is involved in, or interested in becoming involved in, the field of Quality Assurance or for those already involved and wishing to broaden their knowledge of system management. This course aims to enable the student to understand the actual working of a quality system without having to spend long periods on training away from the work place.

The course contents deals in-depth with the requirements of the major International Quality System Specifications ISO 9001 and ANSI/ASQC Q91.

This course has been recognized by the ASQC Certification Committee for their approval. They will recognize 1 Recertification Unit (RU) for completion of this course.

ISO 9000 Internal Auditor training Course

This ISO 9000 Internal Auditor Training Course has been developed from the ISO 9000 Lead Assessor Course of Moody-Tottrup's European sister company, BMIQA. Their Assessor course is registered with the IQA in the United Kingdom and also accepted by the RAB in the United States.

Currently assessment and ISO 9000 Registrar firms are now taking a closer look at how companies train their employees particularly for managing quality and internal audits. This course provides more than just informal training as the course will evaluate each attendee and also provides an examination.

The course is intended for those organizations who require their own personnel to be trained to carry out audit and assessment tasks within a quality management system environment. This course is suitable for attendees from any organization or business activity.

The requirements specified in ISO 10011 - International Standard Guide to Quality Systems Auditing is used as the guideline and taught throughout the course.

During this course, the principles and requirements of quality assurance management systems as specified in the ISO 9000 series of standards are considered in details in their application for any business concern. The course deals in-depth with the techniques for proper facilitation of auditing internal quality assurance systems.

The course is designed to be participative for all attendees. Examples of audits will be reviewed in case studies and attendees will be evaluated based on their performance during the course. A final examination will also be required at the end of the course to verify each attendee has retained the course objectives.

Successful applicants that pass all of the course and examination requirements will be awarded a Training Certificate and will be credited with 2.0 CEU's.

ISO 9000 Registered Lead Assessor Certification Course

Moody-Tottrup's European sister company, BMIQA, has developed this Registered Lead Assessor Course. It is recognized by the American Society of Quality Control Registrar Accreditation Board (RAB). Also, the course is registered with and approved by the National Registration Scheme for Assessors of Quality Systems administered by the Institute of Quality Assurance as meeting all the training course requirements. It meets the requirements of ISO 10011 International Standard Guide to Quality Systems Auditing, and is Registered with the IQA.

The course is intended for those organizations who require their personnel to be trained to carry out audit and assessment tasks within a Quality Management system environment. This course is suitable for attendees from any organization or business activity.

The requirements specified in ISO 10011 Parts 1 and 3 - 1991 Quality Systems Auditing are taught throughout this course as the basis of required auditing practices.

During this course, the principles and requirements of quality assurance management systems as specified in the ISO 9000 series of standards are considered in detail in their application of any business concern.

Reference is made to other QA standards and specifications commonly used, some of which have International recognition.

Course lectures have been prepared to include a high proportion of attendee participation. This includes exercises designed to emphasize the salient points of the lectures which cover company organization, documentation, design, procurement and quality assurance in the user environment.

Throughout the course, instruction is given in conducting audits and the planning, preparation, execution and follow-up actions required in order to ensure each audit is successful.

Extensive use is made of case studies which are studied each evening by groups of attendees who present their findings on the following morning to all course attendees. The case studies are designed to emphasize each section of the chosen standard and to bring out the techniques of audits.

The performance of each attendee is assessed throughout the course to enable the tutors to address any weak areas and to reach a decision on their ability to carry out audits and to ensure that each attendee has mastered and retained the course material. Both the attendees performance requirements and the examination have to be successfully achieved before a course pass certificate can be awarded.

The course tutors are practicing quality consultants, ISO 9000 Registered Lead Auditors and Registered accomplished trainers who have considerable experience of setting up, auditing, gaining registration of and managing Quality Management Systems which meets ISO 9000 requirements.

This course fulfills the requirements of the RAB for auditors wishing to become ISO 9000 Lead Assessors.

MOYE COMPANY LIMITED
59 Breadner Drive
Suite 102
Toronto, Ontario M9R 3M5
Canada
Phone: 416-248-9187
Fax: 416-248-9187

Moye Company offers unique programs on quality management to companies no matter what stage of development and degree of assistance and services they may require. Moye's 8-step program has been categorized to help companies assess their needs based on where they are on the road to ISO 9000 quality system registration.

CONCEPT STAGE

A company is contemplating the development and ultimately registration to the ISO 9000 Quality Management Standards.

Step 1 - Documentation Review

A review of the existing documentation of a company will assist in determining the viability of seeking ISO 9000 registration and provide a roadmap. A review of your existing documentation will determine if you have the 17 procedures and 14 types of records required as a minimum by ISO 9001.

Step 2 - Awareness

This executive presentation provides insight into the political and international trade implications of ISO 9000. Executives will acquire an excellent appreciation of the benefits of implementing an ISO 9000 program, time to develop and implement a quality system, why your company should become registered, and the time and costs of becoming registered.

STARTUP

Commitment to an ISO 9000 quality system exists but work has not fully commenced.

Step 3 - Quality Training

A course that provides: an overview of the ISO 9000 standards, explanation of ISO 9001, guidance on registration and registrars, and shortcuts to ISO 9000 registration. Training involves participants in the writing of their company's quality manual by means of hands-on experience.

Step 4 - Selling up Implementation Teams

Get the maximum from using the Consensus Principle to develop and implement an ISO 9000 Quality System. Guidelines for setting up the infrastructure for expeditious development and implementation of a ISO quality system will be developed.

INTERMEDIATE

A plateau in the development and implementation of an ISO 9000 Quality System can cause frustration even to the point of a company abandoning development of its quality system.

Step 5 - Development of an ISO 9000 Quality System

Consultants with industry and ISO 9000 experience can make the writing of a Quality Manual and its implementation easy to understand and applicable to your company. Experts are available every step of the way during the development process to make sure you are developing the quality manual and documentation expeditiously and correctly.

Step 6 - Pre-registration Assessment

An onsite visit will determine if a company is ready for ISO 9000 registration. The assessment identifies any deficiencies that may impede a successful registration. Typically, the assessment determines a company's position relative to the ISO 9000 requirements, accepted industry practices, and auditing practices used by registrars. Assessments are performed by experienced auditors.

MATURE

Is the registrar's auditor making reasonable interpretations of the ISO 9000 Standards? Assistance with a Registration Program in Canada, United States and Europe can be provided.

Step 7 - Registration Audit

The registration audit does not have to be a mysterious process. Experts with auditing experience and dealing with registrars can guide you through the registration process. You can rely on their past experience with registrars to help you achieve ISO 9000 registration.

Step 8 - Compliance Audit

Registration of your company's quality system should not be the final goal. Registrars perform a compliance audit to ensure that the company is continuing to meet the ISO 9000 requirements. Failure to continue to meet the requirements can result in the loss of registration. Experts on the ISO 9000 registration process with auditing experience can aid in maintaining registration.

N.C. KIST & ASSOCIATES, INC.
900 EAST PORTER AVENUE
NAPERVILLE, IL 60540
Phone: 708-357-1180
FAX: 708-357-3349

N.C. Kist & Associates, Inc. (NCK), formed in 1972 to meet the growing demands for organized expertise in developing quality programs to comply with requirements of codes and standards, offers a complete range of quality program and improvement services from a single source. The company's consultants are experts with hands-on experience in a variety of industries.

Kist & Associates, Inc. is experienced in quality programs for the manufacturing and service industries. Quality programs are developed to meet industry, national and international codes and standards including ASME, API, ISO 9000/ASQC Q90 series or combinations thereof.

Services of N.C. Kist & Associates:

Development of Total Quality Programs

Meeting one or more of the following Quality Program Standards:
- ASME FAP-I
- ASME NQA-I
- ASME Code, Sections, I, III and VIII
- National Board Inspection Code R, RV & NR
- ISO 9000 Series/ANSI/ASQC Q90 Series
- API Specification Q1
- MIL Standards
- AAR Spec for QAM-1003
- Malcolm Baldrige National Quality Award Criteria
- Quality Manual and Procedure Preparation or Review
- Quality Program Studies, Evaluation and Audits
- Strategic Quality Planning
- Hands-On Implementation Assistance
- Quality Improvement and Preventive Action
- Supplier Qualification and Quality Improvement
- Accreditation Survey Preparation

Customized Training and Seminars in:

- Quality Auditing/Auditor Qualification
- Statistical Process Control
- Problem-Solving Techniques
- Codes and Standards

Philosophy:

- Provide highly-qualified personnel
- Evaluate client needs
- Select and justify objectives
- Schedule consulting services efficiently
- Work "on-site" with client personnel
- Understand client methods of operation
- Develop a program that fits the client's system
- Provide training
- Provide hands-on implementation assistance
- Conduct audits/evaluations to determine program effectiveness

Consulting Services:

N.C. Kist has consulted for and audited manufacturers of wellhead equipment and oil field tubular goods, construction contractors, utilities, architect-engineers, equipment/pump/valve/pressure vessel manufacturers and a wide variety of material manufacturers. Recent audits have been to the requirements of ISO 9001 and 9002. The firm has also evaluated quality programs for geological research, hydrological tests and conducted strategic planning.

N.C. Kist has prepared ISO 9001/9002 Quality Manuals for various industries including organizations providing design, inspection, cleaning and field machining, and manufacturers of specialty paper, electronics, welding material, pipe and tubes, fiber drums, wellhead equipment, rails, fiber reinforced panels, non-toxic pigments and rubber products.

N.C. Kist Consultants participated in the QA Program enhancement at Argonne National Laboratory, including the preparation of Procedures and a QA Matrix. The company has also consulted for the United State Department of Energy and the U.S. Nuclear Regulatory Commission.

Seminar Services:

N.C. Kist has developed a course in ISO 9001/9002 as well as a course and examination in quality auditing which meets ISO 10011. This basic auditing course has been presented to over 50 organizations.

N.C. Kist & Associates Expertise:

Qualified professionals possess considerable experience, expertise and ability to observe practices, analyze situations and develop practical, workable solutions to problems. N.C. Kist is not a "body shop" that loads up the job with unnecessary personnel. The company's consultants stay current in codes and standards requirements by assisting at surveys and participating in quality meetings.

The N.C. Kist consultants are Quality Improvement experts that help clients develop a competitive edge. They do this by:

- Providing expertise, experience and skills that clients may not possess, and by helping them to accomplish objectives to which, quite often, their personnel are unable to devote adequate time.
- Offering an unbiased view that may be difficult to obtain within the company. By being independent, they are able to cut through organizational barriers to provide a fresh outlook, offering new and practical solutions to problems.
- Developing client skills by working with and training client personnel so that they can carry on the Quality Program on their own without continual dependence on the consultant.
- Proposing practical systems when needed, to meet common Quality Program requirements.
- Completing assignments expeditiously by using their expertise and experience to accomplish tasks in much less time than the client which also represents less total cost.

OMNI TECH INTERNATIONAL, LTD.
2715 ASHMAN STREET
SUITE 100
MIDLAND, MI 48640
Phone: 517-631-3377
FAX: 517-631-7360

Formed in 1986, Omni Tech International, Ltd. (OTI) has over 100 senior consulting associates with an average of 30 years CPI (chemical processing industry) experience in a wide variety of managerial/technical positions. Specific knowledge of quality standards, conformance, and auditing typified by the qualifications of Dr. Robert Belfit, Omni Tech president and Mr. Richard Hoff, Jack E. Weiler, Everett R. Eastman, and Steven E. Cobb, among several others. Dr. Belfit was formerly the manager of quality standards for the Dow Chemical Company and developed the training courses now taught by himself and others at Omni Tech. Weiler, Eastman, and Cobb are IQA Lead Assessors and RAB Lead Auditors. Hoff is an IQA Assessor, a RAB Lead Auditor, and a Lead Auditor for the American Iron and Steel institute.

Omni Tech offers a wide range of consulting services to its clients. These services fall into the following general categories:

Quality Systems Optimization
- Standards and Awards (described in full below)
- (Customer Market) Satisfaction Studies

Technology Commercialization
- Research
- Engineering
- Marketing

Environmental & Regulatory
- Health/Safety Compliance
- Industrial Hygiene
- Product Registration
- Environmental Audits
- Air, Water, Waste

Safety & Loss Prevention
- Product Stewardship Audits
- Accidental Investigation

Omni Tech's efforts in the Standards and Awards program fall into two basic categories:

Assessments:
- OTI conducts what are generally known as ISO certification assessments. Once a client has determined that registration under an ISO standard is needed, Omni Tech will assess the client's Quality Manual (if one exists) and Quality Systems to determine how well they comply with the criteria of the specific ISO standard. If these audits indicate that the client's manual and/or systems are not in compliance, Omni Tech will work with the client to develop the Quality Manual and to implement the Quality Systems required.

- The same type of work can be done to help clients comply with Awards criteria.

Training:

- OTI has developed a basic ISO 9000 course which can readily be adapted to cover ISO 9001 or ISO 9002. The course helps train the participant to understand what the standards criteria (which are usually quite generic) actually mean, how to apply the criteria to the participant's kind of business, and to anticipate what an auditor will be looking for when conducting the registration audit.

OTI has also developed an Auditor Training Program designed to prepare individuals to do ISO compliance audits (either in-house or for hire).

Gulf Coast Headquarters:
2600 South Loop W.
Suite 475-K
Houston, TX 77054
Phone: 713-661-7507
Fax: 713-661-2399

P-E HANDLEY-WALKER CO., INC.
17371 IRVINE BLVD.
SUITE 200
TUSTIN, CA 92680-3010
Phone: 714-730-0122
FAX: 714-730-0439

P-E Handley-Walker offers a complete range of consulting services to assist in the implementation of, and in obtaining certification to the ISO 9000 standard

ISO 9000 Consulting Services:

The experience and expertise the staff has gained will enable your organization to move through the certification process quickly and economically. Handley-Walker services are categorized in three phases:

Phase I - System Adequacy Audit:

This phase is designed to establish the effort required to bring existing systems up to ISO 9000 certification level.

- Determine Scope of Registration - ISO 9000 has three parts. It is necessary to determine which is to be used in order to establish the terms of reference of the audit.
- Perform Detailed Quality Systems Audit - Existing systems will be audited to ISO 9000 criteria and non-conformances will be identified.
- Prepare a Detailed Audit Report - Non-conformances will be documented along with recommended corrective action to bring systems into ISO 9000 compliance.
- Conduct Management Seminar - The top management team will be presented with a review of the ISO 9000 standard, areas where existing systems fall short and the corrective action required to achieve certification.
- Develop a Corrective Action Plan - Working closely with local management, a plan will be developed to bring areas of non-conformance into line with the standard.
- Create a Time-Phased Implementation Schedule - Work content in the corrective action plan will be compared with available resources to establish a realistic implementation schedule.

Phase II - ISO 9000 Implementation:

This phase addresses all activities required to implement the Standard to certification ready status.

- Form Project Steering Committee - Establish the organization which will carry the responsibility for achieving certification in the time frame defined.
- Prepare an Outline of Quality Systems Manual - The quality manual specifies how the system is operated and managed, where responsibilities lie and establishes a blueprint for the entire system.
- Conduct Employee Training - Training will be required to fully understand the standard, project manage the implementation and certification process, develop and document procedures and perform internal audits.
- Provide Support in the Preparation of Quality Documentation - In addition to a quality systems manual, ISO 9000 requires documented operating procedures, work instructions and various types of quality records.
- Select a Registration Agency - Selecting the right agency for your business and coordinating with them during the implementation process will expedite certification.
- Perform Implementation Reviews - To ensure departmental efforts meet all requirements of the standard, periodic implementation reviews must be conducted.

- Conduct Internal Quality System Audits - Periodic system audits are essential to build the corrective action history needed to obtain certification.

Phase III - Pre-Registration Audit:

This phase provides an unbiased, independent audit of the entire Quality System to identify any shortcomings that may have been overlooked.

- Perform Pre-Assessment Audit - A qualified lead assessor will conduct a simulated registration assessment to identify any potential problem areas.
- Initiate Corrective Action - Fix problems prior to official third party assessment which will help ensure certification is obtained first time through.

Although Handley-Walker can perform all functions required to successfully implement ISO 9000, the firm's experience and expertise can best be utilized in support of your own internal implementation team. Most clients value the staff's ability to: help interpret the standard vis-a-vis their industry, assist their staff where guidance and advice are needed, provide formal staff training and assist management to facilitate the implementation and certification process.

In the firm's view, it is essential that end users of the system play a major role in its implementation so that commitment, ownership and continuous improvement are well established within the organization. This will ensure certification is maintained over time and that the many financial benefits from a good quality system will be realized in improved bottom-line profitability.

Seminars include:

- ISO 9000 Seminar
- ISO 9000 Management Review
- ISO 9000 Preparation of Quality Documentation
- ISO 9000 Quality Systems Auditing
- ISO 9000 Implementation Course
- ISO 9000 Lead Assessor Certificate Course

U.S. Offices:

Western Region:
17371 Irvine Blvd., Suite #200
Tustin, CA 92680
(714) 730-0122

Eastern Region:
Corporate Plaza, Suite #100
6450 Rockside Woods Blvd.
Independence, Ohio 44131
(216) 328-9341

International Offices:

Dublin, London, Glasgow, Paris, Budapest, Hong Kong, Sydney, Curacao, N.A.

PATTON CONSULTANTS , INC.
4 COVINGTON PLACE
HILTON HEAD, SC 29928-7612
PHONE: 803-686-6650
FAX: 803-686-6651

Since 1976, Patton Consultants, Inc. (PCI) has been recognized as a world leader in practical assistance to management in customer service, equipment maintenance, logistics, quality, and support systems. PCI emphasizes service quality through consulting, seminars, publications and support systems. The firm has worked with the service and logistics organizations of four Baldrige winners and prepared several for ISO 9000 qualification. Patton can assist companies preparing for ISO 9000 certification of total internal and field service organizations and for equipment repair centers.

Consulting:

Patton Consultants' professionals provide a welcome balance of consulting, education and support systems. PCI:

- Understands the need for fundamentals done well
- Recognizes the opportunities for improvement through the application of technology and management science
- Advocates practical, action-oriented results
- Can prepare detailed reports, but emphasize direct presentation with opportunity for discussion
- Can assist with all phases of improvement projects from concept through completion

Every organization has different problems and needs. While your organization probably has many challenges PCI has seen before, there is likely also a unique set of uncorrected problems and opportunities yet to be realized. The first step - and the key to the problem/decision process - is setting objectives and goals. Patton Consultants can help write goals that are understandable, measurable, challenging and achievable. PCI can then help develop strategies, plan, organize, direct, staff, control, budget and manage better.

PCI's formula for success is to analyze the client's situation, compare it to PCI consultants' knowledge of what other similar organizations are doing and coming changes, identify problems as well as opportunities, recommend changes, and help implement improvements.

Consulting programs often include on-the-job fact finding surveys and evaluations, which offer high potential savings. Reports are usually presented face-to-face, with detailed recommendations and in-depth discussion to assure that personal concerns have been adequately considered.

Patton Consultants works within your organization to avoid disruption and build permanent improvement into your operations.

On-going Support:

Patton Consultants' relationship may include a "Continuing Support Agreement." This is a service contract for professional assistance to management. A continuing support agreement provides access to Patton Consultants.

PEAT MARWICK STEVENSON & KELLOGG, BYWATER

2300 YONGE STREET
TORONTO, ONTARIO M4P 1G2
CANADA
Phone: 416-482-4705
FAX: 416-482-5729

Peat Marwick Stevenson & Kellogg offers its Quality Management services in partnership with Bywater, a European-based quality consulting firm. Peat Marwick Stevenson & Kellogg has been offering Quality Management consulting and training services for over 20 years. Bywater is a European-based company dedicated to providing a wide range of consulting and training services in Quality Management to all sectors of industry. Together, the two firms have trained over 15,000 people since 1975. Over 650 registrations to an appropriate ISO 9000-Series standard have been achieved by domestic and international clients with the company.

Peat Marwick Stevenson & Kellogg is an employee-owned firm of Management Consultants that has been serving clients for more than 80 years. Peat Marwick Stevenson & Kellogg is affiliated with Peat Marwick Thorne, chartered accountants and internationally with KPMG (Klynveld Peat Marwick Goerdeler). With KPMG offices in more than 120 other countries, they provide consistent value-added service on a global basis.

The Benefits of Quality Strategy

Peat Marwick Stevenson & Kellogg work with organizations to develop a balanced Quality Management strategy which will lead to long-term change and sustainable benefits. Their approach is based on helping companies develop the process, culture and elements needed to assure competitive advantage. Part of your strategy will be based on looking at the organization as a series of linked processes, designed to achieve customer requirements and bottom-line results.

Professional Services for ISO 9000 Quality Management and Quality Assurance Systems

Their ISO Quality Management and Assurance Practice is built on a proven methodology rather than just a philosophy. This experience eliminates guesswork, trial, and error, and capitalizes on an approach that has produced proven results in more than 450 domestic and international companies. They divide these capabilities into three principal areas:

- Consulting and support services
    - Quality system assessment
    - ISO 9000 quality strategy and detailed planning
    - Enterprise process analysis
    - ISO 9000 quality implementation and support
    - Customized pre-registration assessment

- Customized and public education and training
    - ISO 9000 quality management overview
    - Executive and management workshop on quality
    - Planning and implementing quality systems
    - Integrating and implementing HACCP with ISO 9000
    - Quality documentation and procedure development skills
    - Quality system auditing
    - ISO 9000 Lead Auditor course
    - How to prepare a quality manual for ISO 9001 and 9002

- Self-instruction services for smaller organizations
  - The ByDAC package for ISO 9000 registration
  - The ByWORD package for Total Quality management implementation and ISO 9000 registration

CONSULTING AND SUPPORT SERVICES

Peat Marwick Stevenson & Kellogg quality practitioners are available to assist and work with you in the quality management process leading to ISO 9000 Series registration. In addition to ISO 9000 development and implementation support, they can assist you to prepare for other quality standard registrations such as HACCP, CSA-Z299 Series, MIL-Q-/AQAP, TFE, and many others. They also assist many organizations with their efforts to implement the guidelines of the Malcolm Baldrige Award and the Canadian Award for Business Excellence.

Quality System Assessment

This is a customized three-step program designed to establish the effort required to develop your existing organization to the ISO 9000 Series standard. It includes:

- Determining scope of registration
- Planning and conducting onsite quality assessments
- Gap analysis and assessment of resources required to gain registration

ISO 9000 Series Quality Strategy and Detailed Planning

Peat Marwick Stevenson & Kellogg provide the consulting support necessary for an organization to move from concept to reality. The "Executive and Management Workshops on Quality" forms an integral part of this process. Consulting support consists of:

- Developing action plan and time-phased implementation schedule
- Analyzing your organization's needs and developing workshops to suit your needs
- Working with key decision-makers in your organization to help their understanding of the ISO 9000 Series and quality management
- Working with implementation teams to ensure a practical plan is agreed for all processes and functions within the scope of registration

Process Analysis

As part of your ISO 9000 Series implementation strategy, analyzing your processes will lead to identification of what activities are critical to control. Consulting support will include:

- Working with your senior management to develop a framework for how the core and support processes address customer requirements
- Working with process teams to analyze and improve individual parts of processes

ISO 9000 Series Quality Implementation

This phase is designed to provide organizations with the necessary facilitation and coaching assistance for successful implementation. This phase can include assistance to:

- Plan and form a quality management steering council
- Develop a quality policy
- Provide employees with specialized education and skills training
- Provide on-the-job implementation support
- Provide internal quality systems auditor training

- Assist in selection of certification body
- Conduct a pre-registration assessment

Customized Pre-registration Assessment

This is a customized program, designed to assess the readiness and effectiveness of the implemented quality system. Practitioners will assist your internal auditors to simulate registration audits prior to final examination by the selected certification body. During this phase, they will continue to orient the organization to registration audit procedures and auditors' expectations.

CUSTOMIZED AND PUBLIC EDUCATION AND TRAINING

Peat Marwick Stevenson & Kellogg offers the following courses:

- ISO 9000 Series Quality Management Overview
- Executive and Management Workshops on Quality
- Planning and Implementing Quality Systems
- Integrating and Implementing HACCP with ISO 9000 Series
- Quality Documentation and Procedure Development Skills
- Quality System Auditing
- ISO 9000 Lead Auditor course
- How to Prepare a Quality Manual for ISO 9001 and 9002

Self-instruction Services for Smaller Organizations

The third principal area of services has been designed specifically for organizations that require minimum consulting and/or training support. These services are referred to as the ByDAC and ByWORD packages.

SIGNIFICANT EXPERIENCE

Practitioners have assisted over 450 domestic and international companies to applicable ISO 9000 Series registrations. The following project descriptions provide a sample of this experience.

Manufacturing and Transportation Industry

Peat Marwick Stevenson & Kellogg conducted auditor training courses for a number of clients, including an OEM component manufacturer and an automotive parts manufacturer. Training sessions included an introduction to quality assurance, a review of standards including the ISO 9000 Series, auditing techniques, and intensive workshops and role-play by participants.

They assisted a major aluminum manufacturing plant to gain registration to ISO 9001. The manufacturer was experiencing difficulties in gaining the commitment of their staff. They requested an in-depth interview with a sample of staff and to be fed back the results. This led to a plan to modify certain aspects of senior management behavior and improve communications.

Chemical and Plastics Industry

Professionals assisted a number of chemical manufacturers and distributors to establish Total Quality Management and Quality Assurance programs. They conducted a diagnostic assessment of operations and made recommendations for ongoing quality system development. As part of the program, they provided ISO 9002 training and facilitation. This resulted in registration by the appropriate certification body.

They worked with a number of plastics products and tooling manufacturers and an electronics company to develop and implement total quality management. Each company wanted to position itself as a low-cost producer of high quality products. Peat Marwick assisted in developing a plan to address continuous improvement, support cultural change, identify people/skill requirements for the implementation of ISO 9002. The methodology and process optimization techniques also resulted in tangible benefits of reduced scrap, rework and other productivity gains.

Consumer Packaged Goods Industry

At a major flour milling company, professionals facilitated workshops to set objectives, plan and implement total quality in such a way as to also ensure that they meet the requirements of ISO 9002. They developed an education package which was given to all employees by a variety of people ranging from millers to forklift truck drivers to senior managers. Teams were set up across the organization to examine processes and ensure representation and consistency across 11 sites.

Processing Industry

Effective quality management is a prime objective for a film manufacturing and processing company. Senior management selected Peat Marwick to assist them to take their strategy further. Their role was primarily to train and educate staff in the benefits of quality management and the skills required when implementing a quality system, such as auditor training and procedure writing. Executive and senior management workshops were also undertaken. In preparation for registration to ISO 9002, a series of pre-assessment audits were undertaken after a period of providing guidance and support.

The Peat Marwick Stevenson & Kellogg approach has been recognized by national accreditation bodies worldwide including the acceptance of Lead Auditor and Quality System Auditing courses by the Registrar Accreditation Board (RAB). With the experience and qualified IQA and RAB registered professionals, they can assist you and your organization to gain ISO 9000 registration and maintain your competitive position in the global arena.

PERRY JOHNSON, INC.
3000 TOWN CENTER
SUITE 2960
SOUTHFIELD, MI 48075
Phone: 313-356-4410
FAX: 313-356-4230

Perry Johnson, Inc. (PJI) has rapidly become one of the world's leading Total Quality Management consulting and training firms. Since 1983, PJI's corps of consultants have trained employees of more than 1,300 organizations throughout North America, Europe, Asia, and Australia; implemented TQM in more than 600 facilities: presented seminars to more than 700,000 people and trained in excess of 1,350,000 others by means of its catalog of products, including programmed-instruction workbooks, videotape series and overhead transparency presentations.

PJI holds a contract awarded by the United States Office of Personnel Management to provide TQM services and products to agencies of the Federal Government (OPM-89-2870) and is an approved supplier on the GSA Schedule (GS-02F-7576A).

ISO Consulting:

The members of Perry Johnson, Inc.'s European affiliate have over 10 years of experience in ISO, including registration and auditing. PJI's UK staffers have been living and working with the ISO 9000 for years and have successfully registered more than 100 companies for full certification.

Of course, PJI makes its expertise in ISO registration available to its clients in the United States and abroad. The work necessary to obtain ISO registration - training, consultation, manual writing, etc. - usually requires three to six months per facility, at a cost of around $25,000 each. Alternatively, PJI clients can assume much of the burden themselves by sending key executives to PJI's ISO seminars, or arranging for these seminars to be held on-site.

ISO Training:

PJI also offers a training course for people wishing to become lead ISO auditors. Passing the final exam which concludes this course, fulfills one of the four requirements to be lead auditor. The other requirements are a bachelor's degree, five years of experience in the quality field, and participation in 20 field audits.

Perry Johnson, Inc. looks forward to helping American businesses bring world-class quality to European markets.

Open-enrollment seminars include:

- All about ISO 9000
- ISO 9000 Lead Auditor Training
- ISO 9000 Implementation

PHILIP R. HEINLE QUALITY CONSULTING

763 OLD TOWER ROAD
OCONOMOWOC, WI 53066
Phone: 414-567-2854

Philip R. Heinle has been offering quality systems consulting since the beginning of 1991. He is an ASQC Certified Quality Auditor and Certified Quality Engineer, and his ISO 9000 consulting is based on many years of quality systems management in the manufacturing and service industries. Mr. Heinle customizes his programs for individual clients.

Primary services include:

- Pre-Audits for ISO 9000
- Consulting with Manufacturing and Service Industries to develop ISO 9000 Standards
- Presenting seminars to explain ISO 9000 Certification
- Keynote speaking for Sales Meetings and Associations on the future of ISO 9000

PRESSMARK INTERNATIONAL

P.O. Box 30857
KNOXVILLE, TN 37930-0857
Phone: 615-981-7220
FAX: 615-981-7224

The mission of Pressmark International is to provide customers with immediate cost-effective solutions to short-term problems. Pressmark International provides rapid response and solutions to issues and problems that need experts in that field of knowledge and experience. Pressmark International also uses these experts to assist clients by training personnel when internal experts are not available.

Areas of Expertise

- Audit
- Baldrige
- Culture
- Communications
- Customer Feedback
- Customer Surveys
- Evaluation
- ISO 9000
- Strategic Business Plan
- Strategic Initiatives
- Systems/Procedures

Consultants

Consultants are carefully selected, senior-level personnel who have held policy deployment positions and wish to supplement a prior career.

Training

Developing customized in-house training or hiring your own trainers is costly. Pressmark has retained specialists to conduct target training to meet your needs. Experts also customize materials and delivery.

Media

Pressmark International has researched to find the best resources for management knowledge which they provide through videotapes, books, cassettes, software, presentations, voice processing and other forms of communications. Supplies to support initiatives such as exercises and case studies are also available.

PROCESS MANAGEMENT INTERNATIONAL

7801 E. BUSH LAKE ROAD
SUITE 360
MINNEAPOLIS, MN 55439-3115
Phone: 612-893-0313
FAX: 612-893-0502

In 1991, Process Management International (PMI) and Optimum Systems for Quality Ltd. (OPQ) of the United Kingdom entered into a business venture to develop, sell and deliver ISO 9000 consulting and training services in North America. OPQ is a firm specializing in ISO 9000 consulting. PMI is a leading consulting and training firm specializing in TQM. PMI believes that this combination of TQM and ISO standards experience positions PMI as an effective and efficient resource for organizations seeking ISO registration. This approach also positions clients for benefits beyond the foundation of ISO-based quality systems.

ISO 9000 Implementation Consulting Services:

PMI's experienced quality consultants use a model and an approach to ISO registration developed and proven to be effective in Europe. The key steps include:

- Assessing where the client organization is regarding the appropriate ISO standard and defining what is required to become registered
- Developing an implementation plan
- Installing quality systems that optimize the business and satisfy the ISO 9000 standards: PMI has developed an implementation model to satisfy ISO standards effectively and efficiently
- Developing and implementing an auditing capability to ensure ongoing improvement and compliance with the standards
- Position the business to refine and improve its products/services, quality systems, operating effectiveness, and customer satisfaction

PMI's role in the above process is dependent on the desires and capabilities of the client.

ISO 9000 Training:

- ISO 9000 Management Overview
- Achieving ISO 9000 Registration
- ISO 9000 Auditing

PRODUCTIVITY MANAGEMENT CONSULTANTS

849 HARBOR ISLAND
CLEARWATER, FL 34630
Phone: 813-447-6409

Productivity Management Consultants specializes in providing on-site training and consultation to implement quality management systems of continuous improvement to secure ISO 9000 Certification and/or the Malcolm Baldrige Award, or to achieve other customer ratings such as Ford's Q-1 and General Motors' Targets for Excellence. Each of it's clients receives all the necessary training, training materials and guidance tailored to their specific manufacturing, administrative and service operations.

Company Mission:

To significantly increase the profitability of clients through the application of Quality Improvement technologies.

Services offered:

The firm offers on-site training and implementation of Statistical Process Control (SPC) based Total Quality Management (TQM) systems. It takes it's clients from the quality awareness stage, through training and employee involvement, to a fully implemented Quality Management System with emphasis on cost reduction and customer satisfaction.

Other Services Include:

- SPC/TQM/ISO 9000
- Team problem-solving
- Process improvement
- Measurement process evaluation
- Quality audits and PI 9
- Statistics for managers
- Senior management workshops
- Software for advanced statistical techniques
- Free phone consultation

QUALIFIED SPECIALISTS, INC.

13231 CHAMPION FOREST DRIVE
SUITE 104
HOUSTON, TX 77069
Phone: 713-444-5366
FAX: 713-444-6127

Qualified Specialists, Inc., who have been in business for four years, serves organizations in the service, manufacturing, and operating industries. QSI builds from current business practices to create a strong foundation (ISO 9000) for current or future TQM or Malcolm Baldrige efforts. The same style and focus is incorporated into the training courses. QSI has also founded the ISO Connection, a user group to further assist companies with their quality growth.

QSI Services:

- Consulting
- Staff augmentation
- How to select a registrar software
- ISO pre-assessment
- Quality system development
- ISO/EC and specialized training programs
- The ISO connection
- Complete training center located in Houston, Texas
- On-Site training available

QSI's training programs include:

- Introduction to ISO 9000 and Global Competitiveness
- Recognized Lead Assessor training
- ISO 10011 Internal Auditor training
- ISO 9001/2 Quality System Implementation
- ISO 9000 Executive Overview
- Procedure Writing
- How to be Audited

QUALITAS A.P.S., LTD.
HEAD OFFICE
CHAPEL GARDEN
14 RECTORY ROAD
WOKINGHAM
BERKSHIRE RG11 1DH
Phone: 44 (0) 734 891806
FAX: 44 (0) 734 791253

Qualitas a.p.s. is an international company dedicated to providing the highest standard of quality management consultancy, training and auditing.

From the head office near London, England, and strategically located bases in Northern Ireland, USA, Mexico and Hong Kong, Qualitas a.p.s. serves clients around the world in a variety of manufacturing and service industries achieve certification to BS 5750, ISO 9000, Q90, or EN 29000.

Qualitas a.p.s. consultants are long-standing professionals with considerable hands-on experience in quality assurance from large multinational organizations to small family businesses. The ISO 9000/Q90 consultants have literally decades of experience with American Quality systems as well as Quality systems in Europe and Asia. The staff consultants and instructors include Certified Lead Assessors, CQE'S, CRE'S, and CQA's with full academic and professional credentials.

Qualitas a.p.s. training programs are developed specifically to meet clients' needs and are all lead by qualified trainers. They run on- or off-site, typically in workshop format, and are always highly participative.

The Quality Management courses will train key people in how to develop, implement and maintain a quality system and culture involving ISO 9000, TQM or both.

Quality Skills training in writing procedures and work instructions, auditing, SPC, FMEA, and problem-solving are intended to ensure that personnel are fully equipped to work towards, and maintain a quality system.

Employee Development courses in team building, assertiveness and leadership are designed to complement the Quality Management and Skills training.

Qualitas a.p.s. employs registered Lead Assessors who have experience in conducting system audits for third party registration bodies such as BSI, LPCB, BCSA and HKQAA. This enables Qualitas a.p.s. to take clients through pre-registration audits to assess levels of compliance, identify weak areas and conduct vendor audits to improve supply-side performance.

Qualitas a.p.s. operates internationally across a broad spectrum, with projects successfully completed or in progress with manufacturing, construction, general engineering, steel fabrication, steel and chemicals production, freight forwarding and transport.

QUALITAS USA, INC.
3040 CHARLEVOIX DRIVE SE
SUITE 101
GRAND RAPIDS, MI 49546
Phone: 616-285-4010
FAX: 616-949-2812

Qualitas USA, Inc. is a subsidiary of Qualitas a.p.s. Ltd., which is headquartered in Wokingham, England.

Qualitas USA can provide the following services to assist in implementing an ISO 9000 quality system:

- Benchmark Assessment - This evaluation is normally one day and includes a full detailed report. This report will have a detailed gap analysis of the quality system versus the ISO 9001 standard which will provide invaluable information for developing a logical and effective action plan.

- Action Plan - Based on the initial evaluation report and specific desires of the client, an action plan will be proposed to provide the direction and organized approach to implementing the necessary elements of the quality system.

- Internal Auditor Training - This workshop will prepare your audit team for a quick start on internal auditing.

- ISO 9000 Interpretation and Implementation - This seminar is an overview of the ISO 9000 standards which also investigate cross linkage among elements, interpretation of the language in the standard, and application tips.

- Documentation - This workshop explains in detail the four levels of documentation requirements, how to achieve effective documentation that also meets the standards, and basic writing considerations.

- Final Dry Run Assessment - This is an assessment with a detailed report and suggested corrective action.

- Full consulting Program - The Qualitas full consulting program is useful in preparing companies for ISO 9000 registration. The program includes the training and final assessment in addition to keeping the project on focus and other training and assistance as identified in the initial evaluation.

- Small Business Development Program - This is an effective nine month program of self-help and consultancy fee sharing for companies seeking ISO 9000 of fewer than 100 employees. The program covers the necessary training and planning that is critical for companies desiring to implement a ISO 9000 quality system in a cost effective and expedient manner.

Additional courses available include:
- ISO 9000 Interpretation and Application
- ISO 9000 Documentation
- Internal Auditing

QUALITY DEVELOPMENT ASSOCIATES
BOX 66
OAKVILLE, CT 06779-0066
Phone: 203-274-5644
FAX: 203-274-5644

Quality Development Associates (QDA) provides a full range of activities in support of a manufacturer's goal of ISO 9000/ASQC Q90 registration/certification of their Quality Management System.

QDA has been providing assistance to industry for over 10 years. Personnel are knowledgeable and skilled, having achieved ASQC CQE, CRE certification; and programs are custom-tailored to a client company's requirements.

Services include:

■ Quality System Assessment - Quality Development Associates conduct an overview pre-assessment of the client's facilities, provide a detailed audit report, identify system assets and liabilities, and recommend an appropriate plan of action to achieve ISO/ASQC registration.

■ Development of a Plan of Action - QDA conducts Management Awareness Programs to introduce the ISO standards, where the facility stands against them, and work with the staff to develop a Quality Action Plan to address areas of weakness and develop appropriate corrective action.

■ Implementation and Documentation - The company will assist in the development, implementation and documentation of the Quality System to meet the requirements of ISO. Development of your QA Manual and work procedures will also be assisted.

■ Pre-audit Readiness Survey - An unbiased independent audit of the Quality System will be conducted to determine readiness for the complete third party audit.

■ Follow-up - Continue to be provided with follow-up assistance with ISO 9000/ASQC 90 registration and receive assistance in the resolution of any ongoing program problems and maintenance of the client's program.

QUALITY FOCUS, INC.

P.O. BOX 1492
GOLDSBORO, NC 27533-1492
Phone: 919-734-3090
Phone: 800-992-9079
FAX: 919-734-2927

Quality Focus is a quality engineering/management consulting firm located in North Carolina. The partners are senior members of ASQC, and Certified Quality Engineers and Certified Auditors with all associates being Certified Quality Engineers. Partners and associates have years of experience in the field of Quality Systems and Quality Management in various industries including electrical and automotive supply thus being familiar with many of the requirements of supplier programs (i.e., Q-101, Targets, etc.) and how these interact with ISO standards.

QUALITY FOCUS SERVICES

Training:

- ISO requirements and which standard is appropriate for each client
- Auditing and how to develop an effective audit program per the requirements
- How to write the documentation to meet the requirements of ISO
- In specific techniques that are required (i.e., SPC, Problem-solving, DOE, etc.)
- How to implement ISO effectively and efficiently

Developing Documentation for the ISO Requirements:

Based on the concepts of ISO, Quality Focus uses the hierarchical approach for manuals and supporting documentation that is recommended by registrars.

- Quality Manuals - outline the Quality Policy of the organization
- Departmental Procedure/Process Manuals - support the policy outlined in the Quality Manual with departmental specific requirements to insure that each department is working toward the ultimate organizational objectives
- Procedures - support the objectives of the Departmental Manuals with job specific/task oriented details
- Developing Training Programs to meet the intent of the ISO requirements
- Audit to determine current standard of Quality System vs. selected standard and documenting areas where emphasis is required

QUALITY FOCUS PHILOSOPHY

Quality Focus believes that companies/organizations know how to perform their jobs and deliver Quality products to their customers. Quality Focus also recognizes that companies have weaknesses in systems and documentation (which are strengths of ISO standards). The objective is to assist clients in developing a Quality Management System that will operate efficiently and effectively after implementation incorporating many of the tasks that are currently being performed. This is accomplished by viewing client's current Quality Systems insuring that all elements of the ISO standard are addressed and change/modify only areas where weaknesses mandate.

QUALITY IMPROVEMENT NETWORK, INC.
119 RUSSELL STREET
LITTLETON, MA 01460
Phone: 508-486-0010
FAX: 508-486-0010
QUALNET ACCESS: 508-486-0301

The Quality Improvement Network, Inc. provides ISO 9000/Q90 training consulting, and thrid party auditing services to companies providing goods and services to both local and global markets.

The firm's consultants have much experience with American Quality systems as well as Quality systems in Europe and Asia. The staff consultants and instructors include certified Lead Assessors, CQE's, CRE's and CQA's with full academic and professional credentials.

ISO 9000/Q90 Services include:

- Consulting - with the client to develop a program directed toward ISO 9000/Q90 registration. Or the Quality Improvement Network will do it all - manuals, procedures, forms, record design, and ongoing site support.

- Training - on all aspects of ISO 9000/Q90 training for individuals or teams - from IGA-approved Assessor/Lead Assessor training to preparing for auditors from the registering agency.

- Third Party Auditing - to determine the effectiveness of your systems and their compliance with ISO 9000/Q90. Whether once a month or once a week the Quality Improvement Network will adjust to fit your schedule and your available resources for implementing ISO 9000/Q90.

QUALITY PRACTITIONERS, INC.

3100 RIDGEWAY DRIVE
SUITE 2
MISSISSAUGA, ONTARIO L5L 5M5
CANADA
Phone: 416-569-6431
Phone: 800-667-5748
FAX: 416-569-7651

Quality Practitioners, Inc. (QPI) is a group of quality practitioners who are also accredited auditors with many years of practical hands-on experience in all aspects of quality management. QPI has developed and audited quality systems to all levels of the International Organization for Standardization's ISO 9000 series of quality standards.

Quality Practitioners, Inc. will provide client companies with estimates or proposals for complete or partial Quality Systems for one or multiple locations. No system is too large for the firm to prepare through its tried and true methods of implementation to ISO 9000 Quality Standards.

Quality Practitioners, Inc. is:

- Devoted solely to ISO 9000
- Preparing companies to compete in Europe as well as North America through ISO 9000
- Developing seminars approved by the Canadian government
- Staffed by experienced practitioners of Quality
- Able to evaluate suppliers Quality Systems
- Able to provide confidential pre-registration audits
- Able to provide accredited auditors to industry throughout North America

Seminars include:

- ISO 10011 Auditor/Lead Auditor Training
- ISO 9001 and 9002
- ISO 9003
- The Application of ISO 9000 Standards
- ISO 9000 Assessor/Lead Assessor
- Fundamentals of Quality Management

U.S. Office:

QPI
417 First St., NW
Indian Rocks Beach, FL 34633
Phone: 800-667-5748

QUALITY SYSTEMS, INC.
15770 S. PRISCILLA LANE
OREGON CITY, OR 97045
Phone: 503-657-1624

Quality Systems, Inc. (QSI) provides the consulting, auditing, training and implementation necessary to achieve ISO 9000 certification. The company assists clients in going through the certification process in a systematic and orderly manner, at a reasonable cost and in a minimum of time.

Quality Systems has had experience in the chemical, pharmaceutical, plastic, electronics, foundry and machine shop type industries. For instance, the company has assisted a foundry in getting Caterpillar certification and has assisted an after market, automotive manufacturer with ISO 9000 and Ford certification.

The company is flexible and provides only the amount of additional assistance a client company requires to achieve its goals and objectives. Quality Systems assists its clients in getting to where they need to be in the time frame that they desire.

The Quality Systems Guarantee:

When Quality Systems, Inc. advises that a client company is ready for certification, it backs that statement. If clients don't get certified the first time around, QSI will continue to assist the client in getting those requirements, that are indicated lacking. QSI does this at no additional cost to the client.

Management Overviews:

Quality Systems provides Management Overviews in ISO 9000, Quality, Quality Planning, Total Quality Management (TQM), Quality Function Deployment (QFD), Customer Satisfaction, Cost of Quality (COQ), Design of Experiments (DOE), Statistical Process Control (SPC) and Quality Improvement.

Auditing:

Quality Systems will perform an initial assessment to evaluate where you are in regards to the ISO 9000 series requirements. The audit will cover the four phases of management and will determine the suitability of documentation and the conformity of the documentation to operations. A post-implementation audit will be conducted prior to applying for certification to assure readiness.

Documentation:

Quality Systems can help you assess existing documentation and obtain any additional documentation that may be needed. QSI can write the documentation (no matter how technical) or help the staff write and edit it.

Training:

Quality Systems provide on-site training of management, engineers, support staff and operators. The Management Overviews, indicated previously, are the basis for quality training and implementation. In addition, QSI can provide training in such technical areas as Design of Experiments (DOE) and Statistical Process Control (SPC). QSI can perform all the training or QSI can help you train the trainers.

Implementation:

Implementation is the most difficult part of the ISO 9000 process. Quality Systems recommends the implementation of quality tools such as SPC, during training, rather than training everybody and hoping that it gets implemented later. QSI will assist in the implementation to the extent required for achieving results.

Other Quality Requirements:

Quality Systems can integrate other quality requirements such as award criteria or other certification requirements with the ISO 9000 series requirements. This would help a company decrease the time and cost for implementing any other quality requirements. Examples of such awards would be the Malcolm Baldrige National Quality Award and NASA's Quality and Excellence Award. Examples of certification requirements would be those of Ford or Caterpillar. These award and certification requirements could be easily incorporated with ISO 9000.

Certification:

Quality Systems is in the business to assist a company in getting ISO 9000 certification. Thus, QSI cannot certify you, since a third party certifier is required. The company will help bring you through the whole certification process. QSI will help you prepare for certification and then help find someone accredited to perform the final audit of your facility.

QUALITYALERT INSTITUTE
257 PARK AVENUE SOUTH
12TH FLOOR
NEW YORK, NY 10010-7304
Phone: 212-353-4420
Phone: 800-221-2114
FAX: 212-353-4526

The QualityAlert Institute is a member of the Penton Group of companies which includes Penton Publishing, Penton Learning Systems and Penton Software. Penton Publishing publishes 28 trade magazines including Industry Week and Machine Digest. Penton Learning Systems designs, develops and staffs short-term, non-credit managerial, technical, governmental, financial, telecommunications, and computer courses in conjunction with over 65 major universities throughout the United States, Canada and Europe. Penton Software is a producer of PC-based statistical quality control software.

For more than 12 years, QualityAlert Institute has been dedicated to helping manufacturing, service, health care and government organizations with systems training, consulting and implementation services they need to improve and control the quality of their products and services under a Total Quality Management philosophy. The QualityAlert Institute is not a "generalist" consulting firm or training organization, but a specialist in delivering a unified and integrated training system that provides the key elements - tools, direction, support, and employee buy-in - for a Total Quality Management implementation effort.

The QualityAlert Institute's ISO 9000 Group started over 2 years ago. The group is made up of individuals who are prior executives with Fortune 500 companies and have helped large, mid-size and small companies through the entire ISO 9000/Q90 preparation and registration process.

The working relationship with an ISO 9000/Q90 client always begins with clearly understanding their existing corporate culture, Quality Improvement philosophy, goals and objectives. Quality Alert's goal is to work closely with organizations to design and deliver ISO 9000/Q90 registration assistance services that will compliment any existing quality improvement effort already in place.

QualityAlert has demonstrated the ability to build a bridge between Quality philosophies, principles and concepts and the realities of the corporate work place when implementing the ISO 9000/Q90 series of quality standards.

ISO 9000 offers valuable guidelines to assess an organization's quality goals and can be used to set up procedures to achieve a high level of quality in the products and services offered. This quality, in turn, is used as a competitive tool to lower costs, increase productivity and satisfy customers.

Public and In-House ISO Training:

- Executive Overview
- How to Implement the ISO 9000 Series of Quality Standards in Your Organization
- Auditing to the ISO 9000/Q90 Series of Quality Standards
- Project Management Seminar for ISO 9000/Q90 Implementation Teams
- How to Write Effective ISO 9000/Q90 User Manuals
- Train the ISO 9000/Q90 Trainer
- Additional ISO 9000 Seminars for Specific Industries:
    - ISO 9000 for Software Manufacturers
    - ISO 9000 for Defense and Aerospace Contractors
    - ISO 9000 for Service Organizations
    - ISO 9000 for Good Manufacturing Practices
    - ISO for Suppliers to the Automotive Industry

- On-Site Auditing
- On-Site Implementation Assistance

QualityAlert Institute - ISO 9000 Implementation Strategy Recommendations:

- Top Level commitment
- Organize for success
- Educate committee and top management
- Determine appropriate level of registration
- Implement awareness programs throughout the organization
- Organize ISO teams
- Set goals and develop your plan
- Implement the plan
- Status Check (second or third party assessments)

Other Services:
- Tools/training
- Pre-assessment
- Audit

QUEST CONSULTING GROUP, INC.
34 CHANNING STREET
SUITE 400
NEWTON, MA 02158
Phone: 617-527-7032
FAX: 617-527-0618

Quest Consulting Group, Inc. provides quality assurance management consulting, training, and engineering service. The firm also provides engineering and inspection services for long- and short-term projects to the Aerospace/Defense, Transportation, and Construction industries.

ISO 9000 Implementation and Consulting Services:

- A customized introductory seminar and workshop for executives, including plant tour

- Answers to questions:
    - What is the ISO?
    - What is ISO 9000?
    - How much will it cost to register?
    - What does "registration" to an ISO 9000 series standard mean?
    - How long does it take?
    - What is the best strategy as a company?

- Cost effective follow-up support of tasks as required:
    - Assessments
    - Audits
    - System upgrades
    - Software upgrades
    - Registration process assistance
    - ANSI/ASQC certification

Quest Consulting Group also provides Total Quality Management consulting, implementation and training services, including, but not limited to:

- Documentation review and preparation
- Initial quality systems assessment
- Pre-certification assessment
- Development and implementation of continuous improvement programs and training:
    - Quality awareness
    - Problem-solving
    - Cost of quality
    - Design quality
    - Supplier partnerships
    - Statistical process controls (SPC)
    - Root cause corrective action
    - Marketing quality
    - Benchmarking

Quest Consulting Group Areas of Expertise:

- Avionics Equipment
- Communications
- Expediting
- Hybrid Microelectronics
- Integrated Circuits
- Multilayer Rigid/Flex PCB's
- Non-Destructive Testing
- Optical Components
- Precision Machining
- Pressurized Castings
- Process Equipment and Controls
- Quality Program Evaluation
- Structural/Mechanical
- Vendor Surveillance
- Vessel/Pipe Fabrication
- Welding

What Can Quest Consulting Group Do For Its Clients?

- Quest plans inspection programs to lower overall costs. Programs include written instructions covering:
  - Critical Inspection Points
  - Personnel Assignments
  - Inspection Schedule

- Efficient planning, communication and supervision is effected through supervisory personnel averaging more than 20 years experience
- Problems are resolved through direct and continuing telephone, facsimile, and written communication
- Proper documentation and timely reports are provided

Quest provides broad engineering support. Technical services are performed under the client's direction. However, the broad capabilities of Quest's engineers can be focused on any quality problems discovered.

Quest provides professional personnel. Effective engineering/inspection requires professionals. Quest personnel are full-time, career-oriented and experienced. All are required to participate in corporate training and to remain current on industry specific codes and standards.

Affiliate Company:

An affiliate company, Scott Technical Services, offers third party registrations to ISO 9000 standards.

QUEST USA, INC.
27941 HARPER AVENUE
ST. CLAIR SHORES, MI 48081
Phone: 313-774-9480
FAX: 313-774-2709

Quest USA, Inc., the U.S. affiliate of UK-based Quest International Associates Limited, provides quality system consulting, implementing, and training services to U.S. manufacturing and service firms in all sectors.

Quest's team of European-based consultants focuses on two objectives:

- *To help clients implement ISO 9000 Quality Systems*
- *To help them to become registered to International Quality Systems Standards.*

Quest USA, Inc.'s parent firm, based in Lancashire, England, was formed by Mervyn A. Hewlett in May, 1990 to provide a wide range of services to industry, commerce and government agencies on an international basis. The firm contracts either directly with clients, or as an approved subcontractor to other consultancy groups.

In 1992, to meet the emerging U.S. demand for ISO 9000 consulting and implementing services, Quest USA, Inc. was set up in Michigan, headquarters in metropolitan Detroit.

Quest USA, Inc.'s strategy augments existing elements of total quality management (TQM) already familiar to many U.S. quality people by linking them with, and assimilating them into, the defined and proven quality system structure of ISO 9000. This enhances understanding and dramatically shortens the time and cost needed to implement and register the quality system.

Quest USA, Inc.'s strategy is built upon the following factors:

- A preliminary survey of the problem area to facilitate the planning of a customized implementation program
- Advance agreement on objectives and tactics
- Solutions that work in practice as well as theory
- Systems based upon teamwork at all levels of the business

The program stresses introduction of the International Quality System Standard, depending upon the scope of the operation concerned:

- ISO 9001 - 1987: Model for Quality Assurance in Design/Development, Production, Installation and Servicing
- ISO 9002 - 1987: Model for Quality Assurance in Production and Installation

Quest USA, Inc. also provides "TickIT" Scheme assistance for suppliers of electronic and software related products and services (ISO 9000-3).

Commitment to Full Client Satisfaction

Quest USA, Inc. achieves optimal results for its clients by applying expertise, experience, enthusiasm, energy and a great deal of very hard work. Quest believes in practical action toward clear, agreed upon goals.

The firm's ISO implementation program depends on:

- Team work at all levels of the organization
- Sound practical advice and guidance from the consulting firm
- Ownership of the program retained by the client, at all times
- Specific training input at key stages of the project.

The Quest approach to ISO 9000 Implementation:

Typically obtaining ISO 9000 registration is a nine to twelve month process. The principles of ISO 9000 apply equally in manufacturing, non-manufacturing and service organizations.

Stage 1: Initial Survey and Report
Stage 2: Implementing Program and Action Plan
Stage 3: Preparing the ISO 9000 Steering Team
Stage 4: System Implementation and Guidance
Stage 5: Internal Quality Auditing
Stage 6: Final Audit and Review

R. BOWEN INTERNATIONAL, INC. (rbi)

149 WEST MARKET STREET
YORK, PA 17401
Phone: 717-843-4880
FAX: 717-854-8591

r. bowen international, inc. (rbi) is led by Robert D. Bowen and Randy T. Byrnes, one of the most experienced and successful American hands-on ISO 9000 resource teams. Since 1988, Mr. Bowen and Mr. Byrnes have spent over 15,000 hours actually implementing ISO 9000 quality systems. They have been instrumental in implementing ISO 9000 Standards at:

- *The first U.S. electronics firm certified by an accredited third party assessment agency*
- *The first U.S. connector manufacturer ever certified to ISO 9000 standards*
- *The first U.S. Distribution Center certified to ISO 9000 Standards*
- *The first simultaneous worldwide ISO 9000 implementation process*
- *The first introduction of the ISO 9000 implementation process into many countries in the Pacific Rim*

rbi associates have first-hand, personal experience in implementing ISO 9000 Standards with ...

- *Continuous process technologies*
- *Batch or piece-part technologies*
- *High-tech engineering and manufacturing*
- *Traditional engineering and manufacturing*

r. bowen international, inc. ISO 9000 GAME PLAN

The rbi Purpose: To Implement ISO 9000 In a Way That:

- The process is a building block for continuous improvement
- A fully functioning quality system is operative
- The Initial Assessment of your quality system by an accredited third party assessment agency is successfully completed

The rbi Role: To Provide the Following Services During Implementation:

- Education and Training:
    - Executive Workshop
    - Basic Skills Workshop
    - Special Workshops

- Audits:
    - Startup Assessment
    - Project Assessment
    - Dress Rehearsal Audit
    - Preliminary Assessment
    - Special Audits
    - Certification Audit Support

- Documentation Services:
    - Preparation, editorial control, typing and copying of all quality systems documentation such as the Quality Manual, Operating Procedures, and Work Instructions
    - Review, analysis and support needed to prepare and implement quality systems documentation

- Supplier Services:
    - Education and Training
    - Qualification Assessment

- On-Site Resource Services:
    - Scheduled visits to meet and discuss key issues with site personnel

Your Role: To Provide Direct Leadership

- Implement the Management Review process
- Appoint an ISO 9000 Coordinator
- Define and implement a Quality Policy and implement objectives to support this policy
- Execute responsibilities as described in the Quality Manual

Principal Background

Robert D. Bowen, president of r. bowen international, blends his extensive hands-on ISO 9000 experience together with business objectives. Since 1988, Bob Bowen has worked to implement ISO 9000. As the Senior Technical Resource for ISO 9000 implementation in Du Pont Electronics, he has personally presented ISO 9000 workshops to over 3,000 persons throughout the world. He has worked throughout the United States, Japan, Korea, Taiwan, Singapore and other locations to directly implement ISO 9000. Mr. Bowen was the leader of the team to first introduce the ISO 9000 process into the People's Republic of China.

During his tenure with Du Pont Electronics, ISO 9000 was implemented in over 30 locations worldwide. This process was the first global implementation of ISO 9000 and included over 8,000 persons in 15 countries.

Mr. Bowen has over 19 years as a quality professional and is a Certified Quality Engineer and Certified Quality Auditor by the American Society for Quality Control. He is a senior member of ASQC. He has been awarded honors for technical presentations and published in leading journals.

Mr. Byrnes has over 18 years in the development of a highly successful staffing company. He holds a Master of Science degree and focuses in management of the change process in companies implementing ISO 9000. He combines hands-on experience with leading-edge, creative problem-solving techniques.

R.T. WESTCOTT & ASSOCIATES
263 MAIN STREET
OLD SAYBROOK, CT 06475
PHONE: 203-388-6094
FAX: 203-388-6944

RTWA provides both breadth and depth of services to aid the client in improving customer focus, quality, processes and cost-effectiveness of the organization. RTWA also assists organizations in the journey to the Malcolm Baldrige National Quality Award and/or ISO 9000 registration. A list of the areas addressed follows:

Assessment

- Survey of service Quality and Total Quality Management
- Quality audits (ISO 9000 and Baldrige Award criteria)
- ISO 9000 walk through
- Customer satisfaction survey
- Survey of individual commitment
- Organizational diagnoses
- Complaint/Problem management systems assessment
- Training Needs Analyses
- Program evaluation

Management

- Total quality management processes
- Planning for strategic change - Quality
- Continuous improvement support systems
- Unconditional guarantee System
- Employee Involvement/Participation processes
- Problem-solving circles
- Gain-sharing systems

Organizational Development

- Organizing for TQM
- Management of Change
- Team Building
- Reorganization, restructuring, downsizing

Systems and Programs

- Quality commitment and awareness training
- Process management training
- Quality measurement/tracking systems
- Quality/process improvement programs
- Cycle-time improvement process
- Developmental coaching for continuous improvement
- Performance management, measuring/tracking

- Management, supervisory and team training
- Statistical process control and other quality tools
- Training and application

RTWA serves public and private sector organizations, including large and small businesses in manufacturing and services.

ROBERT PEACH AND ASSOCIATES., INC.
541 NORTH BRAINARD AVENUE
LA GRANGE PARK, IL 60525
Phone: 708-579-3400
FAX: 708-579-1620

Robert Peach, Principal, is a delegate to the International Laboratory Accreditation Conference (ILAC), and is a member of the U.S. Delegation to the ISO TC 176 Committee on Quality Assurance, where he served as Convener of the Working Group that developed ISO Quality System Standard 9004 (ANSI/ASQC Standard Q94). He currently chairs the ASQC's Registrar Accreditation Board.

Mr. Peach has spoken over 200 times to organizations on the subject of Quality Management, is author of the ASQC home study course "Successfully Managing the Quality Function," and has received the Edwards Medal of the ASQC for leadership in the application of modern Quality Control methods. He is a Certified Quality Engineer and Registered Professional Engineer in Quality Engineering.

Who Should Consider the Services of RPA?

- Manufacturing organizations wishing to improve quality without increasing costs
- Organizations already enjoying high quality, but desirous of reducing total quality costs
- Suppliers with major industrial customers who are demanding both higher quality and evidence of a comprehensive Quality Control program
- Manufacturers with mature quality programs, who wish to identify potential areas of further improvement
- Successful, growing companies, whose Quality Control systems have not kept pace with other facets of their organization

How Can RPA Help You?

Robert Peach and Associates, Inc. can evaluate the effectiveness of your company's quality organization and practices, making comparisons to up-to-date techniques available to American and world industry. Based on its review, RPA will identify areas of potential improvement in your quality program.

RPA will advise how to place a revitalized quality program into operation. They will show you how to make maximum use of available resources, minimizing the need for continuous outside aid.

Based on your particular needs, RPA can draw on a wide range of skills from professionals working in American industry, who are available to develop a cost-effective plan for your consideration.

Robert Peach and Associates, Inc. will provide continuing guidance and training in Quality Control techniques during the installation phase of its programs.

ROGER HUNT MANAGEMENT CONSULTING, INC.

3220 SCHOOLHOUSE DRIVE
WATERFORD, MI 48329-4331
Phone: 313-673-7675

Roger Hunt Management Consulting, Inc. specializes in working with clients in preparation for major evaluations of their business and/or quality systems. The firm's aim is to help client businesses utilize existing resources so that they can achieve the best possible ratings from external assessments and audits, since suppliers that receive superior scores are more likely to be considered by customers for additional or possibly even continuing business.

Consulting Expertise and Services:

The firm provides economical quality assurance support services for industrial parts suppliers and other small manufacturing businesses. As Principal Consultant, Roger Hunt's qualifications include:

- 15 years experience in quality-system evaluation and supplier development
- 9 years additional experience in laboratory testing and analysis
- Lead Assessor Registration No. A002969 by The Institute of Quality Assurance
- ASQC-certified Quality Auditor since 1989
- ASQC-certified Quality Engineer since 1986

The firm offers two approaches. First, it can review and interpret the applicable requirements with client employees in an on-site conference room setting. Second, it can conduct thorough pre-assessment surveys and provide remedial recommendations accordingly. Follow-up services such as editorial work on procedures and quality manuals, instruction and coaching on SPC implementation, etc., can also be provided.

ROSE ASSOCIATES
27 WILLOW STREET
MYSTIC, CT 06355
Phone: 203-536-2729

Robert A. Rose is president and founder of Rose Associates. He has over 20 years of quality-related work experience in managerial, manufacturing, services, and administrative positions. He teaches quality and related courses for the American Society for Quality Control, the University of New Haven (graduate and undergraduate). Mr. Rose is a registered Professional Quality Engineer and has been an ASQC Certified Quality Engineer since 1974.

Quality Training:

Rose Associates offers both traditional and customized Quality Training, including appropriate computer software training in:

- Probability and statistics
- Sampling and statistical process control
- Advanced statistical & regression analysis
- Design of experiments
- ASQC certification courses
- Quality costs and problem-solving tools
- Total Quality Management
- Just-In-Time manufacturing
- Malcolm Baldrige Award
- ISO 9000

Quality Services:

As statistical consultants and quality engineers, Rose Associates offers a complete array of Total Quality Management and quality services.

Services include:
- Writing proposals that use quality to focus on: product development, productivity improvement, process control, cost reduction efforts and marketing strategy.
- Increasing return on investments by: minimizing wastes, streamlining operations and maximizing productivity.
- Obtaining immediate project improvement savings then use these savings to finance improvement projects that produce more savings and long-term gains.

SERVICE PROCESS CONSULTING, INC.
76 GEORGE AVENUE
EDISON, NJ 08820-3127
Phone: 908-321-0045
FAX: 908-549-9117

Service Process Consulting, Inc. (SPC) is a management consulting firm that specializes in Total Quality Management. The firm has particular expertise and experience in the Malcolm Baldrige National Quality Award and the International Organization for Standards (ISO) 9000 series of quality standards. SPC has experience working with a diverse range of clients in service and manufacturing industries.

Ian Durand, founder and principal consultant of Service Process Consulting, Inc. has served for more than 5 years as a United States delegate to the ISO Technical Committee responsible for the 9000 series of Quality Standards. He was the lead delegate to the Working Group that developed an international guidance standard for quality management in service organizations. His experience with service organizations had an important influence on the precepts, structure and content of the standard. Mr. Durand now serves as the lead U.S. delegate on an ISO Working Group coordinating the updating of the 9000 series. He conducts seminars throughout the United States on these pivotal quality standards and their importance to U.S. companies.

Consulting Services:

Service Process Consulting, Inc. consults with and provides education to organizations that want to improve their market share and improve their cost performance. These improvements result from:

- Continually improving customer satisfaction
- Reducing non-value-adding work
- Increasing the engagement of all employees in satisfying their direct customers while eliminating causes of errors

SPC provides both in-house, customized educational seminars and ongoing consulting to guide companies to the implementation of quality systems that not only meet the requirements of the ISO standards, but also yield benefits of lower costs and faster cycle time.

SHILAY ASSOCIATES, INC.
1419 WANTAUGH AVENUE
WANTAUGH, NY 11793-2206
Phone: 516-783-7600
FAX: 516-785-5742

Shilay Associates Inc. specializes in Total Quality Management, Strategic Planning, Quality Assurance, Manufacturing, Training, and Organizational Studies.

The three core concepts of ISO 9000 are as follows:

- Achieve and sustain the quality of the product or service to meet stated or implied customer needs.
- Provide confidence to management that intended quality is being achieved.
- Provide confidence to the purchaser that intended quality is being achieved in the delivered product or service.

The Shilay Associates Inc. correction processes are as follows:

- Identify company core values and culture parameters
- Validate (or create) overall policy manual to core values and culture
- Assess current state against ISO criteria considering values and culture
- Establish Steering Group
- Assign non-compliance items to responsible people
- Correct and validate corrections
- Train affected personnel
- Pre-assessment

Shilay Associates Inc. intends to help companies achieve:

- Registration to ISO 9000
- Posture to adapt to future ISO requirements
- Posture to launch full TQM culture change
- Identifiable savings to fund the registration task

SOFTWARE QUALITY ASSOCIATES, INC.

2725 COLISEUM STREET
LOS ANGELES, CA 90018
Phone: 213-292-5288

Software Quality Associates, Inc. (SQA) provides a comprehensive and extensive range of management and technical consultation and staff development and training services for firms that are considering registration of their quality systems to one of the ISO 9000 Quality System Models - where ISO 9000-3 (Part 3), Guidelines for the Application of ISO 9001 to the Development, Supply, and Maintenance of Software would be an integral aspect of registration.

SQA was founded in 1982 to provide management and technical assistance to firms in business and industry (i.e., aerospace, electronics, computers, software, telecommunications, commercial aviation, medical devices, nuclear, etc.) and the government.

Since its inception, SQA have become well-known consultants in the areas of Software Quality Engineering, Software Quality Management, Software Quality Assurance, Software Quality Process Development, Software Quality Assurance Program Assessments and Evaluations, Software Subcontractor and Vendor Assessment and Evaluation, Software Engineering Capabilities Assessments (Software Engineering Institute's Model, ISO 9000 Model, Pressman Model, etc.), and Software Engineering and Software Quality Assurance Staff Development and Training.

Staff development and training assistance has been provided in accordance to Government and industry standards and specifications - including ADA Basics, ISO 9000, ISO 9000-3, DoD-STD-2187A, DoD-STD-2168, MIL-Q-9858A, DO-178A/B, IEEE 730, and NASA SMAP.

SQA'S ISO 9000 CONSULTING SERVICES AND SEMINARS

SQA provides a comprehensive and extensive range of management and technical consultation services and staff development/training services for firms that are considering registration of their quality systems to one of the ISO 9000 Quality System Models - where ISO 9000-3 (Part 3), Guidelines for the Application of ISO 9001 to the Development, Supply, and Maintenance of Software would be an integral aspect of registration.

SQA's services during the ISO 9000 registration are both comprehensive and complete - tailored to meet clients needs during pre-certification, certification, and post-certification. SQA's services includes general consultation, implementation assistance, and staff development and training. In the area of general consultation, their services range from formulation of overall, corporate software quality management and quality assurance goals and objectives, strategic planning, and management planning to pre-certification assessments, or auditing, of software quality assurance, software engineering, and quality auditing functions.

The firm's general ISO 9000-3 consulting services are provided to provide firms that develop, supply, and maintain software with expert advice and directions when ISO 9000 certification is being sought and software is a key factor. These services are provided for firms that develop software as a "stand-alone" product or embedded with a system (i.e., electronic systems, medical devices, etc.); firms that develop software as a software subcontractor or vendor; and firms that maintain software.

ISO 9000-3 CONSULTING SERVICES

Comprehensive consulting services are provided for firms in business and industry that are considering certification of their quality system where computer software is an integral aspect of the firm's services or products. ISO 9000-3 (Part 3) provides guidelines for the applications of the ISO 9000 Series to software development, supply, and maintenance. SQA's software quality management and software quality assurance services encompass the spectrum - from pre-assessment strategic planning, determination of overall goals and objectives, definition of ISO management representative's responsibilities, formulation of steering groups, and areas coordinators - to the assessments of existing software quality management systems and software quality assurance programs in light of ISO 9000-3 requirements; complete analysis, design, and implementation of ISO 9000-3 compliant software quality management and software quality assurance programs; and the post-certification auditing of a previously certified program. SQA also provides a complete and comprehensive series of ISO 9000-3 training courses, including introduction to ISO 9000-3, implementation of ISO 9000-3 software quality management and assurance programs, auditing of ISO 9000-3 software quality management and assurance programs, and software engineering under ISO 9000-3.

ISO 9000-3 SOFTWARE QUALITY MANAGEMENT/ASSURANCE PROGRAM PRE-ASSESSMENT

SQA provides a qualified, independent look at current corporate/organizational software quality goals and objectives; management philosophy, policies, commitment, and practices; software quality programs' management, personnel, standards and procedures, tools/resources; and software quality programs' effectiveness and propensity for continuous process development, management and improvement. This assessment allows firms to realistically view their goals and objectives; management orientation and commitment in light of the requirements ISO 9000-3 and their pursuant certification.

ISO 9000-3 SOFTWARE QUALITY MANAGEMENT/ASSURANCE PROGRAM IMPLEMENTATION

SQA provides comprehensive services for the analysis, development, implementation, assessment, monitoring, and auditing of Software Quality Management and Assurance Programs that are compliant with the requirements of ISO 9000-3 (Part 3), Guidelines For The Applications of ISO 9001 to the Development, Supply, and Maintenance of Software. These services are available where consideration is being given to registration of a firm's software quality management/assurance program to one of the ISO 9000 models (i.e., ISO 9001 [ANSI/ASQC Q91], ISO 9002 [ANSI/ASQC Q92], or ISO 9003 [ANSI/ASQC Q93]). SQA's services are performed to ensure a fully compliant, cost-effective, and efficient Program, which embodies the flexibility and adaptability necessary to accommodate other international and domestic software quality management/assurance standards.

ISO 9000-3 SOFTWARE QUALITY MANAGEMENT/ASSURANCE AND SOFTWARE ENGINEERING COURSES

SQA has developed a series of software quality management and assurance, and software engineering curricula, which includes ISO 9000 Software Engineering and Software Quality Curricula; DoD Software Engineering and Curricula; FDA Software Engineering and Software Quality Curricula, etc. The ISO 9000 curricula consists of the following series of ISO 9000-3 courses:

- Introduction to ISO 9000-3
- Implementation of ISO 9000-3
- Auditing ISO 9000-3 Software Quality Programs
- Software Subcontractors Assessments/Evaluations: ISO 9000-3
- Software Engineering: ISO 9000-3
- Software Project Management: ISO 9000-3
- Software Configuration Management: ISO 9000-3
- Software Documentation: ISO 9000-3

SOFTWARE QUALITY ASSOCIATES (SQA) TECHNICAL STAFF

SQA's Technical Staff consists of a cadre of skilled and qualified Software Quality Assurance Managers, Engineers, and Auditors with extensive experience in the areas of software engineering and software engineering capability evaluations and assessments; software quality program management and software quality program development, implementation, and assessment; and software quality assurance staff development and training. Members of the Technical Staff have proven experience in working with both National and International standards - including DoD-STD-2167A, DoD-STD-2168, MIL-S-52779A, FDA's GMP'S, DO-178A/B, NASA's SMAP, NUREG 0856, NUREG/CR-4640, AQAP-13, AQAP-14, and ISO 9000/ISO 9000-3. Members of the Technical Staff have an average of 20 years of professional experience, and many have advanced degrees and participate in the review process for software engineering and software quality standards. SQA's clients consist of an impressive list of well-known firms in Business and Industry, and various Governmental departments and agencies.

SPINDLER CONSULTING ASSOCIATES
P.O. Box 195
THIENSVILLE, WI 53092
Phone: 414-242-6446

Spindler Consulting Services offers consulting in quality management including total quality management systems to satisfy a variety of standards including ISO 9000, improvement programs in quality and productivity, evaluation and auditing of management programs and systems, and application of the quality sciences.

James R.R. Spindler, Principal, is a Fellow of the ASQC, and holds ASQC, CQA and CQE certifications. He teaches courses in quality for organizations including MRA, ASME, ASQC, and the University of Wisconsin Graduate School.

Management and Engineering Type Courses and Seminars:

- Total Quality: A Management Overview
- Quality Planning for Product Design/Development
- Quality Planning for Process Development
- Documenting the Quality Program (Quality Manual)
- Quality Auditing (emphasis may be on systems auditing or product/process auditing)
- Overview of Quality Engineering and Management Methods
- Quality Costs
- Quality Control in Purchasing
- ISO 9000: A Foundation for Total Quality

Statistics Courses and Seminars:

- Basic SPC
- Beyond Basic SPC
- SPC for Job Shops and Short Runs
- Measurement Evaluation (or Repeatability and Reproducibility Studies)
- Statistical Analysis and Design of Experiments (Process Improvement and DOE)
- DOE for Simple, Everyday Experiments
- Statistical Sampling
- SPC in Administrative Applications
- Statistics Overview for Top Management

College Courses:

- Quality Management and Engineering
- Statistical Quality Control
- Statistical Analysis

STAT-A-MATRIX INSTITUTE

2124 OAK TREE ROAD
EDISON, NJ 08820-1059
Phone: 908-548-0600
FAX: 908-548-0409

The STAT-A-MATRIX Group of Edison, New Jersey, has been helping companies meet national and international standards since 1968. With its worldwide staff of professionals, with an average of over 25 years of industrial experience, STAT-A-MATRIX is in a unique position to help clients compete in the global market:

- *The organization has already assisted hundreds of companies achieve ISO 9000/BS 5750 registration.*
- *The staff of over 30 consultants is qualified to provide every aspect of ISO 9000 training, self-assessment, documentation, implementation, and pre-registration assistance.*
- *The Executive Consultants include members of the international committees that review and update the ISO 9000 standards and scores of related codes, regulations, and standards.*
- *The Lead Assessor Certification Course for ISO 9000 auditors is registered by the UK's Institute for Quality Assurance (IQA) as an approved training course.*

CONSULTING SERVICES

ISO 9000 Registration Program:

STAT-A-MATRIX offers a complete package of consultancy services to enable organizations to implement ISO 9000 quality standards and obtain registration. The process consists of five phases designed to bring an organization into total compliance:

- Phase I - Quality System Audit - Conduct an overview audit; provide detailed audit report; identify an appropriate plan of action to achieve ISO registration
- Phase II - Plan of Action - Conduct a management awareness program to introduce the ISO standards; establish the Quality Action Plan to address areas of weakness and develop appropriate remediation
- Phase III - Implementation and Documentation - Develop, implement, and document a quality system to meet the requirements of ISO 9000
- Phase IV - Pre-Audit - Conduct an unbiased, independent, pre-assessment audit of the entire system to identify problem areas
- Phase V - Follow-Up - Assist with ISO 9000 registration and resolution of ongoing problems

ISO 9000 Start-Up Program:

For companies who know where they have to go and want to get a "jump-start" toward ISO 9000 registration, STAT-A-MATRIX offers a start-up process that effectively combines Phases I and II described above. The program takes one to two weeks, depending on the size and complexity of the operations. At the end of this program, client's are ready to go into Phase III, Implementation and Documentation.

- One-Day Management Orientation - Includes a brief walkthrough of your facility and review of your quality system, followed by an ISO 9000 briefing for up to 20 people. This briefing can also be run as a stand-alone program.
- ISO 9000 Training - Two to three days of intensive training for up to 10 people (all of whom have taken the one-day orientation). The group is taught the requirements of the ISO standards, how to document and implement a quality system, and how to audit their own operations for compliance.
- Quality System Audit - Led by a STAT-A-MATRIX consultant (or consultants), members of the group spend one to three days auditing their own facilities.

132

■ Plan of Action - Based on their audit report, and coached by the STAT-A-MATRIX consultant, the group prepares a plan of action for ISO documentation and implementation.

EDUCATION SERVICES

STAT-A-MATRIX has been providing education and administering examinations to satisfy multiple global standards for certification of lead auditors since 1973. Since the inception of the ISO 9000 standards in 1987, STAT-A-MATRIX has been on the cutting edge, helping companies meet these demanding requirements.

Current seminar titles are listed below. Any of these can be customized to be given on-site to meet a particular organization's needs.

■ ISO 9000 Internal Auditor Training
■ IQA Registered Lead Assessor Certification
■ ISO 9000 Management orientation
■ ISO 9000 Management Planning Session
■ ISO 9000 Awareness Program
■ ISO 9000 for Defense Contractors
■ ISO 9000 and the Medical Device GMP
■ Integration of ISO & Baldrige Concepts
■ ISO 9000 Quality System Preparation
■ ISO 9000 Quality Standard Interpretation
■ ISO 9000 Quality Assurance Systems

All courses will be taught by an IQA registered Lead Assessor/Assessor. Ninety percent of the STAT-A-MATRIX ISO instructors are approved by IQA to present the Lead Assessor Certification program. All instructors have a minimum of 25 years of quality/industry experience.

STAT-A-MATRIX is the only U.S.-based organization approved by IQA to present the Lead Assessor Certification Training.

PERIODICAL

A newsletter published three times a year is available free to those who request it. The Stat-A-Matrix News is designed to provide timely information on quality issues such as ISO 9000, TQM, MBNQA, and other quality systems.

TOM BAIR & ASSOCIATES, INC.
ROUTE 3, 1575 STEELE PIKE
VERSAILLES, KY 40383
Phone: 606-873-3077

Tom Bair & Associates, Inc., a Quality Control Service Company was started by Tom Bair who has worked in the field of Quality & Reliability for over 34 years (25 years for Texas Instruments Inc. and 9 years with Eagle Picher Industries).

Tom has had experience with large and small companies from manned space flight launch teams and all of the major automobile manufactures to small five man fabrication shops. His experience has been equally divided between commercial and military type industries. With this broad experience, Tom is in a position to guide and direct companies that need help in improving their Total Company Quality Management programs. He is a graduate of Kansas State University at Pittsburgh and has a masters degree in Quality Systems Management from the University of Dallas. He has also had courses from Dr. J.M. Juran and several courses based on the Phil Crosby and Dr. Deming's teaching. He is a senior member of the American Society for Quality Control and has served on various Vendee-Vendor and supplier related committees.

Tom is especially qualified to assist companies with Quality System surveys and evaluations due to having direct involvement with supplier evaluations for 28 of the 34 years that he has been in the field of quality.

The organization provides the following services:

- Supplier Quality System Surveys/Evaluations for compliance to MIL-I-45208, MIL-Q-9858, MIL-Std-45662A and ISO 9000 Series
- ISO 9000 guidance to become registered
- Supplier certifications for both systems and piece parts
- Total Quality Management system development
- Training: Statistical Process Control (SPC)
    - Root Cause Failure Analysis, 8-Step Plan
    - Supplier Quality Improvement
    - Basic Hand Soldering
- Source Inspection, Basic Inspection First Part and sort operations
- Quality & Employee involvement posters

All services get the "BEAR" stamp of approval

- Basic Inspection, assembly, and sort with overnight delivery
- Supplier corrective action and follow-up with root cause failure analysis report
- Source Inspections and product or process trouble-shooting
- Supplier surveys
    - MIL-I-45208
    - MIL-Q-9858
    - ISO 9000
- Total company quality evaluations
- Quality systems, procedures, and training
    - Incoming inspection
    - Process controls
    - Purchased part certification
    - Supplier certification
    - Total Quality Control
    - Total site cost of quality

- Instruction, guidance, or training
    - First article inspection
    - FMEA - Product and process
    - Hand soldering
    - Quality circles
    - Quality Function Deployment
    - Root cause failure analysis
    - Self-managed work teams
    - Serving the customer
    - Workmanship and quality STDs
    - Statistical Process Control (SPC)

VICTORIA GROUP
P.O. Box 536
FAIRFAX, VA 22030
Phone: 703-250-4990
FAX: 703-250-5523

The Victoria Group, based in the UK, has rapidly developed into one of the most highly regarded management consultant teams in the quality field. The principals of the organization have more than 50 years of combined experience in quality services, resulting in the company quickly achieving worldwide recognition.

The Victoria Group offers public programs, in-house training, and private consulting to a vast range of manufacturing and service industries in response to the increasing demand for quality systems training.

Since its inception, The Victoria Group has served the needs of the international community in Australia, New Zealand, Hong Kong, Malaysia, India, Taiwan and the United States.

In July of 1991, The Victoria Group opened an office in the Washington, DC area to become more accessible and responsive to U.S. companies seeking to develop quality assurance systems.

The Victoria Group is committed to principles of excellence and professes that Quality is a total management philosophy dedicated to improving every aspect of both individual and corporate life and performance - that in the final analysis, Quality is about people.

In-House Training

For companies needing a large staff at the same time and place, The Victoria Group offers in-house training tailored to fit your company's specific requirements. Programs will be customized with preliminary assessments made to determine the organization's unique needs. On-site training offers added time for questions and answers and is designed to solve important problems that are critical to the development of the firm's quality system. The financial advantages of in-house training are significant, and savings begin with as few as ten in a group. In-house training is both economical and efficient, saving your firm valuable time and money.

Consulting Services

The Victoria Group offers consultancy programs for companies wishing to create structured quality management systems that are in compliance with International Standards. In addition, for companies that are approaching a registration audit, The Victoria Group offers a comprehensive pre-assessment audit capability. When required, this can be conducted by British Registered Assessors. The Victoria Group also offers an internal auditing service to assist you in the review and updating of your Quality Management System. Vendor audits (pre-contract assessment surveys or compliance auditing) can be carried out either in the U.S. or in the UK.

Public Seminars: Quality Systems Training Program

The Victoria Group has designed an educational program to improve the understanding and utilization of the ISO 9000 Standards and subsequent Certification within an organization at its various departments. Through this program you will learn what your company must do to become certified.

This training program is administered by CEEM, a Virginia-based company that provides information to industry and government professionals through open-enrollment conferences, briefings, and seminars, as well as through its publications.

Public seminars include:
- Achieving Certification
- Documentation
- Internal Auditor
- Lead Auditor Training

WOLF ADVISORY INTERNATIONAL, LTD.
14 SOUTH DUKE STREET
LANCASTER, PA 17602
Phone: 717-299-6653
Phone: 800-220-4092
FAX: 717-299-6211

Wolf Advisory International, Ltd., founded in Lancaster in 1983, goes beyond training to work with clients in actually implementing the enhancements required to meet ISO 9000 certification or to implement a Total Quality Management environment.

Clients include the Fortune 500 and regional firms. Wolf Advisory International, Ltd. seeks to form a partnership with their clients. They believe their value to the client comes not from impressing them with what they know, but in helping them improve areas of their business. All clients are important and deserve attention regardless of size or potential business. Wolf Advisory believes the best way to grow their business is by doing what is right and fair.

ISO 9000 support includes:

- GAP Analysis
- GAP Plan
- Executive Education
- Lead Auditor Training
- Internal Auditor Training
- Documentation Training
- Pre-Audit Assessment
- Facilitation and Implementation Support

Among the other areas of support offered are:

- Strategic Systems Plans
- Computer Aided Systems Engineering (CASE)
- Computer Integrated Manufacturing
- Applications Selection/Development

WORD-WRIGHTS INCORPORATED
1000 JAMES STREET
SYRACUSE, NY 13203
Phone: 315-471-0400
FAX: 315-478-3442

Word-Wrights' services related to ISO focus on helping a company to understand the standards, plan the documentation system, and write the necessary documents.

As such, their services complement the expertise of in-house quality managers, ISO project leaders, and internal auditors. In addition, they may be active collaborators with external quality consultants.

ISO-related services Word-Wright can:

- Conduct briefings or consult with appropriate people in your company. They can help you answer the following questions:
    - What does each ISO standard cover?
    - What do the elements of the selected standard require of the company?

- Consult with key people to develop the documentation system. Questions to be answered include the following:
    - How many "tiers" should the system have?
    - What should be included at each tier?
    - How should the documentation be controlled?

- Audit all or part of the company's documentation. This audit answers the following questions:
    - Do the necessary documents exist to address each of the elements of the selected ISO standard?
    - Do the documents cover the required controls for each element?
    - Do the documents use a consistent approach for content format and style?
    - Are the documents logical, clear, and readable?

- Conduct group, small-group, and one-on-one training and provide coaching as personnel write the necessary documentation.

WRIGHT KILLEN & CO.
5847 SAN FELIPE
HOUSTON, TX 77057
PHONE: 713-783-1800
FAX: 713-783-5784

Wright Killen & Co. is a consulting firm serving primarily the petrochemical, chemical, refining and related industries. One of the practice areas of Wright Killen & Co. is the Total Quality Management (TQM) practice which includes ISO 9000 implementation assistance.

All Wright Killen & Co. consultants have several years experience implementing ISO 9000 quality systems in operating companies, as well as training and experience in TQM principles.

Services:

Services provided are management overview, implementation and internal auditing training; pre-assessments to develop specific implementation plans; and ongoing advisory role to assist clients throughout the certification process. Wright Killen's philosophy is to develop customized approaches that meet individual clients' needs.

Papers and Publications:

- "ISO 9000 Certification; Maintenance Role," Plant Services Magazine, November 1991
- "Just Talk To Me," Quality Progress, February 1991
- "Certification Requirements of ISO 9000," presented at a special session of the International Maintenance Institute, held for ISO 9000 topics
- "Texas Petrochemical Plant Gets Certification," Oil and Gas Journal, May 1991
- "The Role of Maintenance in ISO 9000", presented at the 1990 NPRA Refinery and Petrochemical Plant Maintenance Conference, San Antonio, Texas, May 1990
- "E & P Companies, Suppliers Move To International Standards," Oil & Gas Journal, May 1991

WRIGHT QUALITY/RELIABILITY PLANNING
6 Susan Road
Marlborough, MA 01752-1535
508-481-2631
Fax: 508-481-2631

Wright Quality/Reliability Planning is a consulting practice that works with companies and performs services in all areas of Quality and Reliability Planning.

Donald Wright, Principal, holds a BGS in Electronics and Mathematics degree and an MS in Systems Management, and has thirty plus years experience as an engineer in design, reliability physics, reliability mathematical modeling, software reliability modeling and measures, Failure Mode Effects and Critical Analysis (FMECA), quality measures, Quality Function Deployment (QFD), Design of Experiments (DOE), Taguchi methods, ISO 9000 series consulting, and teaching in the fields of quality and reliability.

The following quality assurance consulting and training organizations did not submit descriptions to be included in this Sourcebook, however, all were active advertisers for their services in the past year.

Most of these organizations offer a full range of consulting and training services in the areas of pre-assessment, lead auditor training, quality manual documentation, and general consultancy required before a company is ready to be audited against ISO 9001, 9002, 9003 or equivalent series.

AMREP International
1813 El Camino Real, Suite 10
Burlingame, CA 94010
Phone: 415-692-8537
Fax: 415-692-8538

Advanced Quality Engineering
5460 Norwood Lane N.
Plymouth, MN 55442
Phone: 612-553-9064

Affiliated Consulting Services
6515 S. Adams Court, Suite 1
Littleton, CO 80120
Phone: 303-771-0369

BSI Quality Assurance
10521 Baddock Road
Fairfax, VA 22032
Phone: 703-250-5900
Fax: 703-250-5313

Barber Consulting Resource, Inc.
4900 N. Wheeling Avenue
Muncie, IN 47304
Phone: 317-286-4349
Fax: 317-284-3076

Beacon Hill Technologies, Inc.
14 Beacon Street
Boston, MA 02108
Phone: 617-227-7887
Fax: 617-227-6845

Berthelot's Consulting E.T.C.
600 Bayou Boulevard
Pensacola, FL 32503
Phone: 904-438-2934

Bondinson & Associates, Inc.
16479 Dallas Parkway, Suite 390
Dallas, TX 75248
Phone: 214-931-5402
Fax: 214-931-0796

Burns Quality Systems
Box 963
Marshalltown, IA 50158
Phone: 515-753-7434

CEEM
10521 Braddock Road
Fairfax, VA 22032
Phone: 703-250-5900
Fax: 703-250-5313

CMI Concepts Co.
6920 Tanglewood Street
Lakewood, CA 90713-2836
Phone: 310-420-7468

Canatech Consultant Group, Inc.
2434 Bolen Bay
Regina, Saskatchewan S4V 0V6
Canada
Phone: 306-789-5091
Fax: 306-789-5091

Carman Group, The
1600 Promenade Tower, Suite 950
P.O. Box 835088
Richardson, TX 75080
Phone: 214-669-9464
Fax: 214-669-9478

Center for Corporate Learning
762 Miguel Avenue
Sunnyvale, CA 94086-3412
Phone: 408-773-0442

Charles R. "Chuck" Carter & Associates
6400 Barrie Road No. 1101
Edina, MN 55435-2317
Phone: 612-927-6003

Clinical Research Systems, Inc.
4503 Moorland Avenue
Minneapolis, MN 55424
Phone: 612-835-4018
Fax: 612-832-5806

Co-ordinate Measurement
7250 Commerce Drive, Unit H
Mentor, OH 44060
Phone: 216-975-9970

Commercial Scale Co., Inc.
95 Bowles Road
P.O. Box 265
Agawam, MA 01001
Phone: 413-786-8810
Fax: 413-786-8351

Consultant Services Institute
651 W. Mt. Pleasant Avenue
Livingston, NJ 07039
Phone: 201-992-3811

Continuous Improvement Technology
113 McHenry Road, Suite 211
Buffalo Grove, IL 60089
Phone: 708-634-6207
Fax: 708-634-6207

Corporate Resource Group of Connecticut, The
180 Belden Hill Road
Wilton, CT 06897
Phone: 203-761-9707

Cost Technology Associates
3443 Huntington Terrace
Crete, IL 60417
Phone: 708-758-7922

Creative Quality Solutions
7437 Kenwood Avenue
Wauwatosa, WI 53213
Phone: 414-771-2499
Fax: 414-771-2499

DataNet Technologies, Inc.
1270-F Rankin Street
P.O. Box 307
Troy, MI 48099-0307
Phone: 313-588-0150
Fax: 313-588-3735

David Hutton & Associates
82 Strathcona Avenue
Ottawa, Ontario K1S 1X6
Canada
Phone: 613-567-1511
Fax: 613-567-2272

David Mahlke Associates
5791 Michael Drive Northeast
Clear Rapids, IA 52402
Phone: 319-393-7754

Decision Group
P.O. Box 15005
Charlotte, NC 28211
Phone: 704-552-4770
Fax: 704-365-5523

Destra Consulting Group, Inc.
1655 Walnut Street, Suite 330
Boulder, CO 80302
Phone: 303-444-9619
Fax: 303-444-2570

Det Norske Veritas Industry, Inc.
16340 Park Ten Place, Suite 100
Houston, TX 77084
Phone: 713-579-9003
Fax: 713-579-1360

Donald M. Turnbull
3596 Jane Drive
Midland, MI 48642
Phone: 517-835-5076

Donald W. Marquardt & Associates
1415 Athens Road
Wilmington, DE 19803
Phone: 302-478-6695
Fax: 302-478-9329

EBB Associates Inc.
Box 8249
Norfolk, VA 23503
Phone: 804-588-3939
Fax: 804-558-5824

ETI Corp.
5870 S 194th Street
Kent, WA 98032
Phone: 206-340-4343
Fax: 206-872-8269

Eastern Michigan University Center for Quality
34 N. Washington Street
Ypsilanti, MI 48197
Phone: 313-487-2259
Fax: 313-481-0509

Ecco Gaging Systems, Inc.
1270-F Rankin Street
P.O. Box 307
Troy, MI 48099-0307
Phone: 313-588-8830
Fax: 313-588-3735

Edu-Tech Industries
881 Dover Drive, Suite 14
Newport Beach, CA 92663
Phone: 714-540-7660
Fax: 714-540-8345

Educational Data Systems, Inc.
One Parklane Boulevard, Suite 701w
Dearborn, MI 48126
Phone: 313-271-2660
Fax: 313-271-2698

Erin & Associates
723 Woodshire Way
Dayton, OH 45430
Phone: 513-429-3339

Ernst & Young
55 Almaden Boulevard, 4th Floor
San Jose, CA 95115
Phone: 408-947-6574
Fax: 408-947-4971

Excellence in Training Corp.
11358 Aurora Avenue
Des Moines, IA 50322-7907
Phone: 515-276-6569
Fax: 515-276-9476

F.X. Mahoney & Associates
2000 S. Dairy Ashford Road, Suite 230
Houston, TX 77077
Phone: 713-496-0455
Fax: 713-496-6439

Fed-Pro, Inc.
5615 Jensen Drive
Rockford, IL 61111
Phone: 815-282-4300
Fax: 815-282-4304

Federal Marketing Services, Inc.
4100 N. Rockton Avenue
Rockford, IL 61103
Phone: 800-654-6161
Fax: 815-654-6198

G.R. Technologies (USA), Inc.
P.O. Box 810638
Boca Raton, FL 33481-0638
Phone: 407-995-4881
Fax: 407-995-0613

GOAL/QPC
13 Branch Street
Methuen, MA 01844
Phone: 508-685-3900
Fax: 508-685-6151

George R Brearley
1916 NW 42nd Place
Gainsville, FL 32605
Phone: 904-375-4830

George Washington University
801 22nd Street NW
Acedemic Center, Room T-308
Washington, DC 20052
Phone: 202-994-6106
Fax: 202-785-3382

Georgia Institute of Technology
Atlanta, GA 30332-0800
Phone: 404-853-0968
Fax: 404-853-9172

Global Engineering Documents
2508 McGraw Avenue
Irvine, CA 92714
Phone: 800-854-7179
Fax: 714-261-7892

Grady & Associates
40C Lake Street
Wincester, MA 01890
Phone: 617-721-5770

Gunneson Group International
112 Kings Highway
Landing, NJ 07850
Phone: 201-770-4700
Fax: 201-770-4786

H.W. Fahrlander & Associates
640 Downing Drive
Richardson, TX 75080-6117
Phone: 214-783-1216
Fax: 214-783-6043

Harrington Group, Inc.
3208-C E. Colonial Drive, Suite 253
Orlando, FL 32803
Phone: 407-275-9841
Fax: 407-281-4941

Harrison M. Wadworth & Associates
660 Valley Green Drive Northeast
Atlanta, GA 30342
Phone: 404-255-8662
Fax: 404-250-1493

Henning Quality Services
145 Highvue Drive
Venetia, PA 15367
Phone: 412-941-6512

Herbert Monnich & Associates
8710 Summit Pines Drive
Humble, TX 77346
Phone: 713-852-2118

Hertzler Systems, Inc.
Formerly Paul Hertzler & Co., Inc.
17482 Eisenhower Drive
P.O. Box 588
Goshen, IN 46526
Phone: 219-533-0571
Fax: 219-533-3885

Hester Associates, Inc.
210 A Orleans Road
North Chatham, MA 02650
Phone: 508-945-4860
Fax: 508-945-4862

Hogan Quality Institute
16479 Dallas Parkway, Suite 390
Dallas, TX 75248
Phone: 214-931-7597
Fax: 214-407-0796

IIT Research Institute
201 Mill Street
Rome, NY 13440
Phone: 315-339-7068
Fax: 315-339-7002

IQS, Inc.
20525 Center Ridge Road, Suite 400
Cleveland, OH 44116
Phone: 800-635-5901
Fax: 216-333-3752

ITC
13515 Dulles Technology Drive
Herndon, VA 22071-3416
Phone: 703-713-3335
Fax: 703-713-0065

Impaq Organizational Improvement Systems
1744 W. Katella, Suite 3
Orange, CA 92667
Phone: 714-744-8941
Fax: 714-744-1034

Indiana University at South Bend
Division of Continuing Education
P.O. Box 7111
South Bend, IN 46634-7111
Phone: 219-237-4261
Fax: 219-237-4428

Institute for International Research
437 Madison Avenue, 23rd Floor
New York, NY 10022-7001
Phone: 800-999-3123
Fax: 212-826-6411

Institute of Industrial Engineers
25 Technology Park
Norcros, VA 30092
Phone: 404-449-0460
Fax: 404-263-8532

Integrated Technologies, Inc.
9855 Crosspoint Boulevard, Suite 126
Indianapolis, IN 46256
Phone: 317-577-8100

International Quality & Productivity Center
209 Cooper Avenue, Suite 7
Upper Montclair, NJ 07043-1850
Phone: 800-882-8684
Fax: 201-783-3851

International Quality Technologies
4010 Moorpark Avenue, Suite 102
San Jose, CA 95117
Phone: 408-249-1625

JBL Systems, Inc.
41570 Hayes Road
Clinton Twp., MI 48038
Phone: 313-286-3800
Fax: 313-286-5446

JCM Enterprises
4900 Blazer Parkway
Dublin, OH 43017
Phone: 800-835-5526
Fax: 614-792-1607

JP & Associates
5010 Cherrywood Drive
Oceanside, CA 92056
Phone: 619-945-9714
Fax: 619-945-9714

James P. O'Brien & Associates
18730 Arcadia Place
Brookfield, WI 53045
Phone: 414-783-5218

Jamohr U.S.A. Enterprises, Inc.
P.O. Box 144
Jefferson, NY 12093
Phone: 800-452-6657
Fax: 607-652-3382

John A. Keane & Associates
575 Ewing Street
Princeton, NJ 08540
Phone: 609-924-7904
Fax: 609-924-1078

John Kidwell & Associates
116 Skimmer Way
Daytona Beach, FL 32119
Phone: 904-756-2504
Fax: 904-788-1472

Johnson-Layton Co., The
8811 Alden Drive, Suite 7
Los Angeles, CA 90048
Phone: 310-859-2321
Fax: 310-274-3044

Jonathon Cope Associates, Inc.
1930 Indian Trail
Lake Oswego, OR 97034
Phone: 503-636-3709
Fax: 503-636-1578

KMR Group
420 N. Wabash Avenue, 4th Floor
Chicago, IL 60611
Phone: 312-670-2200
Fax: 312-670-2215

Karrie Alen & Associates
1085 Tasman Drive, Suite 726
Sunnyvale, CA 94087
Phone: 408-734-8733
Fax: 408-734-8733

Kinsel & Associates
602 West Avenue
Cartersville, GA 30120
Phone: 404-386-0368
Fax: 404-386-0615

L. Marvin Johnson & Associates, Inc.
822 Montezuma Way
West Covina, CA 91791
Phone: 818-919-1728
Fax: 818-919-7128

Lawrence A. Wilson & Associates
3727 Summitridge Drive
Atlanta, GA 30340
Phone: 404-723-1785
Fax: 404-457-9808

Liberty Consulting Group
6 Drumhill Lane
Randolph, NJ 07869
Phone: 201-361-5952
Fax: 201-361-5939

M.M. Wurtzel Associates
4 Childs Circle
Framingham, MA 01701
Phone: 508-872-1407

MC Instrument Repair, Inc.
2791 Universal Drive
Saginaw, MI 48603
Phone: 517-793-0377
Fax: 517-793-3997

MLI/CGI
31 Milk Street
Boston, MA 02109
Phone: 617-482-5545
Fax: 617-482-7037

Management Sciences International
2120 Lebanon Road
Lawrenceville, GA 30243-5131
Phone: 404-962-9915

Manufacturing Advisory Service
P.O. Box 304
Newburgh, IN 47629-0304
Phone: 800-695-8394
Fax: 812-853-9522

McDonald & Associates, Inc.
2511 E. 46th Street, Suite A-4
Indianapolis, IN 46205
Phone: 317-549-0055

McElrath & Associates, Inc.
6101 Cresent Drive
Edina, MN 55436
Phone: 612-927-4785

McHale Quality Systems
P.O. Box 681093
Indianapolis, IN 46268
Phone: 317-251-7563

McWilliams Quality Consulting
RR1, Box 541
Avinger, TX 75630
Phone: 903-755-3134
Fax: 903-755-2208

Mentor Group
8663 Tyler Boulevard
Mentor, OH 44060
Phone: 216-255-1445
Fax: 216-255-5900

Mescon Group, The
90 Executive Parkway S., Suite 100
Atlanta, GA 30329
Phone: 404-728-0110
Fax: 404-728-9862

Multiface, Inc.
6721 Merriman Avenue
Garden City, MI 48135
Phone: 313-421-6330
Fax: 313-421-1142

NK Consultants
P.O. Box 453
Hebron, KY 41048
Phone: 606-586-9788

National Business Technologies
1805 Cypress Drive
Irving, TX 75061
Phone: 214-579-9494
Fax: 214-438-9149

National Instruments
6504 Bridge Point Parkway
Austin, TX 78730-5039
Phone: 512-794-0100
Fax: 512-794-8411

National Quality Integrators
P.O. Box 20094
Washington, DC 20041
Phone: 703-689-0618
Fax: 703-689-0618

Navneet Enterprises
5151 Nishga Court
Mississauga, Ontario L5R 2M7
Canada
Phone: 416-890-7204

New-Tech Consulting, Inc.
9 Burnham Street
Cincinnati, OH 45218
Phone: 513-851-6256
Fax: 513-851-0165

OSU/OKC
Business/International Relations
900 N. Portland
Oklahoma City, OK 73107
Phone: 405-945-3278
Fax: 405-945-3397

Oil & Gas Consultants International
P.O. Box 35548
Tulsa, OK 74153-0448
Phone: 918-742-7057
Fax: 918-742-2272

Olympic Performance, inc.
7002 SW Nyberg Street
Tualatin, OR 97062-8205
Phone: 503-692-5573
Fax: 503-692-5254

Organizational Dynamics, Inc.
25 Mall Road
Burlington, MA 01803
Phone: 800-634-4636
Fax: 617-273-2558

Papa & Associates
50 Sheppard Avenue W., Suite 300
North York, Ontario M2N 1M2
Canada
Phone: 416-512-7272
Fax: 416-512-7272

Participation Associates
2555 N. Clark Street
Chicago, IL 60614
Phone: 312-935-5858
Fax: 312-935-3588

Paul Hertz Group, Inc., The
7990 S.W. 117th Avenue, Suite 100
Miami, FL 33183
Phone: 305-598-2601
Fax: 305-270-0627

Penton Software/Quality Alert Institute
257 Park Avenue S., 12th Floor
New York, NY 10010-7304
Phone: 800-221-3414
Fax: 212-353-4527

Philip Crosby Associates, Inc.
3260 University Boulevard
P.O. Box 606
Winter Park, FL 32793-6006
Phone: 407-677-3000
Fax: 407-677-3055

Phillips Quality Consultants, Inc.
2105 Damascus Church Road
Chapel Hill, NC 27516
Phone: 919-933-9075

Pister Group, Inc., The
P.O. Box 38042
550 Eglington Avenue W.
Toronto, Ontario M5N 3A8
Canada
Phone: 416-886-9470
Fax: 416-764-6405

Powers Consulting, Inc.
6107 Knox Avenue S.
Minneapolis, MN 55419
Phone: 612-861-4794

Precision Measurement Laboratories
201 W. Beach Avenue
Inglewood, CA 90302
Phone: 310-671-4345
Fax: 310-671-0858

Prime Process Management
5315 W. 74th Street
Edina, MN 55439
Phone: 612-835-1913
Fax: 612-835-2458

Process Integrity, Inc.
P.O. Box 153066
Arlington, TX 76015
Phone: 817-472-6694
Fax: 817-468-0008

Productivity & Quality Consultants International
11802 Fidelia Court
Houston, TX 77024
Phone: 713-781-6255
Fax: 713-973-2055

Productivity Enhancement
P.O. Box 295
Montvale, NJ 07645
Phone: 201-930-8717

Productivity Improvement Center
Durham College
2000 Simcoe Street N.
Oshawa, Ontario L1H 7L7
Canada
Phone: 416-576-2000
Fax: 416-728-2530

Q.A. Systems, Inc
441 Devon Street
P.O. Box 3090
Kearny, NJ 07032
Phone: 210-998-2627
Fax: 201-998-4292

QCI International
P.O. Box 1503
Red Bluff, CA 96080-1503
Phone: 800-527-6970
Fax: 800-527-6983

QMI, Div of the Canadian Standards Assoc
Mississauga Executive Center
Two Robert Speck Parkway, Suite 800
Mississauga, Ontario L4Z 1H8
Canada
Phone: 416-272-3920
Fax: 416-272-3942

QMMT Associates
P.O. Box 3471
Greenville, NC 27836
Phone: 919-757-0667

QNR Associates
1052 Partridge Drive
Palatine, IL 60067
Phone: 708-776-7703
Fax: 708-776-7703

Qualicon AG
Industrie Neuhof 21
Kirchburg, 3422
Switzerland
Phone: 011-4134-455-845
Fax: 011-4134-455-581

Qualifications Consultants, Inc.
3212 Winding Way
Dayton, OH 45419
Phone: 513-293-3377
Fax: 513-293-0220

Qualitran Professional Services, Inc.
P.O. Box 295
Stroud, Ontario L0L 2M0
Canada
Phone: 800-461-9902
Fax: 705-722-0324

Quality Breakthroughs
1407 S. 7th Street
Brainerd, MN 56401
Phone: 218-829-0661

Quality Education Services, Inc.
5200 Roundrock Trail
Plano, TX 75023
Phone: 14-596-6865
Fax: 214-985-0246

Quality International Limited
2716 Orthodox Street
Philadelphia, PA 19137-1604
Phone: 800-524-5877

Quality Management Alliance, The
6400 Barrie Road, No. 1101
Minneapolis, MN 55435-2317
Phone: 612-927-6003

Quality Management Assistance Group
1528 N. Ballard Road
Appleton, WI 54911
Phone: 800-236-7802
Fax: 414-738-7802

Quality Management Associates, Inc.
No. 5 Scottsdale
Salisbury, NC 28146
Phone: 704-637-2299
Fax: 704-637-6181

Quality Management International Limited
55 Morley Circle
Saint John, New Brunswick E2J 2X5
Canada
Phone: 506-633-2060
Fax: 506-633-2060

Quality Management Support, Inc.
P.O. Box 9572
Metairie, LA 70055
Phone: 504-455-1602
Fax: 504-885-8502

Quality Management Systems, Inc.
P.O. Box 781
Palm Harbor, FL 34682-0781
Phone: 813-785-1688
Fax: 813-786-7920

Quality Network, The
TQN Publishing
110 Linden Oaks Drive
Rochester, NY 14625
Phone: 716-248-5712

Quality Plus Engineering
4052 N.E. Couch
Portland, OR 97232
Phone: 800-266-7383

Quality Resources International
1521 Georgetoen Road, Suite 203
Hudson, OH 44236
Phone: 216-650-2767
Fax: 216-528-0029

Quality Sciences Consultants, Inc.
22531 S.E. 42nd Court
Issaquah, WA 98027-7241
Phone: 206-392-4006
Fax: 206-392-2621

Quality Services International
5550 W. Central Avenue, Suite G
Toledo, OH 43615
Phone: 419-535-9555
Fax: 419-535-1370

Quality Techniques, Inc.
552 Washington Avenue
Pittsburgh, PA 15106
Phone: 412-279-0730
Fax: 412-279-3382

Quality Technologies, Inc.
2512 Second Avenue #308
Seattle, WA 98121
Phone: 206-441-0707

Quality Technology Co.
1270 Lance Lane
Carol Stream, IL 60188
Phone: 708-231-3142

Quality Visions
7315 Duluth Avenue
Milwaukee, WI 53220
Phone: 414-321-3869

Qualtec Quality Services, Inc.
11760 U.S. Highway 1, Suite 500
N. Palm Beach, FL 33408-3029
Phone: 407-775-8300
Fax: 407-775-8301

Qualtech of Racine, Inc.
2200 Clark Street
P.O. Box 1527
Racine, WI 53401
Phone: 414-637-1212
Fax: 414-637-5285

Quexx International Limited
3043 Aries Place
Burnaby, British Columbia V3J 7G1
Canada
Phone: 604-421-2491
Fax: 604-421-2491

Quong & Associates, Inc.
54 Fortuna Avenue
San Francisco, CA 94115
Phone: 415-922-2957
Fax: 415-931-4699

R.D. Garwood, Inc.
501 Village Trace, Building 9
Marietta, GA 30067
Phone: 800-241-6653
Fax: 404-952-2976

RAU & Associates
25 Timberly Drive
Lake Charles, LA 70605
Phone: 318-477-0758
Fax: 318-478-9440

RBS Consultant In Quality
319 Friendship Street
Iowa City, IA 52245
Phone: 319-337-8283
Fax: 319-338-3320

RC Associates
3746 Saratoga Drive
Downers Grove, IL 60515
Phone: 708-969-5541
Fax: 708-963-1558

Ralph D. Call Q Consultant
226 Hope Road
Tinton Falls, NJ 07724
Phone: 908-542-3028
Fax: 908-542-3028

Rand E. Winters Consulting Group
3677 Portman Lane
Grand Rapids, MI 49508
Phone: 616-247-1232
Fax: 616-452-8374

Rath & Strong, Inc.
92 Hayden Avenue
Lexington, MA 02173
Phone: 617-861-1700
Fax: 617-861-1424

Richard Chang Associates
41 Corporate Park, Suite 230
Irvine, CA 92714
Phone: 714-756-8096
Fax: 714-756-0853

150

Richard Tyler International, Inc.
7202 Benwich Circle
Houston, TX 77095
Phone: 713-974-7214
Fax: 713-855-0503

Rochester Institute of Technology
Center for Quality & Applied Statistics
P.O. Box 7887
Hugh L. Carvey Building
Rochester, NY 14623-0887
Phone: 716-475-6990
Fax: 716-475-5959

Ron Cristofono Co.
SPC Training & Implementation, Inc.
131 Mack Hill Road
Amherst, NH 03031
Phone: 603-673-7262
Fax: 603-672-6428

Russell Technologies, Inc
4909 75th Street
Edmonton, Alberta T6B 2S3
Canada
Phone: 403-469-4461
Fax: 403-462-9378

SGS Industrial Service
400 N. Sam Houston Parkway E., Suite 800
Houston, TX 77060
Phone: 713-591-5800
Fax: 713-591-5825

STELTECH
1375 Kerns Road
Burlington, Ontario L7P 3H8
Canada
Phone: 416-528-2511
Fax: 416-332-9067

Sanders Quality Associates, Inc.
820 Gessner, Suite 940
Houston, TX 77024
Phone: 713-465-8772
Fax: 713-465-9742

Scott Technical Services
34 Channing Street, Suite 400
Newton, MA 02158
Phone: 617-527-7032
Fax: 617-527-0618

Serendipity Consulting Services
9972 Marquan Circle
Molalla, OR 97038
Phone: 503-829-5921

Silton-Bookman Systems
20410 Town Center Lane, Suite 280
Cupertino, CA 95014
Phone: 800-932-6311
Fax: 408-446-0731

Solaris Systems
1230 S. Lewis Street
Anaheim, CA 92805
Phone: 714-563-4300
Fax: 714-563-4355

Solution Specialists
8460 Dygert Drive
Alto, MI 49302
Phone: 616-891-9114
Fax: 616-891-9114

Southeastern Quality Consultants
800 Laurel Avenue
Black Mountain, NC 28711
Phone: 704-669-4600

Stanton & Hucko
540 Midtown Tower
Rochester, NY 14604
Phone: 716-546-6480

Statimate Systems, Inc.
3216 W. St. Joseph
Lansing, MI 48917
Phone: 517-484-1144
Fax: 517-482-1962

Stochos, Inc.
14 N. College Street
Schenectady, NY 12305
Phone: 800-426-4014
Fax: 518-372-4789

Supplier Research Group
79 Boston Turnpike, Suite 316
Shrewsbury, MA 01545
Phone: 508-842-5223
Fax: 508-798-6606

TQM Consulting
2701 Revere Street, Suite 232
Houston, TX 77098
Phone: 713-523-2312
Fax: 713-520-0495

TQM Group Limited, The
222 Berkeley Street, Suite 1550
Boston, MA 02116
Phone: 617-236-8110
Fax: 617-236-8120

TQM Services
98 Foster Road
Swampscott, MA 01907
Phone: 617-593-4598
Fax: 617-593-4598

TUV Product Services, Inc.
1416 N.W. 9th Street
Corvallis, OR 97330
Phone: 503-753-4438
Fax: 503-753-4510

Technology Development Corp.
5760 S. Semoran Boulevard
Orlando, FL 32822
Phone: 407-381-4518
Fax: 407-381-4517

Third Generation, Inc., The
4439 Rolling Pine Drive
Orchard Lake, MI 48323
Phone: 313-363-1654
Fax: 313-363-3440

Total Quality Associates, Inc.
P.O. Box 47
Lincolnshire, IL 60069
Phone: 800-377-4660
Fax: 708-634-2322

Total Quality Management
500 Oxford Road
Bala Cynwyd, PA 19004
Phone: 215-664-8816

Tri-Tech Services, Inc.
4700 Clairton Boulevard
Pittsburgh, PA 15236
Phone: 412-884-2290
Fax: 412-884-2268

Unified Quality Systems
715- Standish Avenue
Westfield, NJ 07092
Phone: 908-232-1654

Unique Solutions, Inc.
P.O. Box 1711
Royal Oak, MI 48068
Phone: 313-435-5307
Fax: 313-435-5307

United States Testing Co., Inc.
291 Fairfield Avenue
Fairfield, NJ 07004
Phone: 201-575-5252
Fax: 201-575-8271

**University of California Extension
Business & Management**
3120 De La Cruz Boulevard
Santa Clara, CA 95054
Phone: 408-748-2951
Fax: 408-748-7388

Vragel & Associates, Inc.
8950 Gross Point Road
Skokie, IL 60077
Phone: 708-470-2531
Fax: 708-470-3507

W.A. Golomski & Associates
20 E. Jackson Boulevard, Suite 850
Chicago, IL 60604-2208
Phone: 312-922-5986
Fax: 312-922-4070

W.R. Wayman & Associates
3722 Twin Oak Court
Flower Mound, TX 75028
Phone: 214-539-0335

Warne C. Stauss Consultant, Inc.
3240 N. Manor Drive
Lansing, IL 60438
Phone: 708-474-5290

William J. Hill, PE
7 Kramer Lane
Weston, CT 06883
Phone: 203-544-9035

William M. Hayden Jr. Consultants
P.O. Box 56022
Jacksonville, FL 32241-6022
Phone: 904-260-7700
Fax: 904-260-7701

Working Smarter, Inc.
P.O. Box 56
Manchester, PA 17345
Phone: 717-266-7234
Fax: 717-266-7234

REGISTRAR
SECTION

A.G.A. QUALITY, A SERVICE OF INTERNATIONAL APPROVALS SERVICES
8501 EAST PLEASANT VALLEY ROAD
CLEVELAND, OH 44131
TEL: 216-524-4990
FAX: 216-642-3463
CONTACT: CORBY J. LOCKE (X.8311)

OVERVIEW

American Gas Association (A.G.A.) Laboratories, founded in 1925, was the first U.S. third-party agency to develop and implement a quality system registration program to the ISO 9000 (ANSI/ASQC Q90) Series Standards. A.G.A. Quality was formed as a division of the A.G.A. in response to the needs of manufacturers requiring independent auditing and verification to the ISO 9000 standards. International Approvals Services was launched in mid-1993 as a joint venture between A.G.A. Laboratories and CGA Approvals, Inc. of Canada to provide comprehensive service to clients selling products in both the U.S. and Canada.

SCOPE

A.G.A. Quality's product testing capabilities include electric and oil fired products, gas appliances and related accessories. To date, 29 manufacturers and service organizations of most major industries have been certified by A.G.A. Quality. Over 200 million regulated and non-regulated products and appliances bear A.G.A.'s star seal of certification.

ACCREDITATION

A.G.A. Quality's quality system registration program is accredited by the Registrar Accreditation Board (RAB) and the Raad voor de Certificatie (RvC). A.G.A. signed Memorandums of Understanding with DQS in agreement with DIN in Germany, AFAQ in France, and VEG in the Netherlands. Bilateral agreements are being pursued with Japan, England, Denmark, Australia and New Zealand.

ABS QUALITY EVALUATIONS, INC.
16855 NORTHCHASE DRIVE
HOUSTON, TX 77060-6008
TEL: 713-873-9400
FAX: 713-874-9564
CONTACT: BILL SULLIVAN

OVERVIEW

Headquartered in Houston, ABS Quality Evaluations, Inc. (ABS QE) is a member of The American Bureau of Shipping Group of Companies, Inc. (ABS Group). Founded in 1862, the American Bureau of Shipping is one of the leading marine classification societies, with over 200 offices in 90 countries. ABS diversified outside of the marine industry and has offered a wide variety of third party quality system assessment services since 1973. In 1990, ABS Quality Evaluations, Inc. (ABS QE) was formed to handle all third party assessment and certification programs, including ISO 9000. Companies seeking quality system registration are evaluated and certified according to requirements set by the ISO 9000 (ASQC Q90) series of standards. Upon certification, companies are given the authorization to display the ABS QE Quality Mark and those of its accreditors.

SCOPE

Among the wide variety of industries ABS QE is accredited to certify are:

- Architectural & eng'g activities
- Chemicals & allied products
- Electronic & electric equip.
- Fabricated metal products
- Fishing, hunting, & trapping
- Industrial machinery
- Instruments & related products
- Lumber & wood products
- Metal mining
- Miscellaneous repair services
- Miscellaneous manufacturing industries
- Oil & gas extraction
- Paper & allied products
- Petroleum & coal products
- Primary metal industries
- Research & development services and related technical consistency
- Rubber & misc. plastics products
- Stone, clay & glass products
- Textile mill products
- Transportation equipment
- Transportation services
- Water transportation

ACCREDITATION

ABS Quality Evaluations, Inc. is accredited by the Registrar Accreditation Board (RAB) in the United States, the Dutch Council for Certification, the Raad voor de Certificatie (RvC), in the Netherlands, and by INMETRO in Brazil.

Lead assessors are trained and registered by the Institute of Quality Assurance (IQA). All of the audit teams are lead by Institute of Quality Assurance (IQA) trained and registered lead assessors.

Surveillance audits are performed twice per year on certified facilities to ensure continued compliance with the ISO 9000 series standards.

OTHER PROGRAMS

ABS QE also offers industry assessments to a number of quality system standards, including those developed for the ABS Quality Assurance and Quality Accreditation Programs. In addition, ABS Quality Evaluations, Inc. provides auditing services for the quality certification programs of a number of industrial groups. Among these groups are the American Institute of Steel Construction (AISC), the Steel Structures Painting Council (SSPC), the American Petroleum Institute (API), and the Steel Plate Fabricating Association (SPFA).

AMERICAN ASSOCIATION FOR LABORATORY ACCREDITATION (A2LA)

656 QUINCE ORCHARD ROAD, #304
GAITHERSBURG, MD 20878-1409
TEL: 301-670-1377
FAX: 301-869-1495
CONTACT: PETER UNGER

OVERVIEW

The American Association for Laboratory Accreditation (A2LA) is a non-profit association founded in 1978. A2LA accredits testing laboratories and conducts seminars for its scientific members.

SCOPE

A2LA has offered ISO 9000 quality system certification since December 1990. It operates under a Memorandum of Understanding with the Environmental Protection Agency (EPA) to certify environmental reference materials. Reference materials suppliers are required to be registered by A2LA to the ANSI/ASQC Q91 OR Q92 (ISO 9001 OR 9002) quality system standards.

ACCREDITATION

A2LA signed a Memorandum of Understanding (MOU) with the U.S. EPA's Environmental Monitoring Systems Laboratory at Cincinnati (EMSL-Cincinnati) which establishes a relationship between A2LA's Certification Program for A2LA Certified Reference Materials and U.S. EPA's Cooperative Research and Development Agreements (CRADA) for EPA Certified Reference Materials. A2LA has an agreement with National Quality Assurance, USA, Inc. (NQA) for joint accreditation of laboratories and the registration of quality management systems.

AMERICAN EUROPEAN SERVICES, INC.

1054 31ST STREET, NW
SUITE 120
WASHINGTON, DC 20007
TEL: 202-337-3214
FAX: 202-337-3709
CONTACT: ERIC THIBAU

OVERVIEW

American European Services, Inc. (AES) is the U.S. subsidiary of the APAVE Group, founded over a century ago in France. APAVE actively participated in organizing AFAQ, the French Quality Assurance Association, through COPREC-AT, the professional association of French testing laboratories. APAVE maintains active participation in AFAQ and constantly interacts with businesses to evaluate their changing needs. It is, therefore, ideally positioned to analyze requests and reconcile them with the criteria needed to secure AFAQ certification.

AES, as a member of the APAVE Group, provides technical assistance, training and consultation services. SEQUAL, an independent wholly-owned subsidiary of APAVE, was created in 1987 to conduct certification activities. SEQUAL conducts safety- and quality-related assessments for product certification, personnel accreditation, and quality system certification. The necessary documentation is processed for AFAQ approval and certification.

SCOPE

The accredited scope covers all industries.

ACCREDITATION

AFAQ is a member of the European Quality System Assessment and Certification Committee (EQS), an association of the major European certification bodies. AFAQ has signed mutual recognition cooperation agreements with DQS in Germany, SQS in Switzerland, and QMI in Canada. These agreements assure worldwide recognition of certification awarded to registered companies. All SEQUEL auditors are registered and trained through AFAQ.

AT&T QUALITY REGISTRAR

To reach AT&T Quality Registrar, call 800-521-3399 (Union, New Jersey) or contact one of the following:

JOHN MALINAUSKAS
650 LIBERTY AVENUE
UNION, NJ 07083
TEL: 908-851-3058
FAX: 908-851-3158

DAVID SWASEY
2600 SAN TOMAS EXPRESSWAY
SANTA CLARA, CA 95051-1366
TEL: 408-562-1370
FAX: 408-562-1366

JOHNSON CHENG
23RD FLOOR, 3 EXCHANGE SQUARE
8 CONNAUGHT PLACE
CENTRAL HONG KONG
TEL: 852-846-2823
FAX: 852-810-0564

SANN RENE GLAZA
1945, CHAUSSEE DE WAVRE
1160 BRUSSELLS
BELGIUM
TEL: 322-676-3596
TEL: 322-676-3596

OVERVIEW

AT&T Quality Registrar (AT&T QR) has registered quality systems using the ISO 9000 standards since June 1991. Before 1991, AT&T QR's auditors performed hundreds of second party audits for AT&T using ISO 9000 standards, ANSI Z1.15 standards, AT&T and Bell System Quality standards and military standards.

AT&T QR has principal offices in New Jersey, Pennsylvania, California, Hong Kong, Singapore, Taipei, Tokyo, Ireland, and Brussels. Satellite offices are located in Florida, Georgia, Massachusetts, New York, Ohio, Illinois, North Carolina, Colorado, and Oklahoma.

ACCREDITATION:

The registration program currently registers quality systems of service organizations and the producers of:

- Chemicals and plastics
- Distribution of electrical and electronic products
- Electrical equipment, electronics communication Equipment and systems
- Fabricated metal products
- Industrial machinery and computer equipment
- Instruments and related products
- Miscellaneous software services
- Primary metal industries
- Printing and publishing
- Rubber and plastics products (cable & wire)
- Textile products

ACCREDITATION

AT&T QR received its accreditation from the Registrar Accreditation Board (RAB) in June 1991.

AV QUALITE, ASSOCIATED WITH GROUP AIB-VINCOTTE

2900 WILCREST
SUITE 300
HOUSTON, TX 77042
TEL: 713-465-2850
FAX: 713-465-1182
CONTACT: TERRY HEAPS

OVERVIEW

AIB has been a company concerned with safety and quality in the workplace since its establishment in 1890. Vincotte has had experience working with the same type of issues since 1872. These two firms merged in 1989 to form AIB-Vincotte (AV), which in addition to the ISO 9000 registration services office, AV Qualite, in Houston, has eight other offices in Belgium and one in Abu Dhabi. AV has dealt with standardized quality systems since 1969.

SCOPE

AV professionals have extensive experience in areas such as:

- Advanced technology systems
- Calibration of test and measuring equipment
- Chemical manufacturing
- Chemical, mechanical, and electrical testing
- Civil engineering projects
- Food
- Industrial projects
- Information technology
- Medical devices
- Nondestructive testing
- Nuclear safety
- Petrochemical equipment
- Power generation

ACCREDITATION

AV is a notified body to the Commission of the European Communities (EC) in the framework of more than 50 directives. AV is recognized by Belgian authorities and has audited the quality system of all suppliers (more than 600) of regulated equipment for the Belgian nuclear program.

AV is the leading certification body of Belgium and has been accredited for quality system certification by the National Accreditation Council of Belgium (NAC-QS). AV has signed recognition agreements with: QMI (Canada), DS (Denmark), DQS (Germany), SFS (Finland), NSAI (Ireland), N.V. KEMA (The Netherlands), IPQ (Portugal), AENOR (Spain), SQS (Switzerland), BSI-QA (United Kingdom), and JMI (Japan).

As a member of the European Network for Quality System Assessment and Certification (E-Q-Net), AV's certificate is supported by the remaining fifteen members which include the leading certification bodies of Europe: BSI-QA, AFAQ, DQS, DS, N.V. KEMA, SIS, SQS, AENOR, CISQ, IPQ, NSAI, OeQS, SFS, NCS, ELOT.

BELLCORE QUALITY REGISTRATION

6 CORPORATE PLACE
PISCATAWAY, NJ 08854
TEL: 908-699-3739
FAX: 908-336-2220
CONTACT: EDWARD BARABAS

OVERVIEW

Bell Communications Research (Bellcore), the largest research consortium in the United States, provides quality system registration in accordance with the ISO 9000 series of standards. Built on the foundation of the former century-old Bell System, Bellcore was formed in 1984 as a result of the Bell System breakup. Bellcore supports the Bell Operating Companies with research, standards, software, product analysis, quality assurance and other services. Bellcore engineers have extensive experience in software and hardware quality assurance, quality system auditing, production processes, international standards, and telecommunications.

SCOPE

Bellcore issues ISO 9000 registrations to telecommunications industry suppliers including the following Standard Industrial Classification (SIC) categories:

- Administration of environmental quality
- Apparel and other textile products
- Chancels and allied products
- Communications
- Electronics and other electric equipment
- Fabricated metal products, except machinery and transportation equipment
- Furniture and textiles
- Industrial and commercial machinery and computer equipment
- Instruments and other related products
- Leather and leather products
- Lumber and wood products
- Miscellaneous repair products
- Paper and allied products
- Primary metal industries
- Rubber and miscellaneous plastic products
- Software
- Stone, clay, glass and concrete products
- Textile mill products
- Trucking and warehousing

ACCREDITATION

Bellcore quality registration services are accredited by the Registrar Accreditation Board (RAB). Auditors and Lead Auditors are certified by RAB.

BRITISH STANDARDS INSTITUTION QUALITY ASSURANCE

IN THE US:
BRITISH STANDARDS INSTITUTION, INC.
8000 TOWERS CRESCENT DRIVE, STE 1350
VIENNA, VA 22182
TEL: 703-760-7828
FAX: 703-760-7899

IN THE UK:
BSI QUALITY ASSURANCE
PO BOX 375
MILTON KEYNES MK14 6LL
TEL: 0908-220-909
FAX: 0908-220-671

OVERVIEW

British Standards Institution Quality Assurance (BSI) is the United Kingdom National Standards body. BSI sets standards, tests, and offers a system of quality assurance measured against British Standard (BS) 5750/ISO 9000/EN29000, in which their own compliance is guaranteed.

SCOPE

BSI's engineers are capable of testing to foreign standards or a company's own standards. The Kitemark is awarded to products meeting BS 5750 requirements. The Registration and Kitemark schemes are displayed by BSI registered firms in almost every sector of industry.

ACCREDITATION

BSI is accredited by the Raad voor de Certificatie (RvC) and by the National Accreditation Council for Certification Bodies (NACCB).

BUREAU VERITAS QUALITY INTERNATIONAL (NA) INC.
NORTH AMERICAN CENTRAL OFFICES
509 NORTH MAIN STREET
JAMESTOWN, NY 14701
TEL: 716-484-9002
FAX: 716-484-9003
CONTACT: GREG SWAN

OVERVIEW

Bureau Veritas Quality International (BVQI) is a third party assessor and registrar of quality management systems and products to ISO 9000/Q90/EN29000. BVQI is headquartered in London and is a subsidiary of Bureau Veritas in Paris founded in 1928. BVQI (NA) is headquartered in Jamestown, New York to adhere to the needs of North American firms seeking registration.

SCOPE

BVQI is recognized for its competence in all manufacturing and service sectors.

ACCREDITATION

BVQI is accredited by the Raad voor de Certificatie (RvC) in Holland, National Accreditation Council for Certification Bodies (NACCB) in the UK., Registration Accreditation Board (RAB) in the U.S., TGA in Germany, SWEDAC in Sweden, SAB in Switzerland, BENOR in Belgium (cannot be issued by BVQI outside of Belgium), and SINCERT in Italy. National accreditation in several other countries is currently pending. BVQI structures it's Internal Quality System in compliance with the European Standard EN45012 so that suppliers achieving Certification may have international mutual recognition.

CANADIAN GENERAL STANDARDS BOARD
QUALITY SYSTEMS DIVISION
222 QUEEN STREET, SUITE 1402
OTTAWA, ON CANADA K1A 1G6
TEL: 613-941-8657
FAX: 613-941-8706
CONTACT: CLAUDETTE TREMBLAY OR JAMES LITTLEJOHN

OVERVIEW

The Canadian General Standards Board (CGSB), a Government of Canada Special Operating Agency (SOA), evolved in 1934 as an organization involved in standards writing and quality concerns. CGSB has worked as a part of the National Research Council, the Department of Defense Production, and most recently as a Directorate of Supply and Services Canada. As a third party auditing authority, CGSB has been qualifying and certifying companies' products to national standards for the past 20 years and registering quality systems to the ISO 9000 series for over four years.

SCOPE

CGSB has developed over 1600 standards for products and services ranging from children's clothing and office furniture to non-destructive testing, spanning such industries as computer manufacturing, fabrication and high-volume production. CGSB is required under its accreditation to accept any valid application for audit services.

ACCREDITATION

CGSB is accredited to register quality systems by the Standards Council of Canada (SCC) in accordance with its Criteria and Procedures for Accreditation of Organizations Registering Quality Systems Standard (CAN-P-10), which embodies EN 45012. CGSB has a Memorandum of Understanding (MOU) with NSAI (Ireland) and SIRIM (Malaysia). CGSB uses assessors that meet the ISO 10011-2 qualification criteria for auditing, auditors, and audit programs.

CGA APPROVALS - CANADIAN OPERATION OF INTERNATIONAL APPROVALS SERVICES

55 Scarsdale Road
Don Mills
Toronto, ON Canada M3B 2R3
Tel: 416-447-6468
Fax: 416-447-7067
Contact: John Wolff

OVERVIEW

International Approval Services (IAS) is a joint venture between CGA Approvals, Inc., formerly the Approval Division of the Canadian Gas Association, and the American Gas Association (A.G.A.) Laboratories.IAS was formed in mid-1993 to provide comprehensive services to its customers in both Canada and the U.S.

CGA Approvals in Toronto, Ontario is a standards writing and registration organization serving Canada. It has provided equipment safety testing and certification services for more than 50 years.

A.G.A. Laboratories was the first U.S. third-party agency to develop and implement a quality system registration program to the ISO 9000 series. A.G.A. Quality, in Cleveland, Ohio, is the division of the A.G.A. which provides assessment and certification services to the United States.

SCOPE

CGA Approvals has registered companies in the gas and related industries. A.G.A. Quality's accredited scope includes paper and allied products, petroleum and coal products, and primary metal and related industries. Both registrars continue to expand their scope of registration activities.

ACCREDITATION

CGA Approvals is accredited by the Standards Council of Canada (SCC). A.G.A. Quality is accredited by the Registrar Accreditation Board (RAB) and the Raad voor de Certificatie (RvC). A.G.A. signed Memorandums of Understanding (MOU) with DQS in agreement with DIN in Germany, AFAQ in France, and VEG in the Netherlands. Jointly, bilateral agreements are being pursued with England, Denmark, Australia, New Zealand, and the United Kingdom.

DET NORSKE VERITAS INDUSTRY, INC.
16340 Park Ten Place
Suite 100
Houston, TX 77084
Tel: 713-579-9003
Fax: 713-579-1360
Contact: Yehuda Dror

OVERVIEW

Det norske Veritas Industry, Inc. (DnVII) is a wholly-owned subsidiary of DnV worldwide, headquartered in Houston, Texas. DnV was established in 1864 and has expanded its organization throughout over 100 countries. DnVII offers companies in North America the services of quality system certification in accordance with the ISO 9000 series, half-day seminars which clarify the standard from the perspective of the registrar, and two-day internal auditor courses.

SCOPE

DnV has certified companies in the process automation and control, industrial control, and oil field industries. They have been contracted to certify companies in the chemicals industry and are expanding their scope to other industries such as: pulp and paper, computer hardware and software, electronics, and machinery.

ACCREDITATION

DnV is accredited by the National Councils for Accreditation of Certifying Bodies (NACCB) in the UK, the RvC in the Netherlands, TAG in Germany, SINCERT in Italy, SWEDAC in Sweden, DANAK in Denmark, NA in Norway, FINAS in Finland, and NAC-QS in Belgium. They are currently seeking accreditation in other countries introducing an accreditation scheme.

ENTELA, INC., QUALITY SYSTEM REGISTRATION DIVISION

3033 MADISON AVENUE SW
GRAND RAPIDS, MI 49548
TEL: 616-247-0515
FAX: 616-247-7527
CONTACT: BOB KOZAK OR TIM HUBBARD

OVERVIEW

ENTELA, Inc. Quality System Registration Division (QSRD) is a division of ENTELA Laboratories, Inc. ENTELA, founded as a Michigan corporation in 1974, supports and assists industry internationally as an independent third party, auditing, inspection, and testing firm. ENTELA specializes in chemical, electronic, metal, and plastic component and material industries. Facilities are located in Grand Rapids, Michigan and Taipei, Taiwan.

SCOPE

ENTELA, Inc., QSRD, has a comprehensive scope including:

- Artificial Christmas Trees
- Atomizers (other than medical)
- Badges (Police/Fireman)
- Cigarette Lighters
- Furniture
- Games and Toys
- Handbags, Luggage (except leather)
- Jewelry
- Manufacturer of basic metals
- Manufacturer of chemicals, chemical products, and man-made fibers
- Manufacturer of fabricated metal products
- Manufacturer of plastic and plastic products
- Manufacturer of rubber and rubber products
- Manufacturer of wood and wood products
- Manufacturing (N.E.C.)
- Musical Instruments
- Portable Fire Extinguishers
- Sporting Goods
- Tape Measures
- Tear Gas Devices and Equipment
- Treating Surfaces with Luminous Material

ACCREDITATION

ENTELA received accreditation with the Dutch Council for Certification (RvC) in August 1993. ENTELA, Inc., QSRD operates a certification program that meets the requirements of EN45012. Assessors meet the requirements of ISO 10011 part 2 as well as the IQA/RAB lead assessor criteria.

INTERTEK SERVICES CORPORATION

9900 MAIN STREET
SUITE 500
FAIRFAX, VA 22031
TEL: 703-476-9000
FAX: 703-273-4124 OR 2885
CONTACT: WILLIAM E. AIREY (EXT. 3011)

OVERVIEW

Intertek Services Corporation is part of a family of companies serving most of the Fortune 500 companies in over 400 worldwide locations since 1973. Corporate family member, Intertek Technical Services provides consultancy services. These affiliated companies operate under the name Intertek. Intertek has offered ISO 9000 registrations since July, 1991. With operations in the U.S., Europe, and in the Far East, Intertek's headquarters are in Fairfax, Virginia.

SCOPE

Intertek is qualified to assist companies in the aerospace, aircraft, automotive, computer, communications, electronics, and medical industries obtain certification and registration and to assess suppliers' capabilities and qualifications.

ACCREDITATION

Intertek is accredited to perform Quality Management System certification by the Dutch Council for Certification, the Raad voor de Certificatie (RvC). Intertek operates a formal Certification System that satisfies the requirements of EN45012 and ISO 10011, Part 2. Intertek provides technical specialists to perform or support audits and surveys and evaluate supplier quality assurance.

KEMA REGISTERED QUALITY, INC.
4379 COUNTY LINE ROAD
CHALFONT, PA 18914
TEL: 215-822-4281
FAX: 215-822-4285
CONTACT: THEO STOOP

OVERVIEW

N.V. KEMA in the Netherlands opened KEMA Registered Quality, Inc. in the USA in 1991 in order to assist North American companies in obtaining necessary European Certification for their products as well as ISO 9000 Registration for their Quality Systems.

SCOPE

KEMA performs conformity assessments for the CE-mark requirements in the range of electro-magnetic compatability, medical devices, telecommunications terminal equipment, protection technology and information technology. The KEMA-KEUR mark is granted for product certification of electrical consumer appliances.

ACCREDITATION

KEMA was the first European organization to be accredited by the Dutch Council for Accreditation, Raad voor de Certificatie (RvC). KEMA participates in the European mutual recognition program EQNet and has signed cooperation agreements with Underwriter Laboratories, Inc. (UL) in the United States, the Quality Management Institute of the Canadian Standards Association and JMI Institute in Japan.

LLOYD'S REGISTER QUALITY ASSURANCE, LTD.
33-41 NEWARK STREET
HOBOKEN, NJ 07030
TEL: 201-963-1111
FAX: 201-963-3299

OVERVIEW

Lloyd's Register Quality Assurance, Ltd. (LRQA) is a subsidiary company of Lloyd's Register of Shipping in London, England, with a worldwide network in more than 20 countries. LRQA offers an Internal Quality Auditing (IQA) training course which will satisfy the requirements of the IQA National Registration Scheme for Internal Auditors. Another course offered gives advice on developing, documenting and implementing a quality management system.

SCOPE

LRQA offers ISO 9000 certification for quality management systems in a diverse and extensive range of industries. It is the policy of LRQA to achieve accreditation in every new activity they assess.

ACCREDITATION

LRQA is accredited by the National Accreditation Council for Certification Bodies (NACCB) in the UK and the Raad voor de Certificatie (RvC) in the Netherlands.

MET LABORATORIES, INC.
914 W PATAPSCO AVENUE
BALTIMORE, MD 21230-3432
TEL: 410-354-3300
FAX: 410-354-3313
CONTACT: CARLTON BENNETT

OVERVIEW

MET Laboratories, Inc. (MET) is an independent third-party testing laboratory providing quality systems certification in accordance with ISO 9002 and ANSI/ASQC Q90 guidelines since 1990. MET has over three decades of testing and certification experience.

SCOPE

MET performs environmental, safety, performance, telecommunications, and EMI/RFI testing. The laboratory lists and labels products according to National Safety (ANSI/UL) Standards. ISO 9002 certification is granted to compliant manufacturing processes.

ACCREDITATION

MET is accredited by the National Institute for Standards and Technology (NIST) under the National Voluntary Laboratory Accreditation Program (NAVLAP). Met is licensed by the Occupational Safety and Health Administration (OSHA). Accreditation provides all the credibility which may be required to assure compliance with the standards for the U.S. government.

MOODY-TOTTRUP INTERNATIONAL, INC.

350 MCKNIGHT PLAZA BUILDING
105 BRAUNLICH DRIVE
PITTSBURGH, PA 15237
TEL: 412-366-5567
FAX: 412-366-5571
CONTACT: DALE F. GABAUER

OVERVIEW

Moody-Tottrup International (MTI), Inc., formed in 1911, is a member of RCG International Incorporated, one of the largest multi-national consulting and technical services organizations in the world, with operations expanding into over 50 countries. MTI specializes in Quality Assurance (QA) services, assessment, and certification to the ISO 9000 series of standards. MTI operates in association with Groner Certification AS (GC).

GC was founded in 1991 in Norway to perform third-party certification of quality management systems. GC is a subsidiary of Groner AS, one of the largest independent consultancy firms in Norway, founded in 1923. GC has certified nearly 30 companies since accreditation was received two years ago.

SCOPE

MTI registers the quality systems of companies according to ISO 9000 under GC's scope of accreditation which includes:

- Chemicals
- Civil Engineering
- Cleaning
- Electrical
- Electronics
- Fab/Steel Structures
- Food/Drink
- General Engineering
- Machinery

- Paper/Plastics/Rubber
- Printing of Books and Magazines
- Project Management
- Retail/Consumer Services
- Service Industries
- Software Design
- Stock/Distributors
- Telecommunications
- Transport/Distribution

ACCREDITATION

The MTI group companies located in Canada, Germany, Norway, and the UK have achieved ISO 9000 Certification for their operations. The Canada operations are seeking accreditation with the Standards Council of Canada (SCC). The United States firm is in compliance with ISO 9001 and plans for certification before 1994; it will then seek accreditation by the Registrar Accreditation Board (RAB). MTI's sister company, BMIQA Ltd., located in the UK, is approved by the RAB and the Institute of Quality Assurance (IQA) for their ISO 9000 Lead Assessor course. BMIQA is seeking accreditation as a registrar by the National Accreditation Council for Certification Bodies (NACCB).

Certificates are issued by Groner Certification AS. GC was the first certification body to be formally accredited by the Norwegian authorities.

NATIONAL QUALITY ASSURANCE, USA

1146 MASSACHUSETTS AVENUE
BOXBOROUGH, MA 01719
TEL: 508-635-9256
FAX: 508-266-1073
CONTACT: JAMES P. O'NEIL

OVERVIEW

National Quality Assurance, USA (NQA, USA) is a subsidiary of National Quality Assurance Ltd. (NQA), founded in 1988 in the United Kingdom. The company was launched in response to a need for a low-cost and non-bureacratic third-party certification body to address the needs of the Electrical Installation Contracting industry. Since 1988, NQA has widened its scope of accreditation to 80 different areas, and has registered more than 2000 companies worldwide.

NQA offers registration of quality management systems to ISO 9000, EN29000, and BS5750 series of standards. NQA has offices in the United Kingdom, the United States, Northern Ireland, Scotland, and India. NQA, USA opened its Boxborough, Massachusetts headquarters in 1991, an Atlanta office in May, 1993, and an office in Los Angeles in August, 1993.

All of NQA's assessors are IQA and/or RAB registered.

SCOPE

NQA is one of only six multi-disciplinary certification bodies in the United Kingdom and offers an extensive listing of more than 70 accredited scopes of registration which include manufacturing, processing, raw materials, and transportation. Lead Assessors are IQA registered.

ACCREDITATION

NQA, formerly under the name National Inspection Council Quality Assurance, Ltd., achieved accreditation from the United Kingdom's National Accreditation Council for Certification Bodies (NACCB) in early 1990. The NQA applied to the United State's Registration Accreditation Board (RAB) in February, 1993.

NATIONAL STANDARDS AUTHORITY OF IRELAND

5 MEDALLION CENTER
(GREELEY STREET)
MERRIMACK, NH 03054
TEL: 603-424-7070
FAX: 603-429-1427
CONTACT: RICHARD G. BERNIER

OVERVIEW

National Standards Authority of Ireland (NSAI) is the "Notified Body" to the European Community (EC). A member of the International Organization for Standardization (ISO), they develop and publish standards to meet international demands and remove barriers to trade. NSAI sponsors and works in cooperation with the Irish National Committee of the International Electrotechnical Commission (IEC) to develop electrotechnical standards. NSAI certifies products and quality systems to ISO 9000/EN29000. They operate to the EN45000 series of standards and ISO Conformity Assessment Procedures.

SCOPE

To date NSAI has registered over 800 companies across all sectors of industry. Other services offered by NSAI include NSAI Standards Membership Scheme, ISO 9000/EN29000 Workshops, Auditor Training for Internal Quality Audits, and Verified Manufacturers Testing. Manufacturing industries may apply for an Irish Standard Mark (ISM) License and use the ISM on their product upon conforming to an Irish Standard and a harmonized EN standard. Certified products may use the CE Mark to indicate that it complies with EC Directives, conforming to requirements for health and safety. Electrical and electronic products which conform to IEC or EN electrical safety standards may use the Irish Mark of Electrical Conformity (IMEC).

ACCREDITATION

NSAI is a member of the European Quality System Certification Network (EQNet) and has mutual recognition for its certificates in all EC and EFTA member states. Upon payment of registration fees, companies may obtain registration in all EC and EFTA countries without further assessment. NSAI has a bilateral agreement with the Canadian General Standards Board (CGSB) and is currently working on other bilateral national agreements.

NSF INTERNATIONAL

3475 PLYMOUTH ROAD
PO BOX 130140
ANN ARBOR, MI 48113-0140
TEL: 313-769-5112
FAX: 313-769-0109
CONTACT: GARY PUGLIO

OVERVIEW

NSF International (NSF) has been a third-party certifier of products and services, focusing on public health and environmental quality, for over 50 years. NSF registers quality systems and offers to certify products and services for conformity with consensus standards, product-specific test protocols, and official regulations and specifications. The NSF ISO 9000 registration program assists in standard selection, pre-assessment, facility inspection, registration, and semiannual surveillance audits for compliance.

SCOPE

The NSF scope of accreditation includes the following standard industry categories:

- Chemicals and Allied Products
- Industrial Machinery and Equipment
- Eating and Drinking Places
- Electronic and Other Electric Equipment
- Fabricated Metal Products
- Food and Kindred Products
- Food Stores
- Health Services
- Medical Devices
- Primary Metal Industries
- Rubber and Miscellaneous Products
- Transportation Equipment

ACCREDITATION

NSF is accredited by the American National Standards Institute (ANSI) for its standards development and product certification programs. NSF applied for accreditation with the Registrar Accreditation Board (RAB) in the U.S., in late June, 1993. Memorandums of understanding have been signed with the American Gas Association (A.G.A.) Laboratories and Underwriters Laboratories, Inc. (UL).

OTS QUALITY REGISTRARS, INC.

10700 NORTHWEST FREEWAY
SUITE 455
HOUSTON, TX 77092-7308
TEL: 713-688-9494
FAX: 713-688-9590
CONTACT: ANDREW J. BERGMAN

OVERVIEW

The Oil Technology Services, Inc. (OTS) was founded in 1978 to serve the oil and gas industry in quality assurance, engineering, and software needs. OTS Quality Registrars, Inc. (OTSQR) was founded in 1992 to provide quality system assessment, auditing, and registration. Assessors have expert knowledge in EC Legislation and technical product standards for the manufacturing of upstream oilfield products.

SCOPE

OTSQR assists KIWA in assessing manufacturers of products and equipment of oilfields and oil and gas wells. Together, they assess manufacturers of light and heavy metal, fiberglass pipe, valves, rubber, and testing equipment. The emphasis of the assessment and audit is on the technical production areas.

ACCREDITATION

OTS Quality Registrars, Inc. assesses quality systems to the ISO9000 series of standards with an agreement with KIWA, in theNetherlands. KIWA issues the certificate of compliance. KIWA isacredited by the Raad voor de Certificatie (RvC) and is reputed forits product testing and quality system certification in thebuilding and environmental sectors. OTSQR expects to be fullyaccredited in the U.S. by October 1993.

QUALITY MANAGEMENT INSTITUTE

Mississauga Executive Center
Two Robert Speck Parkway, Suite 800
Mississauga, Ontario L4Z 148
Canada
Tel: 416-272-3920
Fax: 416-272-3942
Contact: Catherine Neville

OVERVIEW

Quality Management Institute (QMI) is a division of the Canadian Standards Association (CSA). QMI offers workshops, manuals and systems checklists for the development of quality systems. A national auditor certification program is provided for independent assessment. QMI audits registration applicants against ISO 9000, Z299, and Q9000 series of Standards.

SCOPE

All major industries

ACCREDITATION

QMI is accredited by the Standards Council of Canada (SCC) and operates in accordance with international standard ISO 10011 and European standard EN45012. QMI has a bilateral agreement with a number of organizations such as JMI in Japan, AFAR in France, BSI in the United Kingdom and KEMA in Holland.

QUALITY SYSTEMS REGISTRARS, INC.

13873 PARK CENTER ROAD
SUITE 217
HERNDON, VA 22071-3279
TEL: 703-478-0241
FAX: 703-478-0645
CONTACT: SCOTT R. KLECKNER

OVERVIEW

Quality Systems Registrars, Inc. (QSR) is the first U.S. company accredited to certify quality systems to the ISO 9000/Q90 quality systems standards.

SCOPE

QSR is qualified to perform quality system registration among diverse industries including:

- Electrical Equipment
- Food, Beverage and Tobacco
- Furniture
- Mining and Quarrying
- Optical Equipment
- Pharmaceuticals
- Publishing and Printing
- Real Estate
- Refined Petroleum Products
- Rubber and Plastic Products
- Textiles
- Wholesale and Trade

ACCREDITATION

Quality Systems Registrars, Inc. is accredited by the Registrar Accreditation Board (RAB) in the United States and the Dutch Council for Certification (RvC) in the Netherlands.

QUEBEC QUALITY CERTIFICATION GROUP

70, RUE DALHOUSIE, BUREAU 220
QUEBEC, QUEBEC G1K 4B2
CANADA
TEL: 418-643-5813
FAX: 418-646-3315

OVERVIEW

The Quebec Quality Certification Group (GQCQ), a non-profit third-party registrar, is a division of the Quebec Standard Bureau (BNQ), a constituent of the Quebec Industrial Research Center. GQCQ certifies quality systems which conform to one of the ISO 9000 series of standards or equivalent. Representatives of organizations concerned with registration actively advise GQCQ regarding policies and actions to take in the market.

SCOPE

GQCQ is accredited to register the quality systems of companies in most all manufacturing and service industries. Audits are performed according to the ISO 10011-1 standard. Independent partners of highly qualified auditors form an Auditor Qualification Committee (AQC) to qualify GQCQ auditors in accordance with ISO 10011-2.

ACCREDITATION

The Standards Council of Canada (SCC) has granted GQCQ accreditation in accordance with its Criteria and Procedures for Accreditation of Organizations Registering Quality Systems (CAN-P-10).

SCOTT QUALITY SYSTEMS REGISTRARS, INC.
40 Washington Street
Wellesley Hills, MA 02181
Tel: 617-239-1110
Fax: 617-239-0433
Contact: Warren K. Riddle

OVERVIEW

Scott Quality Systems Registrars, Inc. (SQSR) was recently incorporated as a separate legal entity from Scott Technical Services, Inc., to provide assessment, certification, and surveillance of quality management systems. Several companies, in diverse industries, have contracted to use SQSR as the certifying body for certification and registration to the applicable ISO 9000 or EN 29000 Series Quality Standard to date.

SQSR's certification system is managed by personnel with extensive experience in the quality discipline, performing functions such as auditing, quality engineering, and quality management from both an engineering and manufacturing standpoint. This experience involved a broad spectrum of commercial and government products, and includes ISO 9001 and 9002 Quality Systems development and implementation, including training, for companies in several diverse industries.

SCOPE

Initially, SQSR plans to provide its certification system services to the following industries:

- Aerospace and Defense
- High-tech electronics
- Medical devices
- Machinery and equipment
- Pulp and paper
- Rubber and plastics

ACCREDITATION

SQSR has applied for accreditation as a registrar from the Dutch Council for Certification (RvC). Auditors are certified by ASQC's Registrar Accreditation Board (RAB) and/or the Institute of Quality Assurance (IQA).

SGS INTERNATIONAL CERTIFICATION SERVICES CANADA, INC.

90 GOUGH ROAD, UNIT 4
MARKHAM, ONTARIO L3R 5V5 CANADA
TEL: 416-479-1160
FAX: 416-479-9452
CONTACT: DIANE PRYDE

OVERVIEW

SGS International Certification Services (SGS ICS), Ltd. provides independent assessment and registration services worldwide. The United Kingdom office, SGS Yarsley ICS, has provided technical expertise and systems to affiliates in Europe, Asia and the Pacific, Africa, the Middle East, South America and North America. SGS Yarsley ICS has been providing assessment and registration services since 1985. SGS ICS Canada, Inc. was founded in July 1992 and officially opened in January 1993, offering assessment, registration services and training seminars.

Each SGS ICS national affiliate has achieved or is in the process of achieving accreditation status with the national certification body where one exists. In addition to the assessment and registration services, each SGS ICS office offers a series of ISO 9000 training seminars. Of these, the Internal Auditor and Lead Assessor courses are registered with the IQA Registration Board, UK.

SCOPE

SGS ICS has trained assessors covering 234 industry SIC codes. The number of registered companies worldwide is in excess of 2,000.

ACCREDITATION

SGS ICS Canada, Inc. is an accredited registrar with SCC (Canada) and NACCB (UK). Registration is also provided under accreditation from RvC (Netherlands) and NAC-QS (Belgium), through SGS European Quality Certification Institute E.E.S.V., Belgium. Accreditation status with RAB (USA), through SGS ICS Inc., US, is expected in late 1993. Accreditation status with JAS-ANZ (Australia/New Zealand), through SGS ICS Inc., Australia, is expected in late 1993.

SGS INTERNATIONAL CERTIFICATION SERVICES, INC.
1415 PARK AVENUE
HOBOKEN, NJ 07030
TEL: 201-792-2400
FAX: 201-792-2558
CONTACT: LOIS W. O'BRIEN (X.322)

OVERVIEW

The SGS Group was founded in 1878 and has become the largest inspection and verification organization in the world. An affiliate is the United States Testing Co., Inc., of which SGS International Certification Services, Inc. (SGS ICS Inc) is a subsidiary. SGS ICS Inc offers registration of quality management systems to the ISO 9000 and EN29000 series of standards. SGS has a network of international offices. Offices in the United States are located in Houston, Texas; Los Angeles, California; and the head office is in Hoboken, New Jersey.

SCOPE

SGS ICS Inc's experience is that ISO 9001 or ISO 9002, if properly interpreted, may be applied to any business. They believe these standards provide the level of assurance sought by purchasers. SGS range of services include testing, training, vendor surveillance, inspection, loss adjustment, and quality control. Assessment and quality system registration services are provided to companies in all sectors of industry, including government agencies.

ACCREDITATION

SGS ICS Inc provides ISO 9000 series registration services under accreditation granted to SGS International Certification Services, Ltd., UK, by the National Accreditation Council for Certification Bodies (NACCB). Certification is also provided under accreditationgranted to SGS European Quality Certification Institute E.E.S.V., Belgium, by the Dutch Council for Certification (RvC) and the Belgian National Accreditation Committee (NAC-QS).

SMITHERS QUALITY ASSESSMENTS, INC. SQA
425 MARKET STREET
AKRON, OH 44303-2099
PHONE: 216-762-4231
FAX: 216-762-7447

OVERVIEW

Smithers Quality Assessments, Inc. (SQA) is a wholly-owned subsidiary of Smithers Scientific Services, Inc., headquartered in Akron, Ohio.

SCOPE

The main activities of Smithers Quality Assessments, Inc. (SQA) are: thrid-party audits and certification services to the ISO 9000 International Standards for Quality Management; conduct quality management assessments for firms in the tire, rubber, automotive, plastics, textiles, chemical, carbon black, elastomeric. medical devices, marine, motor vehicle parts and accessories, wheels, equipment manufacturing and bearing and gears industries; provide evaluation and objective evidence of quality system compliance to recognized standards; assure SQA evaluations are impartial and thorough and that the compnay's SQA registration and ISO 9000 certification are recognized worldwide.

ACCREDITATION

Smithers Quality Assessments, Inc. SQA is accredited by the Dutch Council for Certification (RvC)

STEEL RELATED INDUSTRIES QUALITY SYSTEM REGISTRARS
2000 CORPORATE DRIVE
SUITE 450
WEXFORD, PA 15090
TEL: 412-935-2844
FAX: 412-935-6825
CONTACT: PETER B. LAKE

OVERVIEW

SRI is an independent third party which audits and registers the quality systems of manufacturing, service and steel related industries to an ISO 9000 standard. SRI is not-for-profit and is affiliated with the American Iron and Steel Institute.

SCOPE

SRI is accredited to register the quality system of companies that provide products or services in these steel related industries: mining, petroleum products, chemical, refactories, ferrous and nonferrous metals and metal fabrication, machinery and equipment, instruments, transportation, wholesale trade, storage and warehousing, design and engineering, consulting, testing and analyses.

ACCREDITATION

SRI is accredited by Registrar Accreditation Board (RAB) of the United States and in February, 1993 received accreditation by the Raad voor de Certificatie (RvC) of the Netherlands. SRI's lead assessors meet the requirements contained in ISO 10011, EN 45012 and ISO Guide 48.

TRI-TECH SERVICES, INC., AUDITORS/REGISTRAR DIVISION

4700 CLAIRTON BOULEVARD
PITTSBURGH, PA 15236
TEL: 412-884-2290
FAX: 412-884-2268
CONTACT: JOSEPH A FABIAN

OVERVIEW

Tri-Tech Services, Inc., formed in 1987, primarily provided quality consulting, third party audits, and supplier surveys as a Quality Assurance Engineering Consulting firm. In 1992, the Auditors/Registrar Division was formed to avoid a conflict of interest with other services provided by the other divisions and to provide ISO registration.

SCOPE

Tri-Tech Services, Inc., Auditors/Registrar Division, provides ISO 9000 series registration in industries which include chemicals, construction, fabricated metal products, instruments, machinery, mining, paper and allied products, petroleum products, primary metals, rubber and plastic products, refractories, textile mill products, and wholesale trade and services.

ACCREDITATION

Tri-Tech Services, Inc., Auditors/Registrar Division, is accredited by the Registrar Accreditation Board and auditors meet the accreditation body's Certification Program for Auditors of Quality Systems as well as the guidelines of ISO 10011. The division has a cooperation agreement with A.E.S./SEQUAL, France.

TUV AMERICA
5 Cherry Hill Drive
Danvers, MA 01923
Tel: 508-777-7999
Fax: 508-777-8441
Contact: Mark B. Alpert

OVERVIEW

TUV America is a wholly owned subsidiary of TUV Bayern Sachsen. Originally established in 1870, the TUV organization now employs more than 18,000 people worldwide. TUV Bayern Sachsen represents the largest TUV subsidiary employing more than 4,500 people offering a wide range of expertise in almost every engineering and technical discipline.

SCOPE

TUV Bayern Sachsen is a state-accredited European organization authorized to perform mandatory and voluntary inspections, tests and ISO 9000 Quality Systems Registrations on behalf of the Federal Republic of Germany and the EC. TUV technical expertise includes:

- Automotive equipment
- Control equipment and computers
- Electrical and electronic equipment
- Industrial machinery
- Medical equipment
- Nuclear power plants
- Plastics
- Refineries and pipelines
- Service industry
- Software development
- Steam boilers and pressure vessels

ACCREDITATION

TUV America offers certification services to the ISO 9000 series of standards under the guidelines of the Germany TUV Certification Board (TUV CERT). Accreditation has been received from the TAG within the framework of the German Accreditation Board (DAR), under the auspices of the German Department of Commerce (BMWi). DAR is the responsible German accreditation authority for third party test laboratories, inspection agencies, and certification bodies.

TUV RHEINLAND OF NORTH AMERICA, INC.
12 COMMERCE ROAD
NEWTOWN, CT 06470
TEL: 203-426-0888
FAX: 203-426-3156
CONTACT: JOSEPH DECARLO

OVERVIEW

TUV Rheinland of North America, Inc. (TUV Rheinland) has offered product testing and inspection services in North America since the early 1980s. The parent company, TUV Rheinland in Koln, Germany, has offered the same services for more than a century.

Since 1989, when TUV Rheinland began offering ISO 9000 registration services, they have registered 25 North American companies and 400 worldwide. Implementation of the ISO 9000 series and internal audit training, as well as pre-assessments and final assessments of manufacturers' Quality Assurance Systems to ISO 9000/EN 29000 are among the services offered. TUV Rheinland registers compliant companies through the Germany TUV Certification Board (TUV CERT) based in Bonn, Germany, of which it is a member.

SCOPE

TUV Rheinland specializes in auditing the following industries:

- Electronic
- Industrial
- Medical
- Pressure vessel

TUV Rheinland in Germany also has expertise in automotive and steam and pressure related industries.

ACCREDITATION

TUV CERT certificates are received by companies achieving quality system registration. TUV CERT is accredited in Germany by the German Accreditation Council (DAR), the official German accreditation authority for third party certification bodies. TUV's certification system satisfies the requirements of EN 45012 and ISO 10011-2. TUV Rheinland of North America is actively pursuing registration through the Registration Accreditation Board (RAB) in the United States. All auditors are BSI and TUV CERT accredited.

UNDERWRITERS LABORATORIES OF CANADA
7 CROUSE ROAD
SCARBOROUGH, ON M1R 3A9 CANADA
TEL: 416-757-3611
FAX: 416-757-1781
CONTACT: HOWARD SPICE X248

OVERVIEW

Underwriters Laboratories of Canada (ULC) inaugurated its Quality Assurance Registry in 1991, and recently created the Quality Registry Division to operate the program. The registration service was initially offered to ULC's existing client base in the fire and life safety industries. ULC has been active in product certification, including factory follow-up service and quality control, across Canada since 1920 by letters patent issued by the Canadian government.

SCOPE

The Quality Registry Division of ULC offers assessment and registration to the requirements of ISO 9000 as well as the related national standards of Canada (the Q9000 and Z299 series) in industries primarily relating to the following:

- Building materials
- Burglary protection
- Electronics
- Fire protection
- Flammable liquids and gases equipment
- Fuel burning equipment
- Marine equipment

ACCREDITATION

Underwriters Laboratories of Canada is proceeding with accreditation by the Standards Council of Canada (SCC), which is the federal government agency responsible for Canadian accreditation of quality systems registrars. The SCC represents Canada in the International Organization for Standardization and is working toward international recognition of nationally accredited quality system registrars.

UNDERWRITERS LABORATORIES, INC.

1285 WALT WHITMAN ROAD
MELVILLE, NY 11747-3081
TEL: 516-271-6200
FAX: 516-271-8259
CONTACT: JILL SCHMITT (X.733)

OVERVIEW

Underwriters Laboratories, Inc. (UL) is an independent, non-profit organization that has conducted quality evaluations of manufacturers' quality systems in the interest of public safety since 1894. UL is reputed for its product testing, safety certification, and quality assurance. In 1989, UL began offering quality system registration services to ISO series standards. Since that time, the Registered Firm Mark has been received by more than 320 registered facilities.

UL has nearly 200 inspection centers located in Hong Kong, Japan, the United States, Korea, Singapore, Taiwan, and other countries. The four major UL test facilities are located in Northbrook, Illinois; Santa Clara, California; Research Triangle Park, North Carolina; and Melville, New York.

SCOPE

UL's engineering staff investigates more than 14,000 different product types. The UL scope of accreditation spans a wide variety of industries such as:

- Basic metals and fabricated metal products
- Coke and refined petroleum products
- Electrical and other electronic equipment
- Industrial and commercial machinery
- Information technology equipment
- Measuring, analyzing and controlling instruments
- Pharmaceuticals
- Pulp, paper and paper products
- Rubber and plastic products
- Wholesale trade-durable goods industries

ACCREDITATION

UL is accredited as a registrar by the Raad voor de Certificatie (RvC). Through memorandums of understanding, UL has established a global network of 12 quality system registrars for organizations who which to obtain single or multiple registrations. These agreements are with the British Standards Institution (BSI), the Bureau of Commodity Inspection and Quarantine (BCIQ) of Taiwan, JMI Institute of Japan, NSF International, N.V. KEMA of the Netherlands, Quality Management Institute (QMI) of Canada, Singapore Institute of Standards and Industrial Research (SISIR), Standards Australia (SA), Standards Institution of Israel (SII), the Standards and Industrial Research Institute of Malaysia (SIRIM), and INMETRO of Brazil.

UL serves as the U.S. National Supervising Inspectorate (NSI) for the International Electrotechnical Commission Quality Assessment System and as the Systems Supervising Inspectorate (SSI) for the National Electronic Components Quality Certification System.

WARNOCK HERSEY PROFESSIONAL SERVICES, LTD.
128 ELMSLIE STREET
LASALLE, QUEBEC H8R 1V8
CANADA
TEL: 514-366-3100
FAX: 514-366-5350
CONTACT: GILES GAUTHIER

OVERVIEW

Warnock Hersey Professional Services, Ltd. established the WH Quality Registration Program in 1991. The program is available to all interested parties and is founded on many years of experience in quality systems assessment and auditing of suppliers, on behalf of clients. Warnock Hersey is an established independent product testing, inspection and certification organization in Canada and the U.S., with a history dating back to 1898.

SCOPE

Warnock Hersey offers assessment and registration of quality systems implemented by suppliers of goods/services to satisfy ISO 9000 series standards including ISO 9004-2, AQAP or MIL series standards and others.

Quality systems registration is available to suppliers in the fields of consulting services, manufacturing, distribution, and servicing, construction/installation. Industry sectors to which registration services are offered include the following:

- Agriculture and food materials/equipment
- Aviation/aerospace
- Building products and related
- Concrete, ceramic, glass and refractory products
- Electrical/electronic products
- Fuel burning equip.(gas/oil/wood)
- Hydrocarbons, chemicals, and petrochemicals
- Machinery, process equipment, tanks, instrumentation
- Military industry
- Mining, metallurgy and metal products
- Nuclear industry
- Plumbing products
- Polymers and related products
- Pressure vessels and piping
- Pulp and paper
- Road and bridge construction
- Shipbuilding
- Textile and leather industry
- Transportation equipment and services
- Utilities
- Wood products

ACCREDITATION

Warnock Hersey is accredited by the Standards Council of Canada (SCC), which is the federal government agency responsible for Canadian accreditation of quality systems registrars. The SCC represents Canada in the International Organization for Standardization and is working toward international recognition of nationally accredited quality system registrars.

SEMINAR
SECTION

ALL ABOUT ISO 9000

PERRY JOHNSON, INC.
Phone: 313-356-4410
Cost: 245.00
This seminar will familiarize you with the ISO requirements for certification, which is strongly suggested for organizations wishing to conduct business with the European Economic Community.

Course content:

Introduction: ISO 9000 Quality Systems Standards

- Overview of the EEC
- How the ISO 9000 Standards were determined
- Purpose
- Benefits
- Comparison with traditional quality practices

How to Develop ISO 9000 Series Plans

- Available resources

The Registration Process

- Types of registration programs
- Internationally recognized american registration programs
- The fundamentals of the registration process
- Technical requirements: ISO 9000-9004
- Understanding and achieving the goals
- Tips and tricks for minimizing expense

Auditing Programs
- Purpose of audits
- How to commence the auditing process

Continuing ISO 9000 Developments Worldwide

How to Positively Impact the ISO 9000 Standards Process
For: Personnel involved in Quality efforts.

AUDITING TO ISO 9000

CENTER FOR ENERGY & ENVIRONMENTAL
MANAGEMENT (CEEM)
Phone: 703-250-5900
Cost: 1495.00
ISO 9001 Quality System Requirements:

- Management responsibility
- Quality in design
- Documentation requirements

- Purchasing
- Product traceability quality in production
- Inspection and testing
- Handling and storage
- Training and corrective action
- Internal auditing

The Audit Cycle:

- The audit system
- Audit program
- Process breakdown
- Audit environment
- Strategy
- Checklists
- Attributes and practices
- Nonconformities
- Categories
- Recording
- Evaluation
- Reporting the audit
- Corrective action
- Post-activities
- Follow-up

AUDITOR'S PLAIN-ENGLISH GUIDE TO ISO 9000

MIS TRAINING INSTITUTE INC.
Phone: 508-879-7999
Cost: 395.00
Notes: This seminar is also offered on-site. Organizations seeking to capitalize on the growing business opportunities coming out of the new European Economic Community must first verify the quality of their products. To do so, they must meet a series of stringent ISO 9000 Quality Standards set by the Geneva-based International Organization for Standardization. Because comprehensive internal quality audits every six to twelve months are integral to ISO certification, internal audit departments are uniquely positioned to be the driving force behind their organizations' ISO efforts. This seminar will describe what needs to be done to become a major player on the ISO team. In easy-to-follow language, participants will gain an understanding of quality systems along with a working knowledge of ISO 9000 Standards.

Course covers:

- The fundamentals of the ISO 9000 Series of Standards
- How this international quality standard impacts internal audit and the organization
- The steps you must take to prepare for and conduct an internal quality audit

COMPUTER TOOLS FOR ISO 9000 IMPLEMENTATION

EXCEL PARTNERSHIP INC. IN CONJUNCTION WITH TUV RHEINLAND OF NORTH AMERICA INC.
Phone: 203-426-3281
Cost: 795.00
This is a course that provides a thorough understanding of the ISO 9000 Standard - and how to meet the requirements using the IQS system. This workshop reviews the ISO 9000 Series from introduction and background through the necessary steps for registration. Through lectures, role-playing, workshops and case studies, attendees gain a thorough understanding of the ISO 9000 Series. Also, a high degree of class participation and interaction is encouraged.
For: This course is of value to people who are looking to gain an understanding of ISO 9000, who are seeking an integrated approach to quality management systems, or who are looking to computerize their system after having already implemented ISO 9000.

DEVELOPING COMPREHENSIVE ISO 9000 DOCUMENTATION

INFORMATION MAPPING INC.
Phone: 617-890-7003
Cost: 1495.00
Notes: This seminar is also offered on-site. Participants will master a structured set of guidelines, principles, formats, and tools to create ISO 9000 documentation that addresses your readers' needs - something important to ISO 9000 auditors who will judge your documentation on how it meets those needs.

Course covers how to:

- Manage the entire ISO 9000 documentation process
- Understand ISO 9000 and the documentation requirement for each element
- Create complete, accurate, accessible and easy-to-update ISO 9000 documents

For: People who need to understand what resources are necessary to meet ISO 9000 documentation requirements; people who need to understand what the documentation requirements are - and what they mean, and people who are charged with developing the document control and record processes.

DO'S, DON'TS & MAYBE'S OF ACHIEVING ISO 9000 CERTIFICATION

PRODUCTIVITY INC.
Phone: 800-966-5423
Cost: 895.00 Non-member; 795.00 Member
ISO 9000 Standards are becoming accepted as the World's de facto quality standards. And as acceptance spreads, companies that have Certification look for suppliers that are Certified.

Course covers:

- What you have to change - and what you don't have to change - for Certification
- How to properly prepare - and avoid over-preparing - for the ISO 9000 Audit
- How to respond to ISO's key elements
- How to write procedures
- How to create a Quality Manual that not only meets the requirements of the ISO standards, but also serves as a high-caliber document for your quality management system
- How to look at the auditing process "through the auditor's eyes" so you can identify noncompliances, write audit reports and present audit findings to management

DOCUMENTATION: PREPARING QUALITY MANUALS & PROCEDURES

TUV RHEINLAND OF NORTH AMERICA INC. IN CONJUNCTION WITH EXCEL PARTNERSHIP INC.
Phone: 203-426-0888
Cost: 795.00
To become registered to ISO 9000, every company must prepare and maintain a system of documentation in accordance with the guidelines of the ISO 9000 Series. Attendees gain an in-depth understanding of the structure, approach, and methodology for compiling a manual that is workable and usable, as well as meets the ISO 9000 requirements. This course will help you decide where the important information resides and which employees can provide the answers needed to make the manual effective.

Course covers how to:

- Comply with the ISO 9000 Series
- Incorporate existing safety, environmental, and other regulations
- Integrate existing procedures at your facility
- Ensure customer satisfaction with your product/service

For: Quality Assurance personnel, line managers, and supervisors who are required to document their quality systems and practices into manuals and procedures that comply with the ISO 9000 Series. This course is equally suitable for delegates from companies that wish to become independently registered to ISO 9000 and for those companies that recognize the value of operating a controlled management system within the structure of internationally recognized criteria. No particular industrial emphasis is given - nor is it meant to be. The principles are as applicable to manufacturing as to service industries.

DOCUMENTING AN ISO 9000 QUALITY MANUAL

BRYANT COLLEGE CENTER FOR MANAGEMENT DEVELOPMENT
Phone: 401-232-6200
Cost: 295.00
Notes: This seminar is also offered on-site.
This program covers an in-depth review of ISO 9000 requirements and methods for documentation. It offers the opportunity for the participants to experience the entire range of documentation they will encounter during the implementation effort in their own company. Frequent opportunity is provided for the participants to draft examples of the documents they will actually use within their organization. Upon completion of this course, you will have generated a company quality policy, much of the contents of your quality policy manual, and some quality systems procedures. You will also have detailed the requirements of your own document control system.

Course covers how to:

- Gain easier ISO 9000 registration because you know what to expect
- Learn from the experience of other companies who have tried to document several times
- Learn the most efficient documentation methods for your company

- Learn and realize the enormity of the project before you begin the process
- Learn how to handle questions about ISO training before they are asked
- Prepare a draft-quality manual outline for your training function during class

Topics include:

- Mission statements and quality policies
- The quality manual
- Business system procedures
- Work instructions
- Quality plans
- Records
- Methods for document control

EC MEDICAL DEVICE DIRECTIVES

STAT-A-MATRIX
Phone: 908-548-0600
Cost: 995.00
This course is designed for medical device manufacturers doing business overseas. It describes the European Community's Product Certification System, including the new and proposed directives for medical devices, active implantable devices, and in vitro diagnostic devices. It discusses the role of ISO 9000 in the certification process, and the related EC/FDA regulations.

EFFECTIVE QUALITY AUDITING WORKSHOP

BREWER-KLECKNER EDUCATION SERVICES
Phone: 214-660-4575
Cost: 895.00
This seminar will examine every aspect of the process of auditing quality systems. The seminar will look at factual data on what must be done to become a skilled auditor. The seminar will translate its significance into strategies and tactics to improve the effectiveness of an auditor. The seminar will concentrate on those techniques of performing audits which have proven to be effective. The seminar will explore the understanding of what the audit process is, as well as an understanding of the techniques used to accomplish a competent audit. A 200-page loose-leaf manual will used as a valuable reference on a daily basis.

What you will learn:

- Understanding Quality Systems
- Terms and Definitions
- Audit Principles
- Auditor Qualification
- Audit Program Elements
- Checklists
- Procedures
- Performing the Audit
- Auditing Techniques
- Reporting Audit Results
- Audit Completion
- Modern Quality Trends

For: Individuals who need a complete understanding of the audit process.

EUROPEAN COMMUNITY MEDICAL DEVICE DIRECTIVES

STAT-A-MATRIX
Phone: 908-548-0600
This seminar includes an overview of the EC Medical Device Directives and Product Certification System, including conformity assessment requirements, role of notified bodies, and use of the CE Mark.

Course covers:

- Custom-made devices and clinical devices
- ISO 9000 + EN46000 + EN50103
- Steps to satisfy AIMD
- Four-part classification structure
- ISO 9000 + EN46000 + EN72
- Custom-made devices and clinical devices
- Amendment to Medical Device Directive
- Highlights of EC Working Document
- ISO 9000 + EN46000 + CEN/TC 140
- Investigational use: Annex Eight
- Essential requirements
- Inspections and monitoring
- Role of ISO 9000 with Conformity Assessment

For: Personnel in the medical device industry preparing for new and emerging EC directives.

EXECUTIVE BRIEFING

CENTER FOR ENERGY & ENVIRONMENTAL MANAGEMENT (CEEM)
Phone: 703-250-5900
Cost: 495.00
Notes: This seminar is also offered on-site.
This seminar, designed for senior management, is an overview of the ISO 9000 Series. Through various presentations and round-table discussions, the strategic implications of initiating a company-wide adherence to the ISO 9000 Standards will be covered, as well as information regarding how the international standards are expected to be implemented, e.g., within the European Community.

The subjects covered include:
- Introduction - defining quality and the customer's perception of it
- Background and structure - tracing the development of ISO 9000 and explaining its structure
- Analysis of ISO 9000 - interpreting the standard and detailing its requirements
- Management benefits - the use of ISO 9000 as a management tool
- Economic benefits - the advantages of prevention over appraisal and failure costs
- Route to Certification - an explanation of what your company must do to become certified and how your quality system can be registered by BSi.

EXECUTIVE OVERVIEW ON ISO 9000

AMERICAN INSTITUTE FOR QUALITY & RELIABILITY
AIQR
Phone: 408-275-9300
Cost: 295.00
Notes: This seminar is also offered on-site.
This course gets your company ready for the requirements of an audit for ISO 9000 certification. It benefits managers who are uncertain about the requirements of the different ISO 9000 Series Standards, and who need to understand the resources necessary to prepare for the rigorous audit. Furthermore, it is for those individuals who will be responsible for the preparation and implementation of ISO 9000 certification.

HOW TO BE AUDITED TO ISO 9000

STAT-A-MATRIX
Phone: 908-548-0600
Cost: 845.00
This course is geared towards companies that are implementing ISO 9000 systems and are getting ready for a formal pre-assessment or a third party registration. It uses workshops, videos, and role-playing exercises to back what happens during an audit, what the assessors look for, and how to prepare your organization to be audited.

HOW TO CONDUCT INTERNAL QUALITY AUDITS IN SMALL- & MEDIUM-SIZED COMPANIES

UNIVERSITY OF WISCONSIN MADISON ENGINEERING PROFESSIONAL DEVELOPMENT
Phone: 800-462-0876
Cost: 635.00
This course will help you to implement, maintain and improve your quality system. If your company is implementing an ISO 9000 Quality Program, learning about the auditing process will provide a solid basis to better implement an ISO 9000 Quality System and determine its effectiveness. You can then use the internal auditing process to verify that the changes you make are correct and will meet the ISO 9000 Standards.

Course covers:

- The exact steps necessary to conduct the audit
- A guide through each phase of the audit process with the use of a quality audit checklist
- Realistic and challenging exercises, workshops and role-playing audits

For:
- Managers and directors of quality assurance
- Supervisors of quality control
- Senior management and company owners
- Quality engineers
- Internal and external auditors
- Consultants in ISO
- Suppliers and vendors whose customers are either ISO 9000 registered or who are pursuing registration
- Company management representatives

HOW TO DOCUMENT YOUR ISO 9000 QUALITY SYSTEM

STAT-A-MATRIX
Phone: 908-548-0600
Cost: 845.00
Notes: This seminar is also offered on-site.
This workshop is designed to provide a practical approach to evaluating and preparing the documentation needed to implement an ISO 9000 Quality System. Participants learn how to analyze ISO 9000 documentation requirements and write instructions and system-level procedures. Discussion of procedures preparation and recommended formats, plus workshops on analyzing procedural requirements and planning, writing, and evaluating system-level procedures. Also, discussions and workshops on task analysis, planning instructions, readability factors, and actual writing of job instructions are planned.

Topics include:

- The structure of ISO 9000
- Determining the concepts and their definitions
- How to read and interpret ISO standards
- Determining what documents you need
- Planning and structuring the documented quality system
- The documentation pyramid
- Flowcharting

For: Management, supervisory staff, and professional personnel involved in preparing plans, procedures, and instructions as part of an ISO 9000 documented quality system.

HOW TO IMPLEMENT ISO 9000

THE VICTORIA GROUP
Phone: 800-845-0567
Cost: 1295.00
This program is designed to provide the delegate with the core skills and knowledge to baseline an in-company project for the successful implementation of ISO 9000. Stage one of the four-part ISO training package - the How to Implement ISO 9000 - provides an in-depth interpretation of the Standard; guidance on how to structure documentation to make it easy to use, easy to maintain, and easy to audit; assistance in determining what needs to be documented and what need not be; ideas on how to write a Quality Manual; how to go about finding a Registrar; and negotiating the Registration Audit. The principles and structures of Accreditation, Certification and Registration are covered in detail, as is the importance of understanding the scope of your business and that of the Registrar.

HOW TO PREPARE FOR ISO 9000 REGISTRATION

AMERICAN INSTITUTE FOR QUALITY & RELIABILITY
Phone: 408-275-9300
Cost: 675.00
Topics include:

- Pertinent history and background of the ISO 9000/Q90 Standards
- The contents of the standards and how the auditors interpret them
- What the auditors are looking for

- How ISO 9000/Q90 can fit into a Total Quality Management system
- The benefits of certification to your organization
- What parts of your organization are covered by the standards
- How much is enough
- How to manage the important preparation for the audit
- A process for completing your quality documentation and record system

For:
- Top management deciding whether or not to seek certification for their organization
- Management involved in planning and implementing the audit preparation program
- Professionals who affect the quality of customer products
- And, all other personnel, quality professionals, managers, and executives who realize the importance of personally understanding quality in the world arena and want to understand the ISO standards and their impact on the future of business exchange

HOW TO SUCCESSFULLY INTEGRATE BAR CODING INTO MANUFACTURING, DISTRIBUTION & RETAIL OPERATIONS

AMERICAN MANAGEMENT ASSOCIATION
Phone: 518-891-1500
Cost: 1140.00 Non-member; 1000.00 Member
Topics include:

- Review the most important bar code symbologies
- Pick up printing and scanning technologies and options
- Review industry standards - including a look at new developments that will be a key part of ISO 9000

For: Directors, managers, supervisors, and technical and MIS professionals with responsibilities for key disciplines such as inventory and production control, production planning and scheduling, industrial engineering, warehouse, retail, and related technical operations. Anyone involved with the design and implementation of automatic identification systems should attend. If you are looking for practical ways of integrating bar coding into your organization, this seminar will prove very beneficial.

I.S./ISO 9000/EN 29000 QUALITY MANAGEMENT SYSTEM WORKSHOP

NSAI NATIONAL STANDARDS AUTHORITY OF IRELAND
Phone: 603-424-7070
Cost: 895.00
The workshop is designed to familiarize participants with all of the clauses and requirements of the ISO 9000/EN 29000 Standards and their application in actual operation. The workshop is interactive and is structured around a two-part case study which highlights the main requirements of the ISO 9001 and ISO 9002 Standards. It reflects actual problems encountered in preparing for and participating in an assessment to either standard. NSAI designed this course to serve as a foundation for understanding the principles and requirements for meeting ISO 9001 and ISO 9002 Quality Management System Standards.

For: Management serious in developing systems to meet these international quality standards will want their top executives, engineers, marketing specialists, sales managers, quality managers, manufacturing and service managers, to attend this interactive program.

IMPLEMENTATION & REGISTRATION TO ISO 9000

TUV RHEINLAND OF NORTH AMERICA INC. IN CONJUNCTION WITH EXCEL PARTNERSHIP INC.
Phone: 203-426-0888
Cost: 795.00
Free movement to products and services in a global economy, and especially in the European Community, is enhanced through compliance with the ISO 9000 Series of Quality Management Standards.

Course covers:

- ISO 9000 Series requirements and applications
- Background and developments of the standards
- Third party assessment and registration
- Accreditation and Certification Systems, both in the U.S. and the European Community

For: All levels within an organization from senior management to line personnel will benefit from attending this course as it is designed to inform companies of the requirements and provide a thorough analysis of the ISO 9000 Series. This course is equally suitable for delegates from companies that wish to become independently registered to ISO 9000 as for those companies that recognize the value of operating a controlled management system within the structure of internationally recognized criteria.

IMPLEMENTING ISO 9000
BRYANT COLLEGE CENTER FOR MANAGEMENT DEVELOPMENT
Phone: 401-232-6200
Cost: 295.00
Notes: This seminar is also offered on-site.
This program probes implementation strategies, the organization of the quality system, organization and accomplishment of the implementation effort, registrar selection, required documentation, internal auditing, and registration audit management.

Course covers how to:

- Reduce effort and costs of nonconformance
- Reduce overhead from unnecessary tasks
- Enhance your response to customers' needs and expectations
- Gain control over day-to-day operations
- Direct management's focus away from fire fighting to business management
- Meet internationally recognized business management practices
- Impress/satisfy your customers
- Gain market advantage
- Improve market share

Topics include:

- Quality system implementation
- Establish a management review committee
- Document the system
- Consolidate the people, processes, and documentation
- Registration strategy
- Register your company

IMPLEMENTING ISO 9000
MARQUETTE UNIVERSITY DIVISION OF CONTINUING EDUCATION
Phone: 414-288-7345
Cost: 295.00 Non-member; 260.00 Member
The International Standards Organization (ISO) has established a quality standard to be used by its member nations. Many ISO member nations (including the European Community) are requesting registration to the ISO standard in order to avoid custom's charges and delays. Others are requiring compliance to the standard to demonstrate quality

proficiency. The rate of these customer requests is increasing. This course will help participants plan, develop and manage the implementation of the ISO 9000 Standard.

Course covers how to:

- Self-audit and establish plans for complying to ISO 9000
- Establish teams to develop flow diagrams, write procedures and audit compliance that will truly impact the business
- Use a steering committee to evaluate progress, assign resources and reward achievement
- Evaluate Registered Auditors for costs and linkage with their customers
- Assess procedures for efficiency and effectiveness
- Apply for ISO 9000 registration
- Make the program proactive, i.e., use the program effectively to meet business needs and have some fun throughout the certification process

IMPLEMENTING ISO 9000 QUALITY SYSTEM STANDARDS
RUTGERS STATE UNIVERSITY OF NEW JERSEY ENGINEERING OFFICE OF CONTINUING EDUCATION
Phone: 908-932-4454
Cost: 595.00
The course is delivered in a clear, concise, easy-to-understand manner, with focus on applications of basic principles to practical situations. The attendees will first be divided into a number of teams. Groups of ISO 9001 elements will be described by the seminar leader. After each group of elements is described, the teams will participate in brainstorming sessions in which the structure of their environments will be investigated in relation to the requirements just described. The issues identified during the exercise will be captured and presented to the rest of the attendees.

IMPLEMENTING ISO 9000: ACHIEVING COMPLIANCE & REGISTRATION

EXCEL PARTNERSHIP INC. IN CONJUNCTION WITH TUV RHEINLAND OF NORTH AMERICA INC.
Phone: 203-426-3281
Cost: 795.00
Course covers:

- Background in the development and application of the ISO 9000 Series Standards
- Understanding of the requirements of the standards
- Appreciation of the actions and decisions necessary to gain
- Considerations in documenting the quality system
- Understanding of the assessment and registration process for compliance by a third party

For: Those who need to gain an in-depth understanding of the requirements of ISO 9000, and personnel who may be chosen to assist with ISO 9000 implementation, or for those who expect to become internal auditors.

INTERNAL AUDITING AS REQUIRED BY ISO 9000

TUV RHEINLAND OF NORTH AMERICA INC. IN CONJUNCTION WITH EXCEL PARTNERSHIP INC.
Phone: 203-426-0888
Cost: 795.00
Every company seeking registration under ISO 9000 must continually audit its systems in order to satisfy the requirements of the standard. Properly applied auditing can be a powerful management tool in achieving total quality.

Course covers how to:

- Coordinate an effective audit
- Evaluate the audit team's findings
- Communicate with personnel involved in the audit
- Report the results to management
- Develop and implement corrective action programs

For: Those performing audits, as well as, line managers who will appreciate the concepts and benefits to be gained from auditing. This course is equally suitable for delegates from companies that wish to become independently registered to ISO 9000 and for those companies that recognize the value of operating a controlled management system within the structure of internationally recognized criteria.

INTERNAL AUDITING FOR ISO 9000

AMERICAN INSTITUTE FOR QUALITY & RELIABILITY
Phone: 408-275-9300
Cost: 675.00
Course covers how to:

- Write and present an audit plan
- Draft nonconformances and obtain team acceptance
- Evaluate the documentation, the activities performed, and the effectiveness of the Quality System
- Understand the various types of audits and their significance, i.e. design, management, supplier, product/service, process, internal and external audits

For: CEO's, senior managers, quality managers, quality auditors, assessors, production supervisors, manufacturing engineers, consultants, development engineers, quality engineers, ISO program managers, and all those who are involved in auditing a quality management system to meet ISO.

INTERNAL AUDITING TO ISO 9000

ROCHESTER INSTITUTE OF TECHNOLOGY CENTER FOR QUALITY & APPLIED STATISTICS
Phone: 716-475-6990
Cost: 845.00
Participants will learn the auditing techniques necessary to maintain and improve the effectiveness of an ISO 9000 Quality System. Through formal presentations, workshops and open-forum discussions, attendees will be instructed on the detailed requirements of, and auditing to, the ISO 9000 Series Standards. Whether involved with a manufacturing or service-related company, participants will develop skills, knowledge and confidence to conduct a quality system audit. Participants will be shown how audits are planned and performed, as well as how findings are reported and corrective action is taken. A series of workshops will lead the class through the critical stages of an audit, providing an invaluable opportunity to apply theory in a simulated situation.

Topics include:

- General audit background
- Conducting the audit
- Preliminary review of audit findings

INTERNAL AUDITOR

THE VICTORIA GROUP
Phone: 800-845-0567
Cost: 995.00
It will soon become evident that to compete in the global market, organizations will need to comply with the ISO 9000 International Standards for Quality Management, and become certified. The system audit is a vital tool in Quality System Maintenance according to ISO 9000.

Course covers how to:

- Increase your "hands-on " understanding of the ISO 9000 Series
- Work within the framework of a comprehensive notebook
- Be provided a number of pro forma documents valuable to you later when you are actively engaged in audit activity
- Benefit from the expertise and experience of British training teams

Topics include:

- Workshop exercise in time management and presentation skills
- Discussion of the principles of management systems
- Brief introduction to ISO 9000
- Typical documentation hierarchies
- Needs analysis workshop relating to the audit requirements of an audit program
- Audit program planning
- Audit team selection
- Skills identification workshop
- The opening meeting
- The audit
- Audit observations
- The closing meeting
- The audit report
- Follow-up and close-out

INTERNAL AUDITOR TRAINING

PERRY JOHNSON, INC.
Phone: 313-356-4410
Cost: 895.00
This course trains personnel in the skills and activities necessary to meet the requirements of ISO 9000 Quality System Standards.

Course content:

- Background
- The quality standards
- Accreditation process
- Audit requirements
- Document quality systems: Quality manual, operational procedures, written instructions
- Audit schedules/plan
- Audit checklists
- Conducting internal quality audits
- Typical problems
- Case studies/examples
- Management review meetings

For: All personnel who will be carrying out the internal audit activities required by the relevant ISO 9000 Quality System Standards.

INTRODUCTION TO ISO 9000

MIAMI UNIVERSITY CONTINUING EDUCATION
HAMILTON CAMPUS
Phone: 513-863-8833
Cost: 49.00
ISO 9000, the quality standard adopted by the European Economic Community, the United States, and 80 other countries, will serve as a benchmark for the acceptance of goods and services traded among these countries.

Course covers:

- Definitions, purpose and requirements of ISO 9000
- Description and application of the five sections of ISO 9000
- Certification considerations and requirements
- Available resources

IQA & RAB LEAD AUDITOR/ASSESSOR CERTIFICATION

STAT-A-MATRIX

Phone: 908-548-0600

Cost: 1495.00

Notes: This seminar is also offered on-site.
This course and examination provide the necessary body of knowledge and skills to cover the requirements for registration, when combined with appropriate documentation of education, experience, and auditor practice.

Course covers:

- Quality Assurance as a proactive concept rather than a reactive philosophy
- What elements comprise a quality system, including the policy, manual, procedures, and instructions
- Participants are taught the requirements of ISO 9001 and the relationships among 9001, 9002 and 9003. A matrix comparison is presented to help explain these relationships
- Using ISO 10011 as a guide, participants are exposed to the different types of assessments
- Through the use of workshops participants learn how to plan an audit activity, develop a checklist, perform a pre-assessment visit, and conduct an opening meeting

For: People who wish to satisfy the requirements for a course and examination, as part of the qualifications for achieving registration as a Lead Assessor (Lead Auditor) under ISO 9000 (ANSI/ASQC Q90).

IQA REGISTERED INTERNAL QUALITY AUDITING

STAT-A-MATRIX

Phone: 908-548-0600

Cost: 1095.00

Notes: This seminar is also offered on-site.
This course provides the necessary body of knowledge to assist participants in developing, implementing, and auditing internal quality system programs that meet the requirements of ISO 9000 (ANSI/ASQC Q90). This course has been registered by the United Kingdom's Governing Board of the National Registration Scheme for Internal Auditors of Quality Systems.

Course covers:

Introduction to Internal Quality Systems Assessment

- Participants are introduced to the elements comprising a quality system
- They learn to interpret the requirements of the ISO 9000 (Q90) Series and what the third party assessment agency looks for
- Participants are taught the relationships among the quality policy, quality manual, system procedures, and instructions
- They learn what to look for in these documents and techniques for evaluating them
- The three audit phases - planning, execution, and follow-up - are examined closely using concepts detailed in ISO 10011.

Planning and Auditing

- Learn how to prepare for an audit and how to manage their resources effectively
- Learn how to review manuals, procedures, and instructions, organize an audit team, develop checklists, prepare an audit plan, and effectively schedule

Conducting the Audit

- Learn to conduct effective opening and closing meetings, deal with confrontation, collect objective evidence, and document observations
- Learn techniques for effective questioning and listening

Follow-Up Activities

- Learn to verify effectiveness and adequacy of corrective action, close out an audit, and schedule and conduct follow-on surveillances

Case Studies and Simulations

- Participants work in group activities with specially prepared case studies and video simulations to gain hands-on experience in conducting effective audits

Certification Examination

- This course offers a one-hour certification examination. This examination meets the U.K. National Registration Scheme for Internal Auditor Training.

For: Personnel who will conduct, manage, or participate in internal (first party) audits. It is also useful for those seeking to register their companies to ISO 9000, since it identifies the elements a third party auditor looks at.

IQA REGISTERED LEAD ASSESSOR CERTIFICATION

STAT-A-MATRIX
Phone: 908-548-0600
Cost: 1475.00
This course and examination provides the necessary body of knowledge and assessment to cover the requirements for registration, when combined with appropriate documentation of education, experience and assessor (auditor) practice.

ISO 9000

UNIVERSITY OF DELAWARE DIVISION OF CONTINUING EDUCATION
Phone: 302-451-1138
Cost: 195.00
ISO 9000 certification is becoming increasingly important for companies which do business with the international community or with other quality organizations in the U.S. ISO 9000 is a systematic methodology for assuring that the organization is making best practices the standard for operations. This course is designed to give managers who will be implementing ISO 9000 an understanding of what the certification process is, how the quality audit process works, and how to plan for ISO 9000 registration.

Topics include:

- What is ISO 9000?
- What is certification?
- Why get certified?
- How long does it take?
- What are the benefits?
- What does it cost?
- What is the quality audit?
- Compliance standards
- What to expect?
- What gets audited?
- Management awareness and education
- Gap assessment
- Closing the gap
- Registration audit
- Ongoing surveillance
- Continuous improvement

ISO 9000 & SOFTWARE DEVELOPMENT

INFORMATION SYSTEMS INSTITUTE
Phone: 301-670-9020
Cost: 795.00
ISO 9000 is a universal quality standard, developed at the International Organization for Standardization (Geneva), and adopted by the 12 EC countries as a way of standardizing quality throughout Europe. About two dozen other countries have also adopted the standard officially. ISO 9000 is a method that can be adopted by any company that wishes to improve its quality. But, more important, countries who wish to do business with the EC - or other ISO nations - must be audited and registered by ISO registrars. ISO 9000-Part 3 (1991) is a generic standard affecting "development, supply and maintenance of software." To satisfy ISO auditors, organizations must have fully documented quality systems and complete procedural documentation that relates to the software development life cycle and the full range of support activities. This documentation must be clear enough for third party auditors to read, understand use as the basis for their assessments.

Course covers how to:

- Describe the origins and objectives of ISO 9000
- State the particular requirements for software development
- Plan the staffing and organization of an ISO implementation group
- Outline/spec the Software Quality Manual
- Outline a hierarchical system of process/procedure/practice documentation
- Write an auditable 2-level procedure (Process/Practice)

Topics will include:

- Origins and recent history of ISO 9000
- The ISO library of standards & publications
- The ISO process: preparation, implementation, registration
- The most ambitious standard: 9001
- Special considerations for software developers (9000-3)
- Definitions
- Documenting life cycle activities (planning-design-acceptance-maintenance)
- Documenting system support (configuration management, records, measures)

- Documenting high-level processes/procedures
- Detailing high-level workflows with auditable practices, instructions, and data forms

ISO 9000 & THE MEDICAL DEVICE GMP

STAT-A-MATRIX
Phone: 908-548-0600
Cost: 595.00
Notes: This seminar is also offered on-site.
This course is designed to introduce the ISO 9000 Standards to personnel in the medical device industry who are familiar with the Medical Device GMP (21CFR820). Attendees receive a text, copies of the specifications, and matrix comparisons of their contents.

Topics include:

- What is ISO 9000?
- How does ISO 9001 compare with the GMP?
- The ISO Quality System
- Going from GMP to ISO

For: Personnel in the medical device industry involved with maintaining or revising their GMP or ISO 9000 Quality System.

ISO 9000...QUALITY MANAGEMENT FRAMEWORK FOR TQM

CENTER FOR ENERGY & ENVIRONMENTAL MANAGEMENT (CEEM)
Phone: 703-250-5900
Cost: 795.00
Participants will learn how to integrate the concepts, principles and practices of Total Quality Management and the ISO 9000 Standards in order to establish, develop, implement and sustain a quality organization.

Topics include:

- Overview of the elements of TQM
- Overview of ISO 9000 Standards
- Introduction to the P-I-A model
- Planning: Initiating and developing awareness of quality; the strategic planning process; identifying and establishing a quality system; identifying the necessary support systems
- Improvement and Innovation: Identify critical or major processes; prioritize processes; identify customers/suppliers/producers for targeted processes; conduct in-depth process analysis; improve and innovate

- Assurance: Well-defined organizational structure; Continuous process monitoring and control; Performance management; System reviews and audits

ISO 9000 AUDITOR/LEAD AUDITOR TRAINING

AMERICAN SUPPLIER INSTITUTE (ASI)
Phone: 313-271-4200
Cost: 945.00
Attendees from this course will gain a thorough understanding of how to coordinate and conduct an effective audit, evaluate the audit team's findings, communicate with personnel involved in the audit, report results to management, and develop and implement corrective action programs. This course combines tutorial presentations with practical workshop sessions. This course is intended for both internal auditors and those seeking to become certified auditors or lead auditors.

ISO 9000 DETAILED STUDIES

G.R. TECHNOLOGIES (USA) INC.
Phone: 407-995-0611
Cost: 750.00
This is an in-depth description of what is in the standard, how to implement a quality system for auditing and the registration procedure. This course is a must for those who will be implementing the standard and preparing the company for audits.

ISO 9000 DOCUMENTATION

THE VICTORIA GROUP MANAGEMENT CONSULTANTS, LTD.
Phone: 800-845-0567
Cost: 995.00
Get a clear vision of the recommended structure and content for Quality System Documentation.

ISO 9000 DOCUMENTATION WORKSHOP

THE CARMAN GROUP INC.
Phone: 214-669-9464
Cost: 995.00
This seminar was developed based on market research and the combined experience of the many companies. The most daunting task facing organizations that are considering ISO certification is the documentation of the Quality Manual and Procedures (Levels 1 and 2) to the ISO standard. This seminar will teach your team how to take the processes currently in place in your company and write them at Levels 1 and 2 to meet ISO

certification standards. The toughest procedures, as defined by ISO registrars, will be written in the workshop.

ISO 9000 FOR DEFENSE CONTRACTORS

STAT-A-MATRIX
Phone: 908-548-0600
Cost: 595.00
Notes: This seminar is also offered on-site.
This course is designed to introduce the ISO 9000 Standards to aerospace and defense contractors currently working to MIL-Q-9858A, MIL-I-45208A, or comparable NASA or NATO requirements. Attendees receive a text, copies of the applicable specifications, and matrix comparisons of the contents.

Topics include:

- Review of ISO 9001, emphasizing impact on defense and aerospace
- A matrix comparison of the two standards
- Anticipated changes to ISO
- What it takes to be registered
- How DoD views registration and third party audits
- Going from 9858A to ISO
- Building on your existing system
- The key differences
- Selecting the right ISO 9000 Standard for you
- The pros and cons of ISO 9000 registration
- How ISO 9000 fits with your other quality initiatives, like TQM
- Current DoD plans for ISO 9000

For: Executives, engineering and manufacturing managers, and quality specialists in the defense and aerospace industries.

ISO 9000 FOR SERVICE ORGANIZATIONS

GEORGE WASHINGTON UNIVERSITY SCHOOL OF BUSINESS & PUBLIC MANAGEMENT
Phone: 202-994-5219
Cost: 600.00
Early ISO 9000/Q90 efforts have primarily involved manufacturing and production organizations. With the global shift toward a service economy, however, an exclusive focus on manufacturing and production organizations makes less and less sense. This course thus addresses a timely question: How can service organizations use the standards to assure customers of the same level of quality management as that provided by ISO 9000/Q90 - registered manufacturing companies? Successfully applying ISO 9000/Q90 in service organizations requires a knowledge of the ISO 9000/Q90 systems, a familiarity with the processes for self-assessment and registration, an ability to interpret the standards in a service environment, and an understanding of what ISO registration means for the organization's leadership. This course provides the necessary background and shows how ISO 9000/Q90 Standards can be implemented in various types of service organizations.

ISO 9000 FOR THE AUTOMOTIVE INDUSTRY

STAT-A-MATRIX
Phone: 908-548-0600
Cost: 595.00
This course is designed to introduce ISO 9000 to automotive parts manufacturers and parts and service suppliers working with Chrysler, Ford, and GM. It provides an in-depth understanding of the standards and registration requirements for the European Community, Asia, and the United States. It includes detailed matrices of ISO 9001 compared to Chrysler's SQA, Ford's Q-101 and TQE, and GM's TFE standards.

Course covers:

- What ISO 9000 means for the auto industry
- The Big Three's approach to ISO 9000
- The ISO registration process
- The third party audit concept
- An analysis of ISO 9001
- Comparison of current industry standards vs. ISO 9001
- Building on your existing system
- Selecting the right ISO standard for you
- How ISO fits with your other quality initiatives
- Current Big Three, EC, and Asian approaches

For: Executives, engineering and manufacturing managers, and quality specialists in the automotive industry.

ISO 9000 FORUM APPLICATION SYMPOSIUM: AN INTERNATIONAL TECHNOLOGY TRANSFER

AMERICAN SOCIETY FOR QUALITY CONTROL
EDUCATION & TRAINING INSTITUTE
Phone: 800-952-6587
Cost: 695.00 Non-member; 545.00 Member
The International Organization for Standardization (ISO) is a worldwide federation of national standards bodies from over 90 countries. ISO is made up of approximately 180 technical committees. Each technical committee is responsible for one of many areas of specialization, ranging from aircraft to zinc. The object of ISO is to promote the development of standardization and related world activities with a view to facilitating the international exchange of goods and services and to developing cooperation in the sphere of intellectual, scientific, technological, and economic activity. The results of ISO technical work are published as International Standards.

The American National Standards Institute (ANSI) was formed in 1918 by five professional/technical societies and three federal government agencies, prompted by a desire to eliminate conflict and duplication in the U.S. voluntary standards development process. Over the years, ANSI has become the overseer of the consensus method of developing standards in this country, as well as being the U.S. Member body of the International Organization for Standardization (ISO) and, via the U.S. National Committee, the International Electrotechnical Commission (IEC). Today, ANSI guides the efforts of the more than 250 major standards-developing organizations.

Founded in 1946, the American Society for Quality Control (ASQC) carries out a variety of professional, educational, and informational programs reflecting the changing needs of business and industry. Composed of more than 120,000 individual members and 950 sustaining members worldwide, ASQC has been the leading quality improvement organization in the United States for almost 50 years. ASQC willingly supports the ANSI consensus method of developing American National Standards and shows its support by being a Member of ANSI. ANSI has accredited ASQC as a standards-developing organization, and all the standards that ASQC develops are American National Standards.

ISO 9000 IMPLEMENTATION

PERRY JOHNSON, INC.
Phone: 313-356-4410
Cost: 1195.00
This course teaches you how to meet ISO requirements, trouble-shoot your operation and make necessary modifications.
Course content:

Registration and Introduction
- The accreditation process
- Requirements for documentation
- Requirements of the standard

Requirements of the Standard

Quality Manual

- Preparing
- Writing
- Documentation

For: All personnel involved in the implementation of ISO requirements.

ISO 9000 IMPLEMENTATION

EASTERN MICHIGAN UNIVERSITY CORPORATE SERVICES
Phone: 313-487-2259
Cost: 495.00
Notes: This seminar is also offered on-site.
Topics include:

- Introduction
- Management
- Systems
- Design control and servicing
- Purchasing
- Operations
- Nonconforming and handling

For: Quality managers/professionals, plant managers, companies considering third party certification/registration, in-house trainers, purchasing managers, lab, research & design personnel, companies considering specifying ISO 9000 for their suppliers.

ISO 9000 IMPLEMENTATION COURSE

EXCEL PARTNERSHIP INC. IN CONJUNCTION WITH
TUV RHEINLAND OF NORTH AMERICA INC.
Phone: 203-426-3281
Cost: 795.00
This course is designed to provide a detailed
analysis of:

- ISO 9000 Series requirements and applications
- Background and development of the standards
- Third party assessment process and the
  registration process
- Accreditation and certification systems in the
  U.S. and Europe
- How to implement ISO 9000

ISO 9000 IMPLEMENTATION COURSE

HANDLEY-WALKER CO., INC.
Phone: 714-730-0122
Cost: 975.00
This workshop instructs project managers how to
implement ISO 9000 in their organization. Upon
completion of the course, participants will gain an
in-depth knowledge of the standard and what is
required of their organization to prepare for and
achieve certification. This workshop involves
participants in the application of guidelines and
techniques for upgrading, documenting and auditing
their quality system through a variety of exercises
and case studies.

Topics include:

- An analysis of the ISO 9000 requirements and
  the implications for your company
- ISO 9000 project planning, scheduling and
  administration
- Selecting and working with a registration
  agency
- Determining and documenting your company's
  scope of registration
- Developing an awareness of ISO 9000 among
  your management, staff and suppliers
- Selecting and training internal resources for
  documenting and auditing the quality system
- Determining the structure, format and content of
  your quality policy, quality manual and
  operating procedures,
- Auditing the existing system and developing a
  corrective action plan

For: Project managers or leaders involved in
implementing quality management systems,
preparing their company for ISO 9000 certification,
or setting up to document and audit their quality
systems

ISO 9000 IN THE APPLICATION SOFTWARE ENVIRONMENT

THE VICTORIA GROUP
Phone: 800-845-0567
Cost: 1295.00
ISO 9000 is an international standard for Quality
Management Systems. Adopted by over 50 nations
around the world, it has become the primary
measure of systems effectiveness in all the major
trading nations. No company can afford to ignore
its impact on trade.

Topics will include:

- Understanding basic quality concepts - quality
  systems and their uses
- The business areas required to be under control
  as described by ISO 9001
- The interface between ISO 9001 and ISO 9000-
  3
- The Accreditation and Certification process in
  the EC and in the U.S.
- The U.K. "TickIT" scheme for certification of
  software developers and current U.S. initiatives
  in software developer certification.
- What does the Standard mean? A line-by-line
  review of the purpose, application and
  interpretation of ISO 9001 coupled with ISO
  9000-3 presented as a series of functional
  workshops, lecture and general discussion.
- Continuation and completion of the analysis of
  the ISO 9001 and ISO 9000-3 Standards, with
  special focus on the software development
  process. The cross-linking between the two
  documents is thoroughly examined, and some
  of the classic models for software development
  explored, together with discussions of other
  software standards and maturity models.
- Other current software development options
  explored, together with some focused
  discussions on individual delegate concerns and
  interpretations.

ISO 9000 INTERNAL AUDIT

G.R. TECHNOLOGIES (USA) INC.

Phone: 407-995-0611

Cost: 750.00

This is a comprehensive workshop to help staff prepare for audits. Participants will receive an audit checklist and learn to prepare audit questions. Several workshops were designed to provide hands-on practice with real-time audits.

ISO 9000 INTERNAL AUDITOR COURSE

EXCEL PARTNERSHIP INC. IN CONJUNCTION WITH TUV RHEINLAND OF NORTH AMERICA INC.

Phone: 203-426-3281

Cost: 795.00

Every company seeking registration under ISO 9000 must continually audit its quality management systems in order to satisfy the requirements of the standard. Properly applied auditing can be a powerful management tool in assisting the quality improvement process.

Course covers how to:

- Coordinate an effective audit
- Evaluate the audit team's findings
- Communicate with personnel involved in the audit
- Report the results to management
- Develop and implement corrective action programs

This course combines tutorial presentations with workshop sessions. Delegates are required to work in groups in the evening to prepare for the case study and role-playing exercises.

ISO 9000 LEAD ASSESSOR CERTIFICATE COURSE

HANDLEY-WALKER CO., INC.

Phone: 714-730-0122

Cost: 1500.00

Upon completion of this course participants will be fully knowledgeable of the ISO 9000 Standard; be trained internal auditors; be competent to conduct assessments of subcontractors and suppliers; be able to prepare their organization for ISO 9000 registration; and understand the economic advantages of quality management systems. This course is registered by the Governing Board of the U.K. Registration Scheme for Assessors of Quality Systems and meets the training requirements for registration of individual assessors under that scheme. A certificate will be awarded to delegates who satisfactorily fulfill the requirements of the course and pass the course examination.

For: Managers installing Quality Management Systems; Auditors who assess suppliers and subcontractors; Managers who are setting up internal teams to audit their own Q.A. systems and; Individuals seeking employment as lead assessors for ISO 9000 certification bodies

ISO 9000 LEAD ASSESSOR TRAINING

PERRY JOHNSON, INC.

Phone: 313-356-4410

Cost: 1495.00

This course teaches the full ISO 9000 accreditation process, including assessing quality manuals, quality procedures, etc. The course is built around a variety of case studies which include an actual quality manual which the students will assess, and concludes with a final examination.

Course content:

The ISO 9000 Accreditation Process
- Applicable standards
- Benefits of certification

Principles of Auditing
- Internal auditing techniques
- Auditing practices

The Managerial Role of the Lead Auditor
- Selecting and preparing your auditors
- Directing the efforts of the auditing team

Quality Manuals, Systems and Documentation
- What must be included
- Acceptable formats
- Monitoring quality management systems

Planning and Performing an Audit
- Pre-audit planning
- Developing checklists
- Reporting your findings
- Corrective action requests
- Noncompliance and nonconformance
- Taking corrective action

Auditing Design and Research and Development Functions

Auditing Service Functions

For: Personnel who wish to become independent assessors.

ISO 9000 MANAGEMENT AWARENESS
G.R. TECHNOLOGIES (USA) INC.
Phone: 407-995-0611
Cost: 375.00
This is a concise overview for senior management and for those who wish to design an implementation plan. This seminar provides a top view to answer such questions as: how much, how long, etc.

ISO 9000 OVERVIEW: A PRACTICAL APPROACH TO QUALITY
GEORGE WASHINGTON UNIVERSITY (CEEP)
CONTINUING ENGINEERING EDUCATION PROGRAM
Phone: 800-424-9773
Cost: 675.00
Published by the Geneva-based International Standards Organization (ISO) in 1987, ISO 9000 is a series of five standards for developing Total Quality Management and a Quality Improvement Process. The ISO 9000 Series is becoming the international standard of quality and facilitates the universal upgrading of individual quality systems throughout the world. The series has been adopted by many nations including the U.S., as their own national standard. Many countries have assigned their own numbers to the standards. In the U.K. the standards are referred to as British Standard 5750. In the U.S., the number is ANSI/ASQC Q90. The European Community has designed the standards EN 29000. To achieve certification, a company must demonstrate it is committed to quality. Third party qualified assessors are used to certify that each company meets the rigorous standards of ISO 9000 before certification is given. This overview course offers numerous opportunities to develop and expand the quest for quality on an international level.

ISO 9000 QUALITY ASSURANCE SYSTEMS
STAT-A-MATRIX
Phone: 908-548-0600
Cost: 595.00
Notes: This seminar is also offered on-site.
This course is designed to introduce participants to the ISO 9000 Series of Standards. It provides an in-depth understanding of the ISO 9000 Standards, describes the concepts of the European Community (EC) and explains when registration to ISO is required or desirable for export. Participants receive a detailed analysis of each requirement of the standards as well as a comparison to help them understand the relationships among the five ISO standards. Attendees receive a text and copies of the applicable specifications.

Topics include:

- What ISO 9000 means to your industry
- The development of ISO
- The EC approach to "harmonized standards"
- The relationship of U.S. Standards to ISO 9000
- The ISO registration process
- The third party audit concept
- Understanding the Requirements
- The five ISO 9000 Standards
- Differences between 9001, 9002, and 9003
- Reading and understanding ISO 9000
- The detailed requirements of ISO 9001
- Possible changes for 1997
- The steps in ISO registration
- What it takes to become registered
- When it's necessary or desirable to register
- Developing the Quality System
- The requirements for ISO 9000 system documentation
- The documentation pyramid
- Planning the documented quality system
- How and when to implement your system
- Getting ready for a third party audit
- What ISO auditors look for
- Typical audit findings

For: Participants who want to understand the requirements of the ISO 9000 Standards, the requirements for a quality system, and how to prepare for ISO registration.

ISO 9000 QUALITY MANAGEMENT SYSTEM DESIGN
MANAGEX INTERNATIONAL
Phone: 714-727-7001
Cost: 695.00
This is a seminar which will explore all aspects of the ISO 9000 Series Worldwide Standardization and Quality System Registration process. You will explore the ISO 9000 (ANSI/ASQC Q90) Series Quality System Standards in detail and see how to apply them to your business.

ISO 9000 QUALITY MANAGEMENT SYSTEM DESIGN

BREWER-KLECKNER EDUCATION SERVICES
Phone: 214-660-4575
Cost: 695.00

This seminar will explore all aspects of the ISO 9000 Series Worldwide Standardization and Quality System Registration process. The seminar will explore the ISO 9000 (ANSI/ASQC Q90) Series Quality System Standards in detail and see how to apply them to business. This seminar will describe how to design or revise quality management systems to meet these new worldwide requirements. This will be done in an interactive lecture environment in which we will present the significance of the registration process and quality management system standards. Participants will receive a comprehensive student manual which includes all of the ANSI/ASQC Q90 Series Quality System Standards.

What you will learn:
- Quality System Certification/Registration Requirements
- Third Party Assessment and Certification Agencies
- Quality System Registration
- ISO 9000 (ANSI/ASQC Q90) Series Standards
- Documenting the Quality System
- Modern Quality Concepts

For: Individuals who need an understanding of the ISO quality system registration process, the ISO quality management system standards, and the marketing impact these will have on organizations providing products or services in the U.S. or exporting to the European Community or other areas of the world where ISO registration may be needed. Many decisions about registration will be market-driven and sales/marketing should understand the benefits.

ISO 9000 QUALITY MANUAL WRITING

G.R. TECHNOLOGIES (USA) INC.
Phone: 407-995-0611
Cost: 750.00

This course will discuss topics on:

- How to design the quality documentation
- QA Manual
- Secondary documentation
- Forms, tags, etc.

ISO 9000 QUALITY SYSTEM DOCUMENTATION

STAT-A-MATRIX
Phone: 908-548-0600
Cost: 845.00

This workshop is designed to provide a practical approach to evaluating and preparing the documentation needed to implement an ISO 9000 Quality System. Participants learn how to analyze ISO 9000 documentation requirements and write instructions and system-level procedures.

ISO 9000 QUALITY SYSTEM DOCUMENTATION

AMERICAN SOCIETY FOR QUALITY CONTROL EDUCATION & TRAINING INSTITUTE
Phone: 800-952-6587
Cost: 820.00 Non-member; 735.00 Member

Once you have a general understanding of how the ISO 9000/Q90 Standards relate to your company, you need to understand how to properly document your quality practices within your company. ISO 9000 Quality System Documentation provides you with the insight to build a quality manual for your company. Proper documentation is a key aspect of becoming ISO 9000 certified, and the ISO 9000 Standards are becoming a model for companies outside the European Community as well. The course covers topics such as form and instruction preparation, document control, and manual maintenance. In this workshop you will practice how to write effective, understandable policies, procedures, work instructions, and records, a key part of passing your ISO audit. Discuss how to handle release, change, and control procedures. See how you can use your already existing standards and procedures to meet the ISO 9000 requirements. Understand the importance of documenting corrective actions, and improve your procedure verification process. By writing and developing the correct quality manual the first time, you will greatly improve your company's chances for continued ISO 9000 certification.

For: ersonnel responsible for writing procedures for ISO 9000 certification.

ISO 9000 QUALITY SYSTEM IMPLEMENTATION WORKSHOP

QUALTEC QUALITY SERVICES INC.
Phone: 407-775-8335
Cost: 1695.00
Notes: This seminar is also offered on-site.
This course will discuss what are the workshop objectives? The overall objective of this course is to provide senior and middle managers with the knowledge, skills and tools needed to prepare their organizations for ISO 9000 registration.

Course covers how to:

- Develop an understanding of the powerful forces driving more and more manufacturing and service organizations toward ISO 9000 registration.
- Provide an understanding of how the ISO 9000 Quality System fits into the broader process of Total Quality Management.
- Develop an understanding of the role of executive management in structuring and supporting an ISO 9000 Quality System.
- Provide participants with a step by step implementation plan for ISO 9000 registration.
- Provide participants with the knowledge and skills to perform an intern self-assessment of their organization against the ISO 9000 Standard.
- Provide participants with a model ISO 9000 documentation package.

For: Manufacturing and service companies that have a quality system in place and need to modify it to meet the requirements of ISO 9001, 9002, or 9003. Participants should include senior and middle managers responsible for Marketing, Production, Engineering, Purchasing, Quality, and Shipping, who are on, or will be on, the ISO 9000 Steering Committee and/or the Implementation Team.

ISO 9000 QUALITY SYSTEMS AUDITING COURSE

HANDLEY-WALKER CO., INC.
Phone: 714-730-0122
Cost: 650.00
This workshop provides all the necessary information, skills and methods for auditing quality systems to the requirements of the ISO 9000 Standard. Participants will gain the knowledge and skills required to compare existing systems and documentation with ISO 9000 requirements and to

assist their company to plan and perform the periodic audits required by the standard.

Course content:

- Principles and Concepts of Auditing
- Types of Audits
- Familiarization with the ISO 9000 Standard
- Preparing the Audit
- Conducting the Audit
- Reporting the Audit

For: Project leaders and team leaders who must schedule and plan an audit program in compliance with ISO 9000. Personnel responsible for performing periodic audits in compliance with ISO 9000 or other quality systems.

ISO 9000 SEMINAR

ROCHESTER INSTITUTE OF TECHNOLOGY CENTER FOR QUALITY & APPLIED STATISTICS
Phone: 716-475-6990
Cost: 700.00
ISO 9000 topics will include:

- History of the ISO 9000 Series Standard
- Relationship of ISO 9000 to other standards
- Use of ISO 9000 for registration of suppliers
- U.S. registration issues
- Benefits of registration
- Scope and applicability of ISO 9000
- Definitions and principal concepts
- Characteristics of quality systems
- Use of standards for quality management
- Use of the standards for contractual purposes
- Quality policy and objectives
- Quality loops
- Structure of a quality system
- Quality manuals and auditing
- Evaluation of the quality management system
- Quality-related cost considerations
- Quality in marketing

For: Personnel with functional responsibility in the fields of quality management, manufacturing, general management, corporate planning, and marketing.

ISO 9000 SERIES OVERVIEW

GEORGE WASHINGTON UNIVERSITY (CEEP)
CONTINUING ENGINEERING EDUCATION PROGRAM
Phone: 800-424-9773
Cost: 675.00
This course demonstrates how organizations can expand their quest for quality on an international

scale using the ISO 9000 Series of Standards. It describes ISO 9000 Series registration action plans, steering teams, and quality program documentation. The course shows how to maximize and validate on-line testing and inspection and procedures for allocating resources to comply with the ISO 9000 Series. Participants learn how to avoid pitfalls in applying the ISO 9000 Series and how to develop ISO 9000 action plans for their own organizations. For: Quality control managers, purchasing managers, and general managers, engineering supervisors, production supervisors, quality assurance engineers, manufacturing engineers, technicians, and members of ISO steering teams.

ISO 9000 SERIES TRAINING COURSE
QUALITY MANAGEMENT INSTITUTE (QMI)
Phone: 416-272-3920
Cost: 650.00
This workshop will provide you with an understanding of the rationale and application of the ISO 9000 criteria. You will receive a copy of the QMI system checklist, together with QMI 25: Definitions and Clarifications for Auditing & Registering Companies to ISO 9001, 9002 and 9003-87. This workshop provides you with selection criteria for choosing the most appropriate standard to satisfy your needs in-house or your requirements for suppliers. As you learn about the ISO 9000 Series of Quality Standards, you will also learn how to develop your own quality assurance manual in accordance with ISO 9001. A documented quality program is a valuable asset for your company and a requirement for Registration of your program with QMI. It provides evidence to your potential customers of your commitment to meet their quality requirements, and provides you with a roadmap to do it right the first time. The workshop provides you with a practical handbook to guide you through the process when you return to your workplace.

Course content:

- The elements of all levels of the ISO 9000 Series of Quality Assurance Standards.
- The role of documentation in Quality Program: Purpose and benefits and types of documentation.
- Steps to prepare your Documentation: How to get started, who to involve and what to do

ISO 9000 STANDARDS & AUDITOR TRAINING
AMERICAN SUPPLIER INSTITUTE (ASI)
Phone: 313-271-4200
Cost: 1445.00
This course is designed to meet the educational requirements for RAB auditor/lead auditor certification. RAB recognition of this complete course, developed by ASI and QPI, was applied for November 1992.

ISO 9000-3 FOR SOFTWARE DEVELOPERS & AUDITORS
STAT-A-MATRIX
Phone: 908-548-0600
Cost: 995.00
Notes: This seminar is also offered on-site.
This seminar prepares the participant to develop, evaluate, implement, maintain, and improve Software Quality Assurance (SQA) programs, including the evaluation processes necessary to meet ISO 9000 Standards. The emphasis is on software defect prevention activities rather than after-the-fact testing.

Topics include:

- ISO 9001 for two-party contractual situations
- ISO 9000-3, applications guidelines for software
- Management responsibility
- Quality systems strategy
- The waterfall model
- Internal quality system audits
- Corrective action
- Contract review
- Purchaser's requirements specification
- Interface specifications
- Development planning
- Inputs to development phase
- Outputs from development phase
- Quality planning and design
- Testing, validation, and acceptance
- Maintenance activities and plans
- Configuration management
- Document and change control
- Quality records
- SQA measurements
- Rules, practices, and conventions
- Purchased software

For: SQA managers and practitioners, and those involved in managing, procuring, developing, operating, or maintaining software systems.

ISO 9000: AN EXECUTIVE BRIEFING WORKSHOP

INSTITUTE FOR PROFESSIONAL EDUCATION
Phone: 703-527-8700
Cost: 1095.00

Approaching the 21st century, management of the global enterprise is a major strategic focus of American corporations. The intensification of global competition has been the principal environmental force shaping this new focus. The new marketplace requires improvements in quality and concurrent improvements in price/performance ratios. Continuous, real-time process improvement is the critical key to achieving and maintaining a world-class enterprise. The ISO 9000 Standards are seen as the platform of choice to manage the smooth migration towards TQM and world-class production systems. A company with an ISO 9000 compliant quality management system provides its customers with independent continuation that it has in operation a well-defined and controlled set of procedures which ensures the consistent quality of its products and services over time. Considering the speed, magnitude and direction of these forces, understanding what ISO 9000 is, how it works and what it means is critical to every business leader in America. This executive briefing workshop is designed to provide participants with a clear understanding of ISO 9000 and its strategic implications.

Topics include:

- ISO 9000: How does it work?
- Registration
- ISO 9000 requirements
- Implementing ISO 9000
- Documentation requirements
- Strategic implications

ISO 9000: BEDROCK OF QUALITY IMPROVEMENT

GEORGE WASHINGTON UNIVERSITY (CEEP)
CONTINUING ENGINEERING EDUCATION PROGRAM
Phone: 800-424-9773
Cost: 2000.00
Notes: This is a live telecast.

This telecast demonstrates how organizations can expand their quest for quality on an international scale using the ISO 9000 Series of Standards. It describes ISO 9000 Series registration action plans, steering teams, and quality system documentation. Participants learn how to avoid pitfalls in applying the ISO 9000 Series and how to develop team-based ISO 9000 action plans for their own organizations. Gain insight into the ISO registration process and learn the value of ISO relative to quality improvement efforts.

ISO 9000: HOW TO ACHIEVE COMPLIANCE & CERTIFICATION IN YOUR COMPANY

AMERICAN MANAGEMENT ASSOCIATION
Phone: 518-891-1500
Cost: 1380.00 Non-member; 1200.00 Member

ISO 9000 certification distinguishes companies around the world for providing highly superior quality. Sign up for AMA's ground breaking ISO 9000 seminar and learn from experts in the field of quality - and in ISO 9000 certification - how to create a game plan for quality that will bring your company both distinction and success.

For: Quality control/assurance managers, engineering supervisors, quality assurance engineers, production supervisors, manufacturing engineers, technicians, plant managers, purchasing managers, members of the ISO steering team, ISO 9000 site coordinators, and all managers concerned with practical application of quality controls.

ISO 9000: IBM IMPLEMENTATION EXPERIENCES & RESULTS

NATIONAL TECHNOLOGICAL UNIVERSITY
Phone: 303-484-6050
Notes: This is a satellite course.

The advent of the European Economic Community has brought on the adoption of national and international quality standards with third party registration. Companies will be required to submit to auditing by licensed quality system auditors in order to be registered as a complying supplier. These international quality standards are referred to as ISO. The ISO 9000 experiences session will discuss issues of interest to the software and hardware quality community as they move forward in obtaining ISO registration. Sessions will be offered regularly over the NTU and IBM satellite delivery system networks.

Course covers how to:

■ Understand how ISO 9000 is coordinated throughout IBM
■ Hear about actual experiences in obtaining registration for a major hardware laboratory and a major software laboratory
■ Be given tips and techniques for implementing a successful ISO 9000 program

For: Technical employees with an involvement and detailed introductory training in ISO registration.

ISO 9000: LEAD ASSESSOR TRAINING COURSE

INTERTEK
Phone: 703-591-1320
Cost: 1495.00
   Course goals include:

■ Satisfies the training requirements for achieving registration by the Institute of Quality Assurance in London, England, as a Lead Assessor
■ Provides an in-depth understanding of the implementation of a Quality Management System to the requirements of ISO 9000 including the Quality Policy, Standard Operating Procedures, and Work Instructions
■ Defines the requirements for auditing a Quality Management System to the ISO 9000 Standards

ISO 9000: MEETING THE WORLDWIDE QUALITY CHALLENGE

COMPLIANCE ENGINEERING
Phone: 508-264-4208
Cost: 895.00
Notes: This seminar is also offered on-site.
Compliance with the ISO 9000 Series of Quality Management Standards is required for access to EC markets for many companies. For others, ISO 9000 certification has become an important marketing specification. This program provides a comprehensive discussion of the ISO 9000 Series of Quality Requirements, as well as details on how to achieve and maintain ISO 9000 certification. The course includes a comprehensive case study exercise to sharpen your understanding of important requirements.

Course covers:

■ The worldwide impact of quality management systems
■ How to evaluate compliance with ISO 9000 requirements
■ The importance of documentation in implementing and marketing a quality management system
■ Audit plan guidelines

For: Engineers involved in design and development of products destined for European and overseas markets, quality control engineers responsible for establishing and maintaining quality management systems at their facility, and managers looking to understand the implications of quality management systems.

ISO 9000: THE WORLD QUALITY STANDARD

CENTER FOR PROFESSIONAL ADVANCEMENT
Phone: 908-613-4500
Cost: 990.00
Notes: This seminar is also offered on-site.
The economic, business and marketing justification for implementing the ISO 9000 process will be reviewed. Differentiation between the ISO 9000 registration process and industry standards including CGMP for the pharmaceutical industry will be discussed, and CGMP will be compared to ISO 9000 showing where modifications must be made between one and the other.

LEAD AUDITING

THE VICTORIA GROUP
Phone: 800-845-0567
Cost: 2195.00
Through this course, senior executives, quality managers and anyone responsible for leading an audit of your own or another company's quality management system will gain:

■ A fuller understanding of the ISO 9000 Series
■ An appreciation of, and ability to cope with, the psychological requirements of both the auditor and the auditee
■ A framework to set up and/or fine-tune your company's Quality Assurance program
■ The expertise and experience of British training teams

This course incorporates formal presentations, open discussions and case study workshops, culminating in a written examination. Successful completion of this detailed hands-on training and the examination

214

fulfill the training requirements for registration of individual assessors under the United Kingdom National Registration Scheme for Assessors of Quality Systems. This program qualification is also recognized by the U.S. R.A.B. The Victoria Group Lead Auditor Training is registered by the Governing Board of the U.K. National Registration Scheme.

LEAD AUDITOR

CENTER FOR ENERGY & ENVIRONMENTAL
MANAGEMENT (CEEM)
Phone: 703-250-5900
Cost: 2195.00
Quality and Quality Assurance - An Overview
Quality Assurance Management Standards:
- History of QA standards
- BS 5750/ISO 9000/Q 90
- Paperwork systems
- Change control
- Management style

The System for Quality Management Audits:
- Audit stages
- Types of audits
- Programming audits

Preparing for the Audit:
- Plan development
- Quality manuals
- Audit program
- Checklist preparation

Performance of the Audit:
- Process of auditing
- Attributes of a good auditor
- Audit team meetings

LEAD AUDITOR COURSE: TO MEET ISO 9000 STANDARDS

CENTER FOR ENERGY & ENVIRONMENTAL
MANAGEMENT (CEEM)
Phone: 703-250-5900
Cost: 2195.00
Notes: This seminar is also offered on-site.
You will gain the information and understanding you need to lead your company toward rapid certification to ISO 9000. Successful completion of this detailed, hands-on training and an examination, fulfills the training requirements for registration of individual assessors under the United Kingdom National Registration Scheme for Assessors of Quality Systems.

MANAGING INFORMATION SYSTEMS PROJECTS

GEORGE WASHINGTON UNIVERSITY (CEEP)
CONTINUING ENGINEERING EDUCATION PROGRAM
Phone: 800-424-9773
Cost: 700.00
Notes: This seminar is also offered on-site.
This course addresses all areas of information systems project management: hardware, software, systems integration, and human resources. It also treats contemporary issues including the Software Engineering Institute's Process Maturity Model, the National Institute of Standards and Technology's Application Portability Profile, and other standards such as GOSIP, POSIX, and ISO 9000.
For: Current and prospective information systems project managers, from government and industry, who have basic project management skills - such as planning, scheduling, earned value, and PERT/CPM - but need to learn advanced practices specific to this challenging field.

OVERVIEW OF THE TWENTY ELEMENTS OF ISO 9000

BRYANT COLLEGE CENTER FOR MANAGEMENT
DEVELOPMENT
Phone: 401-232-6200
Cost: 295.00
Notes: This seminar is also offered on-site.
This program is designed to remove the mystery and misinformation from the subject of ISO 9000. You will gain a basic understanding of the key issues, the impact on ongoing operations, and the implementation workscope. This information will allow you to make informed decisions about the benefits, the commitment, and the plans required to obtain registration. You will cover in detail the content of ISO 9001 and the requirements of all 20 business management system elements. This is an interactive workshop that will allow you to apply your understanding of each element to your particular work situation.

Course covers how to:

- Demystify the world of ISO 9000
- Make informed decisions about your company's future
- Understand how to gain an edge on your competition
- Choose a registrar that is right for your company
- Assign implementation resources efficiently

Topics include:

- An understanding of ISO 9001, ISO 9002, and ISO 9003
- A detailed review of the contents of ISO 9001
- Applying the elements of ISO 9001 to your own business situation
- Conclusion - How does it all apply to your organization?

PREPARING FOR ISO 9000 - INTERNAL AUDITOR COURSE

TRI COUNTY TECHNICAL COLLEGE
Phone: 803-225-2250
Cost: 695.00 Non-member; 485.00 Member
This is a skill building program to develop the skills and techniques used by an ISO 9000 Auditor. Class exercises include planning an audit, the role of the quality manual, the quality plan and the audit process. If possible, an actual mini-audit of a local industry will be performed during the course.

PREPARING FOR ISO 9000 - MANAGEMENT OVERVIEW

TRI COUNTY TECHNICAL COLLEGE
Phone: 803-225-2250
Cost: 250.00 Non-member; 195.00 Member
This is an overview of the ISO 9000 Quality Standards.

Topics include:

- History of the ISO 9000 program
- The benefits of registration
- The scope and applicability of the ISO 9000 quality policy and objectives
- Participative management concepts and more

PREPARING FOR ISO 9000 REGISTRATION

AMERICAN SOCIETY FOR QUALITY CONTROL EDUCATION & TRAINING INSTITUTE
Phone: 800-952-6587
Cost: 740.00 Non-member; 655.00 Member
What is ISO 9000/Q90? The International Standards organization (ISO) is a specialized international agency for standardization, representing an international consensus on good quality management for internal guidance and requirements for external quality assurance. The ISO 9000 Series of Quality Standards (adopted as ANSI/ASQC Q90 in the United States) has been adopted in over 55 countries, as well as by regional entities and industry associations. There is a vast amount of information available about the ISO 9000 Series and how it affects companies with international customers. Today, interest by major industrial customers and marketplace competition have overtaken regulation as the principal forces spurring suppliers to seek registration. This course helps sort it out. It is designed for participants who are beginning to learn about the ISO 9000 Standards and how they apply to their companies. Preparing for ISO 9000 Registration answers your questions about the content and application of the ISO standards. Understand the background, current uses, and future direction of the standards in response to increasing global trade and the economic integration of the European Community. Learn about the increasing importance of the standards in the U.S. marketplace. Learn what quality system registration is, what it involves, when it is appropriate, and how to prepare for it.

QUALITY MANAGEMENT IN THE LABORATORY

CENTER FOR ENERGY & ENVIRONMENTAL MANAGEMENT (CEEM)
Phone: 703-250-5900
Cost: 1195.00
Notes: This seminar is also offered on-site.
This course is specifically aimed at the practical and technical management of a laboratory, but more importantly, it includes a heavy bias toward quality management of laboratory operations - ISO Guide 25. There will be several sessions held throughout the seminar for participants to interact and present their ideas. A comprehensive notebook and group exercises will address topics including laboratory quality concepts, work planning, uncertainty calculations, and QC programs.

Subjects covered:

- The people factor - staff motivation and formal job specifications
- Staff training and development programs
- Laboratory accommodation and environment
- Laboratory equipment management, including calibration
- Laboratory recording and reporting systems
- Test methodology and method manuals
- Purchasing control in the laboratory
- Laboratory quality control - corrective action, review/audit programs
- Preparing a quality manual

QUALITY SYSTEM CERTIFICATION

CENTER FOR ENERGY & ENVIRONMENTAL
MANAGEMENT (CEEM)
Phone: 703-250-5900
Cost: 995.00
ISO 9001 System Requirements & ISO 9004
System Guidelines:

- Management responsibilities
- Contract review
- Quality in design
- Documentation requirements
- Purchasing
- Product traceability
- Quality in production
- Inspection and testing
- Calibration
- Audits
- Statistical techniques
- Nonconformance
- Handling and storage
- Training and servicing
- Quality costs
- Product safety

Quality Documentation:
- Compiling the documentation
- Analyzing requirements
- Getting started
- The Quality Manual

Quality System Certification:
- Inquiry
- Application
- Assessment
- Registration
- Foilow-up

QUALITY SYSTEM CERTIFICATION COURSE: TO MEET ISO 9000 STANDARDS

CENTER FOR ENERGY & ENVIRONMENTAL
MANAGEMENT (CEEM)
Phone: 703-250-5900
Cost: 995.00
Notes: This seminar is also offered on-site.
This course will explain how you can prepare for third party certification to ISO 9000 Standards. A series of presentations and workshops will provide guidance in interpreting standards, explain how to compile the necessary documentation and lead you through a BSi audit/certification process. You will acquire the in-depth knowledge necessary to implement a quality management system complying with ISO 9000. You will also gain insight into the third party audit/certification process.

For: hose wishing to gain an understanding of ISO 9000, responsible for operating a quality management system, or whose company is committed to achieving third party certification. Those who will derive the greatest benefit from this course are:

- Senior Management, Including CEOs
- QC/QA Managers
- Engineers & Chemists
- Consultants & Analysts
- Manufacturing/Production Leaders

QUALITY SYSTEM DOCUMENTATION

CENTER FOR ENERGY & ENVIRONMENTAL
MANAGEMENT (CEEM)
Phone: 703-250-5900
Cost: 1095.00
The course is comprised of a series of presentations that explain how you can best structure and prepare effective quality system documentation. This knowledge is then related to the practical environment through workshops and case studies using small group interaction. Registrants receive a detailed course notebook. Prior to the course you will receive a copy of ANSI/ASQC Q91 and activities which should be completed for the course.

QUALITY SYSTEM DOCUMENTATION

AMERICAN INSTITUTE FOR QUALITY & RELIABILITY
AIQR
Phone: 408-275-9300
Cost: 295.00
Notes: This seminar is also offered on-site.
This workshop will be presented by individuals who have directed the documentation of one or more companies on the way to certification to ISO 9000/Q90. The ISO 9000/Q90 Standard requires that you have your system documented. This workshop will train your employees on how to plan and write your Quality Manual.

SOFTWARE MANAGEMENT IN THE AGE OF ISO 9000

STAT-A-MATRIX
Phone: 908-548-0600
Cost: 995.00
This seminar prepares the participant to develop, evaluate, implement, maintain, and improve Software Quality Assurance (SQA) programs, including the evaluation processes necessary to

meet ISO 9000 Standards. The emphasis is on software defect prevention activities rather than after-the-fact testing.

Course covers:

- ISO 9001 for two-party contractual situations
- ISO 9000-3, Applications Guidelines for Software
- Management responsibility
- Quality systems strategy
- The waterfall model
- Internal quality system audits
- Corrective action
- SQA life cycle activities
- Contract review
- Purchaser's requirements specification
- Interface specifications
- Development planning
- Inputs to development phase
- Outputs from development phase
- Quality planning and design
- Testing, validation, and acceptance

For: SQA managers and practitioners, and those involved in managing, procuring, developing, operating, or maintaining software systems.

STANDARD & CALIBRATIONS LABORATORY: PRINCIPLES & PRACTICE

GEORGE WASHINGTON UNIVERSITY (CEEP)
CONTINUING ENGINEERING EDUCATION PROGRAM
Phone: 800-424-9773
Cost: 1295.00
Notes: This seminar is also offered on-site.
Government and ISO 9000 requirements mandate that standards and calibration laboratories must demonstrate that their measurement results are traceable to the appropriate national, international or consensus standards. Achieving this objective requires the integration of a variety of disciplines many of which are parameter dependent. This course addresses those disciplines that are important to establishment and maintenance of good measurement processes; to quantifying measurement process errors; and the development of a meaningful uncertainty statement. In addition to the traditional areas of metrology, the course covers automation, statistics, measurement quality assurance, and trends in metrology.

Topics include:

- The application of sound measurement principles
- Calibration strategies
- Error analysis
- Statistical techniques to maintain laboratory standards and provide quality to clients

TECHNIQUES FOR AUDITORS - INTERNAL AUDITOR TRAINING: INTERNAL AUDITING TO THE ISO 9000/Q90 QUALITY STANDARDS

BRYANT COLLEGE CENTER FOR MANAGEMENT DEVELOPMENT
Phone: 401-232-6200
Cost: 550.00
Notes: This seminar is also offered on-site.
This program explains why auditing is an essential component of every quality assurance system and how to carry out audits to comply with ISO 9000 requirements. You will be exposed to the role of audits within your quality management system, the role of the auditor, how to organize and execute audits, and how to communicate the results. The course includes several practical exercises in auditing that will enable the attendee to develop immediate skills based on the concepts that have been taught.

Course covers how to:

- Develop a thorough understanding of what is involved with an audit
- Gain control of your organization through the audit process
- Gain an unbiased view of your organization's behavior and performance
- Know how to prepare for an audit
- Identify opportunities for improvement
- Improve intracompany communications
- Identify root causes of problems
- Assess the status and capability of company personnel and equipment
- Provide a basis for identifying training needs
- Save time and money on your certification process

TEN-STEP ACTION PLAN FOR MAKING ISO 9000 THE BEDROCK OF QUALITY IMPROVEMENT

GEORGE WASHINGTON UNIVERSITY (CEEP)
CONTINUING ENGINEERING EDUCATION PROGRAM
Phone: 800-424-9773
Cost: 50.00
Notes: This is a satellite broadcast.
Many U.S. organizations' quality improvement efforts lack a proven, practical, realistic focus - too much theory and not enough application. Developing a quality system consistent with ISO registration is an excellent concrete first step for many organizations. This telecast demonstrates how organizations can expand their quest for quality on an international scale using the ISO 9000 Series of Standards. It describes ISO 9000 Series registration action plans, steering team, and quality system documentation. Participants will learn how to avoid pitfalls in applying the ISO 9000 Series and how to develop team-based ISO 9000 action plans for their own organizations.

UNDERSTANDING & APPLYING ISO 9000

AMERICAN SUPPLIER INSTITUTE (ASI)
Phone: 313-271-4200
Cost: 745.00
This course provides not only a detailed explanation of the ISO 9000 Standards and the registration process, but also practical guidance on preparing for successful audit and registration. You will learn how to get the most out of ISO 9000 to improve your company's quality system.

USING ISO 9000

LOUISIANA STATE UNIVERSITY EXECUTIVE EDUCATION
Phone: 504-388-8545
Cost: 895.00
This seminar will help you bridge the gap between confusion and certification when you decide to apply for ISO 9000 registration. ISO 9000 is a series of standards that outline the requirements for quality management systems. This seminar is a guide to understanding the requirements of ISO 9000, it will provide a step by step approach to the design and implementation of a quality management system.

Course covers:

- Support you in the design of a Quality Management System (QMS)
- Give you an in-depth understanding of the ISO 9000 Series requirements, including the necessary documentation needed
- Use ISO 9004 for Total Quality Management ranging from marketing to technical support
- Cut down the time required to prepare for registration for ISO 9001 or ISO 9002
- Set up an internal audit program for auditing the Quality Management System, including the basic principles for auditing
- Use project planning to determine bottlenecks in the ISO 9000 implementation. Project planning will also be used to predict the time and manpower requirements for ISO 9000 registration
- Teach you about Quality Management Information Systems, how they are used to carry out the tasks of a Quality Management System
- Give you an understanding about how to prepare a documented quality system, including the Quality Manuals and procedures
- Give you an understanding of the certification process, including the external audit, the certification bodies performing the assessment and issuing the certifications

BOOK
SECTION

1993 INTERNATIONAL SERVICE QUALITY & TOTAL QUALITY MANAGEMENT RESOURCE GUIDE & DIRECTORY

LAKEWOOD PUBLICATIONS
Phone: 800-328-4329
Cost: 349.00
Directory includes:

1. The Global Directory

Over 2500 quality- and service-related training and consulting companies, professional associations, governmental bodies, publications and much more. Includes contact information, descriptions of products and services offered, and industries served. A user friendly index helps you identify the companies that can best serve your needs.

Plus, the Global Directory features analysis of the current state of quality improvement in over 45 countries, written by experts in those countries. Also contains general economic and workforce data for each country.

2. Quality Awards

Reviews over 80 quality award competitions in 30 countries, featuring summaries of judging criteria, eligibility requirements, and past winners.

3. ISO 9000

Insightful articles and standards information to aid you in the compliance or certification process.

4. Books & Videos

Reviews of 50 of the best books and videos on hot topics such as benchmarking, leadership, quality, teamwork, empowerment, and customer service.

5. Research & Assessment Instruments Results from the International Survey of Service Quality and Total Quality Management, which compares quality perceptions among managers at companies in North America and Europe. Plus, descriptions of assessment instruments, surveys and other tools to measure and benchmark internal quality.

6. Academic Programs

Information on over 200 academic institutions throughout the world offering research, courses, workshops, and degrees in the field of Total Quality Management.

7. Selected Readings

Current articles from leading publications on topics such as implementing TQM, empowerment and employee development, leadership, process improvement, service quality, the Baldrige award and more.

8. The Global Service and Quality Master Calendar Local, regional and international conferences, seminars and expositions, and symposia around the world during 1993.

9. Selected Proceedings of the 1992 International Service & Quality Forum.

Highlights from the first ISQF Conference, held in Paris, 16-18 November, 1992, which brought together managers and executives from leading multinational organizations.

ALL ABOUT ISO 9000

PERRY JOHNSON, INC.
Phone: 313-356-4410
Cost: 50.00
This workbook was created to familiarize managers, supervisors and other quality-oriented persons about the ISO 9000 quality system standard and its equivalents.

In addition, this workbook can help managers assess the extent to which existing quality systems conform to the ISO 9000 standard. We recommend that managers use this workbook to:

- Become familiar with ISO 9000
- Assess its role in strategic and tactical planning
- Lay groundwork for adoption and/or certification, if desired

Course content:

- All About ISO 9000
- Origins of Quality Standards
- Benefits of ISO 9000
- Components of ISO 9000
- Technical Requirements
- The Certification Process: Documenting the Quality System
- The Certification Process: Finding a Registrar
- The Certification Process: Initial and Annual Assessments

ANSI/ASQC A1-1987: DEFINITIONS, SYMBOLS, FORMULAS, & TABLES FOR CONTROL CHARTS

AMERICAN SOCIETY FOR QUALITY CONTROL
EDUCATION & TRAINING INSTITUTE
Phone: 800-952-6587
Cost: 18.95 Non-member; 16.95 Member
This document provides a standardization of the symbols, concepts, terms, and procedures relating to Shewhart control charts, control charts with warning limits, moving averages and ranges, exponentially smoothed averages, Custom charts, multivariate control, trend control, process capability factors, and the acceptance control chart.

ANSI/ASQC A2-1987: TERMS, SYMBOLS, & DEFINITIONS FOR ACCEPTANCE SAMPLING

AMERICAN SOCIETY FOR QUALITY CONTROL
EDUCATION & TRAINING INSTITUTE
Phone: 800-952-6587
Cost: 17.50 Non-member; 16.00 Member
This document covers the major forms of acceptance sampling schemes for both attributes and variables measures, including extensive comments, explanations, and comparison of the various acceptance sampling approaches.

ANSI/ASQC A3-1987: QUALITY SYSTEMS TERMINOLOGY

AMERICAN SOCIETY FOR QUALITY CONTROL
EDUCATION & TRAINING INSTITUTE
Phone: 800-952-6587
Cost: 18.50 Non-member; 16.95 Member
This text presents basic definitions dealing with quality assurance, quality control, quality programs, and quality systems for general use within U.S. commerce and industry. Utilizes new terms from ISO 8402.

ANSI/ASQC C1-1985 (ANSI Z1.8-1971)

AMERICAN SOCIETY FOR QUALITY CONTROL
EDUCATION & TRAINING INSTITUTE
Phone: 800-952-6587
Cost: 12.95 Non-member; 11.95 Member
This standard concerns the establishment and maintenance of a quality program by a contractor to assure compliance with contract requirements in the areas of quality management design information, procurement, manufacture, acceptance, and documentation.

ANSI/ASQC E3-1984: GUIDE TO INSPECTION PLANNING

AMERICAN SOCIETY FOR QUALITY CONTROL
EDUCATION & TRAINING INSTITUTE
Phone: 800-952-6587
Cost: 12.95 Non-member; 11.95 Member
This standard describes the significant elements that should be considered in the development of inspection activities. It provides generic guidelines for planning and applying a product/process inspection system for construction, manufacturing, operating, or service functions.

ANSI/ASQC Q1-1986 - GENERIC GUIDELINES FOR AUDITING OF QUALITY SYSTEMS

AMERICAN SOCIETY FOR QUALITY CONTROL
EDUCATION & TRAINING INSTITUTE
Phone: 800-952-6587
Cost: $19.50
This document assists in the establishment, planning, and execution of internal and external audits of quality assurance systems. This generic guideline is general enough to be used in different industries and organizations. The guideline has been formulated in conjunction with a careful study of published audit standards, as listed in Appendix "A", and current audit practice in the quality field. Appendix "B" is a bibliography. Some definitions were adopted from the ANSI/ASQC A3-1987 standard.

ANSI/ASQC Q3-1988: SAMPLING PROCEDURES & TABLES FOR INSPECTION OF ISOLATED LOTS BY ATTRIBUTES

AMERICAN SOCIETY FOR QUALITY CONTROL
EDUCATION & TRAINING INSTITUTE
Phone: 800-952-6587
Cost: 24.95 Non-member; 22.95 Member
This is an acceptance sampling system to be used when one or more lots that are isolated or separated from a continuous of lots are submitted for acceptance. For this purpose the quality levels referenced in this standard are indexed by limiting quality (LQ). The LQ represents the quality of a lot the consumer does not wish to accept. The probability of acceptance of a lot which has a quality equal to or worse than the LQ is purpose low. Plans provide for the judgment of lots based on the percent nonconforming or the nonconformities per hundred units. The procedures of this standard differ from those of ANSI/ASQC

Z1.4, which is appropriate for a continuous stream of lots with an AQL (acceptable quality level) specified.

ANSI/ASQC Q90-Q94 1987 QUALITY MANAGEMENT & QUALITY ASSURANCE STANDARDS SERIES

AMERICAN SOCIETY FOR QUALITY CONTROL
EDUCATION & TRAINING INSTITUTE
Phone: 800-952-6587
Cost: $44.95
This new set of American national standards on quality management and quality assurance is identical to the International Standards Organization (ISO) 9000-9004 standards, which are recognized internationally. (Definitions of the key terms and concepts basic to the Q90 Series are included in ANSI/ASQC A3-1987).

The series include:

- Quality Management and Quality Assurance Standards - Guidelines for Selection and Use
- Quality Systems - Model for Quality Assurance in Design/Development, Production, Installation, and Servicing
- Quality Systems - Model for Quality Assurance in Production and Installation
- Quality Systems - Model for Quality Assurance in Final Inspection and Test
- Quality Management and Quality System Elements - Guidelines

ANSI/ASQC Q90/ISO 9000 GUIDELINES FOR USE BY THE CHEMICAL PROCESS INDUSTRIES

AMERICAN SOCIETY FOR QUALITY CONTROL
EDUCATION & TRAINING INSTITUTE
Phone: 800-952-6587
Cost: 20.50 Non-member; 18.25 Member
Length: 112 pages
For those who work in the chemical or process industries, here's the necessary information to apply the ANSI/ASQC Q90-94 quality system model standards to your company. There are at least two reasons why this book is must reading:

- It translates the meaning of the Q90 (ISO 9000) series into CPI terms
- It relates to every activity that affects the quality of the reader's products and services

The book's user-friendly format includes a description, discussion of issues and practices, interpretation, cautions, and application of each element of the standards. The guidelines also include examples of good quality practices to help develop a quality assurance system.
The Chemical Interest Committee of the ASQC Chemical and Process Industries Division, in cooperation with the Total Quality Council of the Chemical Manufacturers Association's CHEMSTAR Division, developed the guidelines. Chemical Interest Committee members also wrote the best-selling Quality Assurance for the Chemical and Process Industries: A Manual of Good Practices.

ANSI/ASQC S1-1987: AN ATTRIBUTE SKIP-LOT SAMPLING PROGRAM

AMERICAN SOCIETY FOR QUALITY CONTROL
EDUCATION & TRAINING INSTITUTE
Phone: 800-952-6587
Cost: 23.50 Non-member; 22.95 Member
This standard provides a procedure for reducing the inspection effort on products submitted by those suppliers who have demonstrated their ability to control, in an effective manner, all facets of product quality and consistently produce superior quality material. This procedure shall not be applied to the inspection of product characteristics which involve the safety of personnel. The standard is to be used on with ANSI/ASQC Z1.4-1981. Annexes A, B, and C augment the usability of the standard by outlining procedures for tailoring to the user's specific situation, by describing a simple method of random selection, and by providing criteria for deciding between skip-lot inspection and reduced inspection under ANSI/ASQC Z1.4-1981.

ANSI/ASQC Z1.4-1981: SAMPLING PROCEDURES & TABLES FOR INSPECTION BY ATTRIBUTES

AMERICAN SOCIETY FOR QUALITY CONTROL
EDUCATION & TRAINING INSTITUTE
Phone: 800-952-6587
Cost: 19.50 Non-member; 17.95 Member
This standard, which corresponds to MIL-STD-105, establishes sampling plans and procedures for inspection by attributes. tables and procedures are completely compatible with MIL-STD-105. It is also compatible and interchangeable with ANSI/ASQC Z1.9-1980 for variables inspection.

ANSI/ASQC Z1.9-1980: SAMPLING PROCEDURES & TABLES FOR INSPECTION BY VARIABLES FOR PERCENT NONCONFORMING

AMERICAN SOCIETY FOR QUALITY CONTROL
EDUCATION & TRAINING INSTITUTE
Phone: 800-952-6587
Cost: 26.95 Non-member; 24.95 Members
This standard, establishing sampling plans and procedures for inspection by variables, corresponds to the military standard MIL-STD-414 and is interchangeable with ISO/DIS 3951. It contains tables and procedures of MIL-STD-414, suitably modified to achieve correspondence with ISO/DIS 3951 and matching with MIL-STD-105 and ANSI/ASQC Z1.4-1981.

AUDIT STANDARDS: A COMPARATIVE ANALYSIS, SECOND EDITION

AMERICAN SOCIETY FOR QUALITY CONTROL
EDUCATION & TRAINING INSTITUTE
Phone: 800-952-6587
Cost: 19.95 Non-member; 17.95 Member
Length: 80 pages
Revised to describe the ISO 10011 standards, this second edition takes the major existing guidelines and standards and summarizes them to direct and support audit activity. The book compares differences between individual documents, and details their strengths and weaknesses. The reader becomes familiar with these documents and can more fully comprehend the standards with which the auditor must comply. The book is presented in a step by step progression of an audits natural flow. The end result is an invaluable service to anyone interested in effective auditing.

DEMYSTIFYING ISO 9000: INFORMATION MAPPING'S GUIDE TO THE ISO 9000 STANDARDS

INFORMATION MAPPING INC.
Phone: 617-890-7003
Cost: BOOK 99.95
Our guide to the ISO 9000 Standards, "Demystifying ISO 9000," explains and clarifies the ISO 9000 standards. If you'd like a complete, easy reference to ISO 9000, Information Mapping's exclusive guide provides clear, detailed information on the ISO 9000 standards.

Book covers how to:

- Select the appropriate conformance model (ISO 9001, 9002 or 9003)
- Understand key ISO 9000 terms
- Interpret the twenty sections of ISO 9001
- Develop strategies for getting registered
- Understand the document control process

DOCUMENTING QUALITY FOR ISO 9000 & OTHER INDUSTRY STANDARDS

AMERICAN SOCIETY FOR QUALITY CONTROL
EDUCATION & TRAINING INSTITUTE
Phone: 800-952-6587
Cost: 24.95 Non-member; 21.95 Member
Length: 200 pages
This book is a must-have for all small- to medium-sized organizations interested in pursuing ISO and other industrial certification. A basic, but very specific "how-to" guide, this book will teach you how to document your administrative procedures from start to finish. Documentation processes are absolute requirements for ISO certification and implementation. The book is your step by step, fully detailed guide to document quality systems.

The author uses everyday life situations and relates them to the documentation process. Organized much like a quality manual itself, this book helps you to understand how to record your procedures and incorporate this documentation with your quality implementation plans. It also contains short summaries to help clarify complex concepts, and also includes forms, flow charts, and documents to assist in building a set of administrative procedures which will help put a quality program into motion for your company or organization.

GUIDEBOOK TO ISO 9000 & ANSI/ASQC Q90

AMERICAN SOCIETY FOR QUALITY CONTROL
EDUCATION & TRAINING INSTITUTE
Phone: 800-952-6587
Cost: BOOK 53.95 Non-member; 45.95 Member
Length: 138 pages
This book is the perfect place to begin your search for understanding ISO 9000. It provides a brief, general, question/answer overview of the ISO 9000 and ANSI/ASQC Q90 standards. In addition, it features the ANSI/ASQC Q90 standards in their entirety. In fact, the whole booklet is priced at just $1.00 more than the regular price of the standards themselves. The question-and-answer format

makes it easy to find answers to key questions about the ISO 9000 standards. Author Ronald J. Cottman has firsthand knowledge about the European quality community and quality systems registration and regulation. This book also explains how to relate the Q90 series to an existing quality system.

HOW TO PASS AN ISO 9000 QUALITY SYSTEM AUDIT

AMERICAN GAS ASSOCIATION A.G.A.
LABORATORIES
Phone: 213-261-8161
Cost: 175.00
Topics include:

- 10 Chronological steps to successful registration
- The purpose of each clause of ISO 9001
- How to write a quality manual
- A 32 page complete quality manual
- 100 Questions the auditor will definitely ask
- The pre-audit...is it necessary?
- The most important ingredient is the employee
- ANSI/ASQC Q91 Standard for Quality systems

HOW TO WRITE YOUR ISO 9000 QUALITY MANUAL

PERRY JOHNSON, INC.
Phone: 313-356-4410
To obtain ISO 9000 certification, you must document your quality system with a Quality Manual. And that's not simple. To satisfy the assessors, your ISO 9000 quality manual must address the right issues, with the right language, in the right format.

PJI's exclusive How to Write Your ISO 9000 Quality Manual trains management teams in the writing of ISO 9000 quality manuals. Your team will learn the basics of the ISO 9000 certification process, ISO 9000 documentation guidelines, the contents of the ISO 9001 standard, and acceptable formats and reference methods. Plus, the workbook helps you assess your own quality system. This can help you find areas of nonconformance with the ISO 9000 standard so that you can fix them long before the ISO 9000 assessors walk in. Replete with examples, the workbook reinforces its training with numerous self-graded quizzes. It's a great way to launch your ISO 9000 program!

All About ISO 9000 Overheads

Now you can train all your people in the ISO 9000 standard with PJI's All About ISO 9000 kit. Our full color, fully scripted overhead transparency presentation gives your staff orientation in the quality system standard which is becoming the international standard for quality.

IMPLEMENTING THE ISO 9000 SERIES

INSTITUTE OF PACKAGING PROFESSIONALS
Phone: 703-318-8970
Cost: 45.00
Length: 262 pages
Highlights ISO 9001, the most involved of the standards, and places the others in proper perspective.

Book covers:

- The major European directives that refer to ISO 9000 and related critical issues such as the political economy of the ISO standards
- Interprets ISO clauses from various industrial viewpoints, including those of service industries, and gives examples of these viewpoints
- Shows which organizational strategy to adopt, how to coordinate implementation, and how to bring about change within a company to implement ISO 9000
- Furnishes examples of how to document Tier Two
- Illustrates the preparation of generic flow charts
- Analyzes in detail the procedures for conducting internal audits and offers sample forms to help maintain the system once it is implemented
- Examines third party audits and supplies case studies with their solutions
- Discusses the latest revisions to the standards, their implications, and future developments
- Eight appendices that provide addresses and phone numbers of governmental agencies specializing in ISO 9000
- Regional addresses of all trade adjustment assistance centers
- A list of registrars
- Sample quality manual
- A list of ISO/IEC guides

Note: Though this book contains much material that can be directly applied to packaging, it is not written exclusively for packaging professionals and does not address packaging issues specifically.

INTERNAL AUDITOR
PERRY JOHNSON, INC.
Phone: 313-356-4410
Cost: 50.00
The ISO 9000 quality system standard requires regular internal audits. In most firms, these audits are carried out by employees who lack auditing training or experience. This programmed-instruction workbook teaches managers at all levels the strategies and tactics of effective quality system auditing in an ISO 9000 environment. Managers learn the characteristics of a competent auditor, effective auditor tactics, techniques for countering auditee tactics and the detailed steps of productive internal audits. The workbook includes an actual case study as well as an appendix which provides instruction in the ISO 9001 quality system standard for those who have not received this training previously.

Course content:

- Introduction to Quality System Auditing
- The Effective Auditor
- Audit Initiation
- Audit Planning
- Audit Implementation (Execution)
- Audit Reporting
- Corrective Action/Follow-up
- Case Study
- ISO 9000 Standards

ISO 10011 SERIES: GUIDELINES FOR AUDITING QUALITY SYSTEMS
AMERICAN SOCIETY FOR QUALITY CONTROL EDUCATION & TRAINING INSTITUTE
Phone: 800-952-6587
Cost: 25.00 Auditing (T1111); 25.00 Qualification criteria (T1112); 19.00 Management of audit (T1113).
The ISO 9000 (ANSI/ASQC Q90) series emphasizes the importance of the quality audit as a key management tool for achieving the objectives set out in organizational policy.

ISO 9000
FACTORY MUTUAL ENGINEERING CORPORATION
Phone: 617-255-4606
Cost: 1.50
Length: 4 pages

Factory Mutual Research Corporation's (FMRC) Approvals Division can now provide ISO 9000 certification services for its customers. This booklet explains how the International Organization for Standardization developed this system of quality standards, which the European Economic Community has adopted as a way of guaranteeing quality among member nations. It also discusses the benefits of ISO 9000 certification and FMRC's role in the certification process.

ISO 9000 & STRATEGIES TO COMPETE IN THE SINGLE EUROPEAN MARKET
GOAL/QPC
Phone: 508-685-3900
Cost: 125.00
Length: 675 pages
This work consists of three parts in two volumes. Part one, Competing in the Single European Market of the '90s, provides the strategic framework for ISO certification, and highlights the changes taking place in Europe today. Part two focuses on the process of ISO 9000/Q90 certification, analyzing step by step implementation to achieve certification. Part three includes the ISO 9000 Series standards, the European Total Quality model, and other relevant documents. This book is a basic resource for any company wanting to achieve ISO 9000 registration.

ISO 9000 BOOK: A GLOBAL COMPETITOR'S GUIDE TO COMPLIANCE & CERTIFICATION
GEORGE WASHINGTON UNIVERSITY (CEEP)
CONTINUING ENGINEERING EDUCATION PROGRAM
Phone: 800-424-9773
Cost: 26.95
A company that competes for lucrative, high-level European business doesn't stand a chance if it hasn't passed the ISO 9000 quality audit, which most Europeans use to judge suppliers and partners. This book provides a clear explanation of what is required for organizations that want to measure up to the ISO certification. It converts what is often perceived as a Herculean task into a foundation for running a good business. The book explains what ISO 9000 is, how to meet the standards for certification, and how to handle the final audit.

ISO 9000 EQUIVALENT: ANSI/ASQC Q90-1987 SERIES QUALITY MANAGEMENT & QUALITY ASSURANCE STANDARDS

AMERICAN SOCIETY FOR QUALITY CONTROL
EDUCATION & TRAINING INSTITUTE
Phone: 800-952-6587
Cost: 52.95 Non-member; 44.95 Member
This new set of American national standards on quality management and quality assurance is identical to the International Organization for Standardization (ISO) 9000-9004 standards, which are recognized international. (Definitions of the key terms and concepts basic to the Q90 Series are included in ANSI/ASQC A3-1987.)

ANSI/ASQC Q90.1987
- Quality Management and Quality Assurance Standards
- Guidelines for Selection and Use

ANSI/ASQC Q91-1987
- Quality Systems - Model for Quality Assurance
- In Design/Development, Production, Installation, and Servicing

ANSI/ASQC Q92.1987
- Quality Systems - Model for Quality Assurance in Production and Installation

ANSI/ASQC Q93-1987
- Quality Systems - Model for Quality Assurance in Final Inspection and Test

ANSI/ASQC Q94-1987
- Quality Management and Quality System Elements - Guidelines

ISO 9000 FACILITATOR: HOW TO WRITE YOUR ISO 9000 QUALITY MANUAL

PERRY JOHNSON, INC.
Phone: 313-356-4410
Cost: 695.00
The ISO 9000 quality system standard includes strict documentation requirements. The chief document is the Quality Manual - which, in the world of ISO, is quite different from what most quality managers are accustomed to. This kit equips ISO 9000 facilitation teams with everything they need to prepare quality manuals which address the issues, objectives and specifics of the ISO 9000 quality system standard. The kit includes 6 copies

of PJI's How to Write your ISO 9000 Quality Manual workbook, which includes self-graded quizzes, sample quality manual text, and an ISO 9000 self-assessment grid. The kit also includes a license which permits purchasers to adapt the wording in the workbook to their own quality manuals, and an official copy of the ISO 9000 standards.

Course content:

- An Overview of ISO 9000
- The Quality Manual
- Management Responsibility
- Quality System
- Contract Review
- Design Control
- Document Control
- Purchasing
- Purchaser Supplied Product
- Product Identification and Traceability
- Process Control
- Inspection and Testing
- Inspection, Measuring and Test Equipment
- Inspection and Test Status
- Control of Nonconforming Product
- Corrective Action
- Handling, Storage, Packaging and Delivery
- Quality Records
- Internal Quality Audits
- Training
- Servicing
- Statistical Techniques
- Your ISO 9000 Self Assessment

ISO 9000 HANDBOOK

CENTER FOR ENERGY & ENVIRONMENTAL MANAGEMENT (CEEM)
Phone: 703-250-5900
Cost: 85.00
CEEM Information Services - publishers of Quality System Update - has teamed up with Robert Peach, a member of the international committee that wrote the ISO 9000 standards, and a host of other insiders and experts to offer the only ISO 9000 resource your company will need - The ISO 9000 Handbook.

Topics will include:

- Background & development of ISO 9000
- The importance of ISO 9000 to the EC and world communities
- Details of the registration process

- Choosing the appropriate standard for your company
- Effectively implementing the standards
- Profiles of all registrars active in the U.S.
- The relationship between ISO 9000 and other quality standards and awards
- ISO 9000's vital links to safety and product liability issues
- ISO 9000 consultants

ISO 9000, 2ND EDITION

SOCIETY OF MANUFACTURING ENGINEERS
Phone: 313-271-1500
Cost: 59.95 Non-member; 54.95 Member
Length: 200 pages
Topics include:

- The Background to the Standard
- Definition of ISO 9000
- The Standards in Detail
- The Manufacturing Elements Involved
- The Initial Steps
- Policy and Commitment
- Procurement
- Design and Change Control
- Production
- Inspection and Test
- Quality Audit
- Certification and Registration
- Digital Equipment International Case Study

ISO 9000-3: SOFTWARE QUALITY ASSURANCE

AMERICAN SOCIETY FOR QUALITY CONTROL
EDUCATION & TRAINING INSTITUTE
Phone: 800-952-6587
Cost: 35.00
This standard presents the guidelines for the application of ISO 9001 (ANSI/ASQC Q91) to the development, supply, and maintenance of software.

ISO 9000: A COMPREHENSIVE GUIDE TO REGISTRATION, AUDIT GUIDELINES & SUCCESSFUL IMPLEMENTATION

OLIVER WIGHT PUBLICATIONS
Phone: 800-343-0625
Author: Greg Hutchins
Cost: 37.50
Length: 288 pages
A comprehensive, yet user-friendly guide to ISO 9000. The author explains ISO 9000, the certification process, compliance standards, and

registration. Readers see the challenges, pitfalls, opportunities and benefits of ISO 9000 registration. And most importantly, the reader is able to evaluate if ISO registration is required for their company.

Course covers how to:

- Reach a higher level of customer acceptance of supplier partnerships based on ISO standards
- Document procedures
- Increase levels of training for all employees
- Place a greater emphasis on customer needs
- Enhance the ability to compete in global markets

Topics include:

- Global Standardization
- ISO Series of Quality Systems Standards
- EC Standards Development
- US Conformity Assessment
- ISO Quality Auditing
- Integrating ISO 9000 with existing quality systems
- The ISO Registration Process

Also included is firsthand advice from ISO registered companies, a sample Quality Manual, and a complete glossary of terms.

ISO 9000: A GLOBAL COMPETITOR'S GUIDE TO COMPLIANCE & CERTIFICATION

ASSOCIATION FOR QUALITY & PARTICIPATION
Phone: 513-381-1959
Cost: 26.95 Non-member; 24.26 Member
The authors demystify the process of complying with this quality standard by laying out the basics of what ISO 9000 is, what it means to your organization, how it fits into your overall quality efforts, and why you may be required to comply. Practical, firsthand advice based upon their experiences at one of the first U.S. companies to become fully certified.

ISO 9000: HANDBOOK OF QUALITY STANDARDS & COMPLIANCE

AMERICAN SOCIETY FOR QUALITY CONTROL
EDUCATION & TRAINING INSTITUTE
Phone: 800-952-6587
Cost: 69.95 Non-member; 59.95 Member
Length: 287 pages
ISO 9000: Handbook of Quality Standards and Compliance answers the burning questions your company is already asking - or should be asking about the ISO 9000 series of quality management and assurance standards. How was ISO 9000 developed? What does it entail? Is this something our customers might care about? How can we comply with the standards at our company? These questions and more are answered in this comprehensive volume.

Topics include:

- The Development of ISO 9000 and Its Proliferation in the Global Marketplace
- Third Party Registration
- ISO 9000 and Total Quality Management
- U.S. Companies' Advice for ISO 9000 Success

Included is the complete ANSI/ASQC Q90 Series of quality management and assurance standards. Also included are glossaries of acronyms and important terms, and directories of quality system registrars.

ISO 9000: PREPARING FOR REGISTRATION

AMERICAN SOCIETY FOR QUALITY CONTROL
EDUCATION & TRAINING INSTITUTE
Phone: 800-952-6587
Publisher: Marcel Dekker Inc.
Cost: 45.00 Non-member; 40.50 Member
Length: 254 pages
This volume offers indispensable information for all who must organize, document or implement a quality assurance system based on the ISO 9000 standards.

Contents include:

- Supplies thorough, up-to-date reviews of the five ISO standards including a paragraph by paragraph explication of the ISO 9001 standard.
- Focuses on essentials for efficient use of the standards.

- Helps make documentation easier by furnishing a model for quality assurance.
- Presents a timetable of cost estimates necessary for management.
- Describes how to approach registration and what to consider when choosing a registrar.
- Delineates guidelines for conducting internal audits.
- Answers the most asked questions.
- Gives insight into recent ISO developments.

Filled with helpful examples and incorporating an ISO questionnaire, ISO 9000 is a highly practical, important resource for all quality managers and directors; industrial, manufacturing process, and design engineers; chief executive officers; company presidents; auditors; registrars; and upper-level under-graduate and graduate students in these disciplines.

ISO 9004-2: GUIDELINES FOR SERVICE

AMERICAN SOCIETY FOR QUALITY CONTROL
EDUCATION & TRAINING INSTITUTE
Phone: 800-952-6587
Cost: 37.00
This part of ISO 9004 (ANSI/ASQC Q94) encourages organizations and companies to manage the quality aspects of their service activities in a more effective manner.

OVERVIEW OF THE ISO 9000 STANDARDS & ISO 9000 FACILITY REGISTRATION

NATIONAL ELECTRICAL MANUFACTURERS ASSOCIATION NEMA
Phone: 202-457-8400
Cost: 40.00 Non-member; 25.00 Member
This booklet presents a basic explanation of the ISO 9000 series of quality system and quality management standards, and briefly describes additional 9000 series standards currently under development. It also discusses the current understanding of the use of ISO 9000 facility requirements for products regulated under the EC 1992 initiative.

PROCUREMENT QUALITY CONTROL, FOURTH EDITION

AMERICAN SOCIETY FOR QUALITY CONTROL
EDUCATION & TRAINING INSTITUTE
Phone: 800-952-6587
Cost: 70.50 Non-member; 62.96 Member
Length: 323 pages
Completely rewritten and updated to make it even more useful for quality and purchasing professionals, the fourth edition of Procurement Quality Control provides all the latest procurement information. A combination of philosophy and methodology written in everyday language helps the reader develop a customized purchasing program with all the elements of a good quality system.

Book Includes:

- ANSI/ASQC Standards Q90-1987, Q91-1987, Q92-1987, Q93-1987, Q94-1987, and ANSI/ASQC Standard C 1-1985
- Previously separate booklets -- How to Conduct a Supplier Survey, How to Evaluate a Supplier's Product and How to Establish Effective Quality Control for the Small Supplier
- Complete index for convenient cross-referencing
- Chapter summaries
- Terminology update

Q-TEACH TRAINING PACKAGE

G.R. TECHNOLOGIES (USA) INC.
Phone: 407-995-0611
Cost: 799.00
Topics include:
- Q-Teach satisfies this requirement conveniently and at low cost to you
- It is necessary to prepare your employees for the Internal and the Certification Quality Audits
- Q-Teach satisfies this requirement by covering all the necessary elements these audits examine, so your staff is well prepared
- Executives to obtain a clear understanding of ISO 9000 requirements
- Technical staff to be able to contribute to development of your company's ISO 9000 program
- Production staff to comply with ISO 9000 requirements in order to satisfy the audit

QUALITY MANAGEMENT BENCHMARK ASSESSMENT

AMERICAN SOCIETY FOR QUALITY CONTROL
EDUCATION & TRAINING INSTITUTE
Phone: 800-952-6587
Cost: 16.95 Non-member; 15.25 Member
Length: 136 pages
Designed as an assessment device, this text consists of a series of checklists that pinpoint specific quality management criteria, including the current standards of the International Organization for Standardization (ISO 9004) and the 1991 Malcolm Baldrige National Quality Award criteria. Through active use of the checklists, readers can compare a company's performance with recognized quality standards.

Russell's work simplifies the planning and conducting of the quality improvement process, highlights specific quality elements for improvement and productivity, helps to direct corrective action, helps to monitor progress, and assures consistency between assessments by providing a permanent record for evaluation. It will also help prepare an organization for quality assurance certification.

In addition to the meticulously cross-referenced tables of criteria, the author provides hints, examples, and questions to ask at every step to ensure improvement in all areas.

Topics include:

- The QMBA and your quality process
- Quality management planning
- Quality manual and practices
- Specification basis procedures
- Sampling practices
- Laboratory standards and practices
- Corrective action
- Process control and SQC

VIDEO
SECTION

BUILDING QUALITY EXCELLENCE WITH ISO 9000

VIDEOLEARNING RESOURCE GROUP
Phone: 313-271-1500
Cost: 745.00 Non-member; 695.00 Member
Length: 90 minutes
Notes: The ISO 9000 Book is also available for 59.95
What does ISO 9000 certification mean to your company?

In Building Quality Excellence with ISO 9000 videotapes, you'll learn from people already involved in all phases of the certification process. You'll learn from people who have helped create ISO 9000. You'll learn from people who enforce ISO 9000. You'll learn from quality managers who have implemented ISO 9000, and gotten their companies successfully certified. You'll learn that it's not as difficult a process as you may have thought. And that ISO 9000 certification offers many residual internal benefits -- cost savings and more employee involvement, for example -- which far outweigh the obvious external benefits such as entry to new export markets, or proving a quality edge over your competitors.

Building Quality Excellence with ISO 9000 starts your company toward getting everyone involved -- from the initial buy-in of corporate management, to the commitment and participation of everyone in your organization. The videotapes show you that much introspection, internal analysis, and documentation are needed, but also that much of what your company's already doing may not need changing to be certified. The videotapes also show how ISO 9000 certification will yield improvements that will ultimately strengthen the quality of your products, and the competitiveness of your company worldwide.

Tape one: The What and Why of ISO 9000
- Dr. Armand Feigenbaum (the author of TQC) explains why quality expectations are an upwardly-moving target for American companies
- Quality audits: The supplier's point of view
- Quality audits: Automotive suppliers discuss their experience with second party audits
- Why second party audits of automotive suppliers are moving toward third party ISO 9000 audits

- How ISO 9000 quality criteria often complement Malcolm Baldrige National Quality Award criteria, and which effort should come first
- Explaining the current popularity of ISO 9000 worldwide
- ISO 9000's philosophy of controlled evolution and continuous improvement in the standard itself
- Why ISO 9000 won't become obsolete
- Why over 60 countries have adopted ISO 9000 as their national quality standard
- The basic structure of ISO 9000 in Europe and the U.S.
- Recent activities of ISO registration and accreditation bodies
- Perspectives on the perceived value of ISO certifications worldwide
- A review of the 20 basic elements of ISO's quality system
- Why it may be difficult to apply ISO's generic quality criteria to either your specific application or your industry, and the planned revisions to this problem
- Guidelines for interpreting ISO's functional components
- The intent of each of ISO's five major sections: 9000, 9001, 9002, 9003, 9004
- A look at the number of ISO certifications worldwide
- A summary of recent proposed modifications to ISO 9000

Tape Two: How to implement ISO 9000
- Criteria for helping you decide whether to pursue ISO 9001 or ISO 9002 certification
- Perspectives from quality managers experienced with ISO 9001 and ISO 9002 certification
- Who should choose the registrar: You or your customer?
- The qualifications you should require in a registrar
- What you need to know about registrar qualifications, accreditations, and fees
- Why some registrars use subcontracted auditors
- The real meaning of "memorandums of understanding"
- How the registrar's company maintains subjectivity, consistency, and credibility
- Perspectives from quality managers experienced with the ISO certification auditing process
- How to recognize whether you need to hire a consultant, or if your company has existing in-

house expertise and/or quality documentation structures

- Perspectives on training, upgrading your company's quality manual, and meeting documentation requirements
- Perspectives on the pre-assessment, whether you need an internal or external quality audit before the actual ISO 9000 audit
- What auditors look for during the audit process
- Insight on the auditor's decision-making process toward awarding ISO certification
- Perspectives from companies with successful audits: What they went through, where they were wrong, right, or overprepared
- How ISO 9000 fits into your company's long-term TQM goals
- Why companies who achieved ISO 9000 certification feel it was well worth the effort and expense
- ISO 9000's impact on improving the perception of US quality and competitiveness in the world marketplace

FUNDAMENTALS OF ISO 9000
STAT-A-MATRIX
Phone: 908-548-0600
Cost: 995.00
For the past few years our training and consulting clients have been asking us for a basic one or two hour overview that can be presented to any of their employees involved in ISO 9000 implementation and auditing. We have always insisted that employee awareness training is best given by the client's own supervisors, managers, or training personnel. Now, in response to your many requests, we have developed a package to help you in that task.

Course includes:

- One set of approximately 50 four-color overhead transparencies (or, if you prefer, 35 mm slides)
- An instructor's guide, which contains copies of the transparencies, the key points for each, background explanatory matter, tips for tailoring, and a copy of the key standards
- (Optional) Participant's workbook for each student, including copies of the transparencies and spaces for notes (This option is recommended for key or lead people.)

For: Members of management, supervision, or human resources with good presentation skills.

What we're offering is a concise package, developed by the senior staff of North America's foremost ISO 9000 training/consulting/educational company. The package is designed to be presented as a 1-1/2 to 2 hour overview, and it can be tailored to any level of employee and any type of industry.

HOW TO PREPARE FOR THE NEW INTERNATIONAL QUALITY STANDARDS: ISO 9000 SERIES
ROCHESTER INSTITUTE OF TECHNOLOGY CENTER FOR QUALITY & APPLIED STATISTICS
Phone: 716-475-6990
Length: 8.5 hours
Cost: 1905.00
This comprehensive videotape program available on ISO 9000 is a cost way to prepare for on which is being to market in the EEC.

ISO 9000
VIDEOLEARNING RESOURCE GROUP
Phone: 215-896-6600
Cost: 295.00
Length: 85 minutes
This video describes a proven approach to the Total Quality Management Process. It outlines the standards and some of the procedures of Quality Assurance required by the international marketplace.

ISO 9000
CENTER FOR ENERGY & ENVIRONMENTAL MANAGEMENT (CEEM)
Phone: 703-250-5900
Cost: $295.00
What will you learn from this important new training package?

- The structure of the International Management System Standard and a review of each section
- The nature, purpose and principles of the International Quality Assurance Management System Standard...with a brief history
- The need for and purpose of a documented Quality Assurance Management System and the three levels commonly involved
- How the "Right First Time" principle and the "Quality Equals Fitness for Purpose" definition apply in a certifiable Quality System
- The purpose and principles of the Standard, and how to apply them in a wide range of companies

- The steps involved in assessment and certification
- The benefits to be gained from applying the principles and requirements of the Standard by management, employees and the organization as a whole
- The role of consultants and advisers in developing a Quality System

ISO 9000 TRAINING PROGRAM

VIDEOLEARNING RESOURCE GROUP
Phone: 215-896-6600
Cost: 245.00
This video provides the tools and knowledge to evaluate the application of ISO 9000 and to start the qualification process.

ISO 9000 - SERIES

EXCELLENCE IN TRAINING CORPORATION
Phone: 800-747-6569
Cost: 595.00
Length: 2-part video / 45 minutes each
This two-part video seminar provides information to help your company understand which ISO 9000 standards apply to companies of all sizes, how to use the ISO standards to enhance your company's competitive market position, and more.

ISO 9000 INTERNATIONAL QUALITY SEMINAR

OLIVER WIGHT PUBLICATIONS
Phone: 800-343-0625
Cost: 595.00
Length: 2 videotapes 45 minutes each
This video seminar covers the essentials of ISO 9000. Featuring the authoritative quality management consultant Ian Durand, the ISO Video Seminar will help your company.

Course covers how to:
- Understand the basics of ISO 9000
- Identify which standards apply to your company
- Prepare for quality system registration
- Interpret and apply ISO requirements
- Document a quality system
- Perform a self assessment

ISO 9000 INTERNATIONAL QUALITY STANDARDS

AMERICAN SOCIETY FOR QUALITY CONTROL
EDUCATION & TRAINING INSTITUTE
Phone: 800-952-6587
Cost: 595.00
With this tape series, an entire company can be educated in the essentials of the ISO International Quality Standards for less than the cost of sending one person to a seminar. This package provides practical information that will help a company:

- Use the ISO 9000 series to build an international recognized quality system
- Register a quality assurance system to enhance a competitive market position
- Understand the evolving ISO 9000 series

The series tells why the ISO 9000 standards are important and what they require. It also describes the quality system registration process and how to begin it as well as quality system documentation. Includes 2 tapes (45 minutes each), workbook and complete set of ISO 9000 International Quality Standards.

ISO 9000 OPERATIONS TRAINING PROGRAM

VIDEOLEARNING RESOURCE GROUP
Phone: 215-896-6600
Cost: 1350.00
Length: 45 minutes
This is a video-based program with interactive workbook designed to teach what ISO 9000 is and how its requirements help ensure quality in process information. It consists of six segments covering topics such as production, marketing, purchasing, documentation, statistical methods and audits.

ISO 9000 SERIES WORKSHOPS

NATIONAL ELECTRICAL MANUFACTURERS
ASSOCIATION NEMA
Phone: 202-457-8400
Cost: 100.00
This VHS video tape presents NEMAs November 1990 program on the ISO 9000 Series Quality Assurance Standards.

Course content:

- What is ISO 9000
- U.S. Government view of ISO 9000, in context of EC 1992
- Compliance to ISO 9000: European perspective and experiences
- Compliance to ISO 9000: U.S. private sector perspective
- NEMA member perspective

ISO 9000 TELECONFERENCE

STAT-A-MATRIX
Phone: 908-548-0600
Cost: 395.00
On March 13, 1992, STAT-A-MATRIX hosted the first nationwide teleconference on ISO 9000. This videotape contains highlights of the conference, including addresses by George Lofgren, President of the Registrar Accreditation Board; Ian Durand, internationally known expert on ISO 9000 and member of the technical committee updating the standards; and Robert Marash, IQA-registered Lead Assessor and recognized authority on developing, documenting, and auditing quality systems. The package includes a 90-minute video tape, a brief audio introduction, and an ISO 9000 reference pamphlet.

ISO 9000

PRODUCTIVITY PRESS, INC. DEPARTMENT 305
Phone: 800-394-6868
Cost: 595.00
Length: 2 videos
This video looks at ISO 9000 from a U.S. manager's perspective and emphasizes the importance of an internationally recognized quality system in a global environment, how to use the standards to enhance your company's competitive market position, and the critical role of senior management in registration.

ISO 9000: A MANAGEMENT BRIEFING

TALICO INC.
Phone: 904-241-1721
Cost: 69.96
Length: 20 minutes
This video is a simplified and pragmatic introduction to the critical international quality assurance standard which has become the basis for reliability and consistency in quality results. It is presented by Fortune 500 quality expert Gene Mondani.

Video Covers:

- ISO 9000 requirements
- How management can develop a quality philosophy by adapting quality management systems to ISO 9000
- The benefits of ISO 9000 certification
- Registration costs and procedures including registration pre-assessment and audits
- How management can apply ISO 9000 principles to improve their competitive position and increase profitability

Materials include: The video and audio cassette, ISO 9000: A Management Briefing.

ISO 9000: AN EXECUTIVE BRIEFING

OLIVER WIGHT COMPANIES
Phone: 800-258-3862
Cost: 195.00
Length: 25 minutes
This video is an overview of the most significant topics and issues of interest to executives and managers. In 25 minutes, Ian Durand reviews the significance of ISO 9000 for companies in the U.S. and discusses the benefits and challenges of ISO registration. Interviews with executives from ISO certified companies are included along with coverage of the registration process itself.

ISO 9000: INTERNATIONAL QUALITY SEMINAR

OLIVER WIGHT COMPANIES
Phone: 800-258-3862
Cost: 595.00
Length: 90 minutes
This is a highly informative video seminar covering the essentials of ISO 9000. Featuring the authoritative quality management consultant Ian Durand.

Video covers how to:

- Understand the basics of ISO 9000
- Identify which standards apply to their business
- Prepare for a quality system registration
- Interpret and apply ISO requirements
- Document a quality system
- Perform a self-assessment
- Align ISO 9000 with existing quality efforts
- Identify specific areas for ISO compliance
- Become acquainted with ISO 9001, the most extensive ISO standard

ISO 9000: THE FIRST STEP TO THE FUTURE

VIDEOLEARNING RESOURCE GROUP
Phone: 215-896-6600
Cost: 495.00
Length: 37 minutes

The ISO 9000 standards impact the way we do business, here in the U.S. as well as in the new Europe. Module 1 (6 minutes) of this program provides a lively overview of the subject, dispelling misconceptions, and addressing management's role. Module 2 (31 minutes) provides substantive information about the requirements, registration process and the costs and benefits of ISO 9000 qualification.

UNDERSTANDING & IMPLEMENTING ISO 9000

H. SILVER & ASSOCIATES
Phone: 310-785-0518
Cost: 595.00
Course content:

- Using Quality As a Global Competitive Weapon
- Structuring Your Company and Quality Systems to Achieve ISO 9000 Goals
- Building a Quality Manual to Fulfill the 20 ISO Sections
- The Case Study - Examples that Really Show You "How To"
- Scheduling Your ISO 9000 Implementation and Certification Plan
- Avoiding the Registration and Implementation Pitfalls

What is the ISO 9000 Series? Where does it apply? How do you certify your company? In this video, you will learn all you need to know to start the ISO 9000 process. How the complex ISO structure fits your product and business mix. How most of the industrialized nations have implemented the standards. How different types of companies must tailor their implementation activities.

Mr. Linnell will show you how ISO 9000 encompasses the setup and operation of your company's management and management systems - not simply your quality assurance and control systems. Mr. Linnell graphically describes how to establish the top-down organization structure you need to fulfill the requirements and implement the real systems and training necessary to achieve certification.

Depending on your company's products, ISO 9000 can address each and every aspect of your business. Its 20 sections apply to a broad range of company processes - from management to marketing, from contract review to purchasing, from process control to inspection, from training to application of statistical techniques. Mr. Linnell explains what sections apply to your company, and how to apply them. He explains the level of quality sophistication you must attain to cost-effectively achieve worldwide certification.

Mr. Linnell teaches by examples - examples that show you the what, where, when, why, and how of meeting ISO 9000 requirements. The video incorporates an integrated case study. You see specific pages from actual Quality Manuals. Learn how these sections addressed and met the requirements. Study the sections in great detail - document control, purchasing, process control, corrective action, and many others. See what other major companies around the world have done to be certified - and what your company must do.

The video goes on to address the key aspect of ISO 9000 - how you are assessed and subsequently registered through third party auditing agencies. Mr. Linnell explains how the certification system really "works", and what the auditors are looking for. He tells you how to find the right auditor for your company, and what to do before and after the audits begin. Most importantly, he shows you how long you can expect the certification process to take - a detailed implementation schedule with time-phasing for all key tasks.

Is ISO 9000 easy to implement? Is certification easy to achieve? No. But, Mr. Linnell shows you where the failures have occurred - where the "traps" lie. You learn how errors in simple activities such as document control and purchasing can cause you to fail. You see examples of process failures, and how they were corrected. You learn what to do - and what not to do. And, how to avoid the "classic error" - the "all paper" system that will never be certified.

To assist you in understanding and implementing the ISO 9000 Series of world quality standards, a complete set of courseware is included with the video. The courseware includes all charts and case study examples used by Mr. Linnell - plus further examples and reference materials to aid you in developing and structuring your Quality Manual and other ISO 9000 documentation.

WHAT IS ISO 9000, & WHY DO I CARE?
VIDEOLEARNING RESOURCE GROUP
Phone: 215-896-6600
Cost: 450.00
Length: 33 minutes
From this video learn how two companies became ISO certified. Explains what their ISO standards are, what the ISO certification process is, where to start, and why implementing the ISO standards can lead your firm to greater profitability and improved control.

SOFTWARE
SECTION

EMBEDDING QUALITY: ISO 9000 COMPUTER-BASED TRAINING

DIGITAL EQUIPMENT COMPUTER USERS SOCIETY
DECUS
Phone: 508-841-3341
Cost: CBT 495.00
Learn the ISO 9000 quality process on your own personal computer. This course is designed to provide organizational and professional skills needed to implement ISO 9000-based quality systems in your workplace.

Computer-Based Training Benefits

- Design supported by Digital members - Learn from expert experience
- Complete ISO 9000 regulations available on-line - Accessible when you need them
- Comprehensive Audit Case Study Example - Helps you understand and apply ISO 9000 concepts
- MS/Windows Self-Paced Instruction - Available at home, at work or on the go

For: This course is for cross-functional teams and individuals including managers, designers, developers, and others and in organizations such as engineering, manufacturing, sales and service.

ISO 9000 CHECKLISTS

G.R. TECHNOLOGIES LTD.
Phone: 416-886-1307
Cost: 125.00
This package provides the internal auditor with a systematic and comprehensive method of conducting an audit. Use the provided hard copy Workbook as is, or modify it to reflect your company's own requirements. Create your own workbook add and modify the questions on diskette to reflect your company's specific operations. Print additional Workbooks in one consistent format. Use the Workbook as a permanent record of the findings during the internal audit. From this record, develop requests for corrective action. The Workbook will serve as a permanent reference document reflecting the company's quality program.

Software contents:

- A Workbook (paper copy)
- A diskette containing 3 Workbooks in WordPerfect format for ISO 9001, 9002 and 9003 respectively

- Questions for each System function in the ISO 9001, ISO 9002, ISO 9003 standards
- Audit trail
- Document reference
- Audit comment
- Rating
- Supplementary notes

Key objectives:

- Provide a guide for the internal auditor
- Provide a true assessment of your quality program
- Permit comparison with other evaluations
- Provide a clear record of evaluation, with assurance that all the necessary requirements have been considered.

P-WRITE-ISO 9000 (FOR WORDPERFECT 5.1 FOR DOS)

G.R. TECHNOLOGIES (USA) INC.
Phone: 407-995-0611
Cost: 399.00
Contents include:

- 8 Core Operating Procedure Manuals that include tables of contents and more than 25 sample procedures ready for you to customize and use
- 8 Optional Operating Procedure Manuals that include tables of contents and basic formatting for structure and guidance

P-Write contains a ready-to-use, 20-page Supplier Quality Survey as part of the Procurement Operating Manual. The rating and survey system will fit most industries with minor or no modifications. Each of the Core Manuals contains a Manual control system and a number of completed procedures that demonstrate typical subjects and degrees of detail. Some useful forms are also included.

Q-CHECKLIST-ISO 9000 (FOR WORDPERFECT 5.1 FOR DOS)

G.R. TECHNOLOGIES (USA) INC.
Phone: 407-995-0611
Cost: 130.00
Q-CheckList provides the internal Quality Auditor with a systematic and comprehensive method of conducting an audit.

Convenient package contains a workbook (printed copy) and a diskette containing workbooks in

WordPerfect 5.1 for DOS format - one each for ISO 9001, 9002 and 9003

You can use the included copy of the Workbook as is, or create your own customized version.

Add to and modify the questions on the diskette to reflect your company's specific operations. Print additional Workbooks in one consistent format.

Topics include:

- Records the findings during the internal audit
- From this record, you can develop requests for corrective action
- Provide a guide for the internal auditor
- Provide a true assessment of your quality program
- Provide a clear record of evaluation, with assurance that all the necessary requirements have been considered
- Questions for each system function in the ISO 9001, 9002, and 9003 standards
- Audit trail
- Document reference
- Audit comment
- Rating

Q-WRITE-ISO 9000 (FOR WORDPERFECT 5.1)

G.R. TECHNOLOGIES (USA) INC.
Phone: 407-995-0611
Cost: 279.00
This software provides the internal auditor with a systematic and comprehensive method of conducting an audit. Use the provided hard copy Workbook as is, or modify it to reflect your company's own requirements.

TQS - 9000: A SOFTWARE GUIDE FOR ISO 9000

OLIVER WIGHT COMPANIES
Phone: 800-258-3862
Cost: 995.00
Software covers:

- TQS-9000 is a complete system for easy implementation of a quality system based on ISO 9001 and 9002 standards
- A powerful, yet easy to use Windows-based program
- Features 7 modules to help you reach your goal of developing an ISO-based quality system

If your company is considering, or is already pursuing ISO 9000 registration, this software package will repay your initial investment many times over. Its 7 Modules are designed to help you move through the ISO 9001 and 9002 standards, (the standards that most companies must comply with for registration), and create an effective, accurate quality system.

Modules include:

- Guidelines for Quality Work
- Tools for Analysis
- Interpretation of the ISO standard
- Sample Quality Manual
- Comprehensive Documentation System
- Internal Audit Checklist ■ Quality Cost Tracking System

TITLE
INDEX

SUBJECT
INDEX

AUDIT PREPARATION

AUDITOR TRAINING

AUTOMOTIVE INDUSTRY

BAR CODING

IMPLEMENTING ISO 9000

CONSULTANT INDEX

CONSULTANT INDEX GEOGRAPHICAL SECTION

NEW HAMPSHIRE

NEW JERSEY

NEW YORK

NORTH CAROLINA

REGISTRAR INDEX SECTION

SOURCE
INDEX

ABS QUALITY EVALUATIONS, INC.
16855 North Chase Drive
Houston, TX 77060-6008
Phone: 713-873-9400
Fax: 713-874-9564

ADVANCED QUALITY ENGINEERING
5460 Norwood Lane North
Plymouth, MN 55442
Phone: 612-553-9064

AFFILIATED CONSULTING SERVICES
6515 S. Adams Court
Suite 1
Littleton, CO 80120
Phone: 303-771-0369

AGA QUALITY, A SERVICE OF INTERNATIONAL APPROVALS SERVICES
A Division of American Gas Association
Laboratories
8501 East Pleasant Valley Road
Cleveland, OH 44131
Phone: 216-524-4990
Fax: 216-642-3463

AMER SUPPLIER INST (ASI)
Publications Sales
1504 Commerce Drive South
Dearborn, MI 48120
Phone: 313-271-4200
Phone: 800-462-4500

AMERICAN ASSOCIATION FOR LABORATORY ACCREDITATION
656 Quince Orchard Road, #304
Gaithersburg, MD 20878-1409
Phone: 301-670-1377
Fax: 301-869-1495

AMERICAN EUROPEAN SERVICES, INC.
1054 31st Street, NW
Suite 120
Washington, DC 20007
Phone: 202-337-3214
Fax: 202-337-3709

AMERICAN GAS ASSOCIATION
1452 Grande Vista Avenue
Los Angeles, CA 90023
Phone: 213-261-8161

AMERICAN INSTITUTE FOR QUALITY & RELIABILITY (AIQR)
P.O. Box 41163
San Jose, CA 95160
Phone: 408-275-9300
Phone: 800-274-4220
Fax: 408-275-9399

AMERICAN MANAGEMENT ASSOCIATION
135 West 50th St
New York, NY 10020
Phone: 518-891-1500
Fax: 518-891-3653

AMERICAN MANAGEMENT ASSOCIATION FYI VIDEO
Customer Service Ctr
Nine Galen Street
Watertown, MA 02272-9119
Phone: 800-225-3215
Phone: 617-926-4600

AMERICAN SOCIETY FOR QUALITY CONTROL
Education & Training Institute
611 East Wisconsin Avenue
Box 3005
Milwaukee, WI 53201-3005
Phone: 800-952-6587
Phone: 414-272-8575
Fax: 414-272-1734

AMREP INTERNATIONAL
1813 El Camino Real
Suite 10
Burlingame, CA 94010
Phone: 415-692-8537
Fax: 415-692-8538

ASSOCIATION FOR QUALITY & PARTICIPATION
801-B West 8th Street
Cincinnati, OH 45203-1607
Phone: 513-381-1959
Fax: 513-381-0070

AT&T QUALITY REGISTRAR
2600 San Tomas Expressway
Santa Clara, CA 95051-1366
Phone: 408-562-1370
Fax: 408-562-1366

AV QUALITE
Group AIB-Vincotte
2900 Wilcrest
Suite 300
Houston, TX 77042
Phone: 713-465-2850
Fax: 713-465-1182

BARBER CONSULTING RESOURCE, INC.
4900 N. Wheeling Avenue
Muncie, IN 47304
Phone: 317-286-4349
Fax: 317-284-3076

BEACON HILL TECHNOLOGIES, INC.
14 Beacon Street
Boston, MA 02108
Phone: 617-227-7887
Fax: 617-227-6845

BELLCORE QUALITY REGISTRATION
6 Corporate Place
Piscataway, NJ 08854
Phone: 908-699-3739
Fax: 908-336-2220

BERTHELOT'S CONSULTING E.T.C.
600 Bayou Boulevard
Pensacola, FL 32503
Phone: 904-438-2934

BONDINSON & ASSOCIATES, INC.
16479 Dallas Parkway
Suite 390
Dallas, TX 75248
Phone: 214-931-5402
Phone:
Fax: 214-931-0796

BOSTON UNIVERSITY CORPORATE EDUCATION CENTER
72 Tyng Road
Tyngsboro, MA 01879
Phone: 508-649-9731
Phone: 800-733-3593
Fax: 508-649-6926

BREWER-KLECKNER EDUCATION SERVICES
2505 Locksley Drive
Grand Prairie, TX 75050
Phone: 214-660-4575
Fax: 214-641-1327

BRITISH STANDARDS INSTITUTION, INC.
8000 Towers Cresent Drive
Suite 1350
Vienna, VA 22182
Phone: 703-760-7828
Fax: 703-760-7899

BRYANT COLLEGE CENTER FOR MANAGEMENT DEVELOPMENT
1150 Douglas Pike
Providence, RI 02917-1283
Phone: 401-232-6200

BSI QUALITY ASSURANCE
10521 Baddock Road
Fairfax, VA 22032
Phone: 703-250-5900
Fax: 703-250-5313

BUREAU OF BUSINESS PRACTICE
24 Rope Ferry Road
Waterford, CT 06386
Phone: 203-442-4365
Phone: 800-243-0876

BUREAU VERITAS QUALITY INTERNATIONAL (NA), INC.
North American Offices
509 North Main Street
Jamestown, NY 14701
Phone: 716-484-9002
Fax: 716-484-9003

BURNS QUALITY SYSTEMS
Box 963
Marshalltown, IA 50158
Phone: 515-753-7434

CALIFORNIA STATE UNIVERSITY LOS ANGELES
Office of Continuing Education
5151 State University Drive
Los Angeles, CA 90032-8619
Phone: 213-343-4900
Fax: 213-343-4954

CANADIAN GENERAL STANDARDS BOARD
222 Queen Street
Suite 1402
Ottawa, Ontario K1A 1G6
Canada
Phone: 613-941-8657
Fax: 613-941-8706

CANATECH CONSULTANT GROUP, INC.
2434 Bolen Bay
Regina, Saskatchewan S4V 0V6
Canada
Phone: 306-789-5091
Fax: 306-789-5091

CARMAN GROUP, INC.
1600 Promenade Tower, Suite 950
P.O. Box 835088
Richardson, TX 75080
Phone: 214-669-9464
Phone: 800-942-6880
Fax: 214-669-9478

CENTER FOR CORPORATE LEARNING
762 Miguel Avenue
Sunnyvale, CA 94086-3412
Phone: 408-773-0442

CENTER FOR ENERGY & ENVIRONMENTAL MANAGEMENT (CEEM)
Box 200
Fairfax Station, VA 22039-0200
Phone: 703-250-5900
Phone: 800-745-5565
Fax: 703-250-5313

CENTER FOR PROFESSIONAL ADVANCEMENT
144 Tices Lane
P.O. Box H
East Brunswick, NJ 08816-0964
Phone: 908-613-4500
Phone: 908-613-4535
Fax: 908-238-9113

CGA APPROVALS - CANADIAN OPERATION OF INTERNATIONAL
Approvals Services (IAS)
55 Scarsdale Road
Don Mills, Ontario M3B 2R3
Canada
Phone: 416-447-6468
Fax: 416-447-7067

CHARLES R. "CHUCK" CARTER & ASSOCIATES
6400 Barrie Road No. 1101
Edina, MN 55435-2317
Phone: 612-927-6003

CLINICAL RESEARCH SYSTEMS, INC.
4503 Moorland Avenue
Minneapolis, MN 55424
Phone: 612-835-4018
Fax: 612-832-5806

CMI CONCEPTS CO.
6920 Tanglewood Street
Lakewood, CA 90713-2836
Phone: 310-420-7468

CO-ORDINATE MEASUREMENT
7250 Commerce Drive, Unit H
Mentor, OH 44060
Phone: 216-975-9970

COMMERCIAL SCALE CO., INC.
95 Bowles Road
P.O. Box 265
Agawam, MA 01001
Phone: 413-786-8810
Fax: 413-786-8351

COMPLIANCE ENGINEERING
629 Massachusetts Avenue
Boxborough, MA 01719
Phone: 508-264-4208
Fax: 508-635-9407

CONSULTANT SERVICES INSTITUTE
651 W. Mt. Pleasant Avenue
Livingston, NJ 07039
Phone: 201-992-3811

CONTEMPORARY CONSULTANTS CO.
15668 Irene Street
Southgate, Michigan 48195-2023
Phone: 313-281-9182
Fax: 313-281-4023

CONTINUOUS IMPROVEMENT TECHNOLOGY
113 McHenry Road
Suite 211
Buffalo Grove, IL 60089
Phone: 708-634-6207
Fax: 708-634-6207

CORPORATE RESOURCE GROUP OF CONNECTICUT
180 Belden Hill Road
Wilton, CT 06897
Phone: 203-761-9707

COST TECHNOLOGY ASSOCIATES
3443 Huntington Terrace
Crete, IL 60417
Phone: 708-758-7922

CREATIVE QUALITY SOLUTIONS
7437 Kenwood Avenue
Wauwatosa, WI 53213
Phone: 414-771-2499
Fax: 414-771-2499

DATANET TECHNOLOGIES, INC.
1270-F Rankin Street
P.O. Box 307
Troy, MI 48099-0307
Phone: 313-588-0150
Fax: 313-588-3735

DAVID HUTTON & ASSOCIATES
82 Strathcona Avenue
Ottawa, Ontario K1S 1X6
Canada
Phone: 613-567-1511
Fax: 613-567-2272

DAVID MAHLKE ASSOCIATES
5791 Michael Drive Northeast
Clear Rapids, IA 52402
Phone: 319-393-7754

DECISION GROUP
P.O. Box 15005
Charlotte, NC 28211
Phone: 704-552-4770
Fax: 704-365-5523

DESTRA CONSULTING GROUP, INC.
1655 Walnut Street
Suite 330
Boulder, CO 80302
Phone: 303-444-9619
Fax: 303-444-2570

DET NORSKE VERITAS INDUSTRY, INC.
16340 Park Ten Place
Suite 100
Houston, TX 77084
Phone: 713-579-9003
Fax: 713-579-1360

DIGITAL EQUIPMENT COMPUTER USERS SOCIETY
333 South Street
SHR1-4/D31
Shrewsbury, MA 01545-4195
Phone: 508-841-3341
Fax: 508-841-3373

DK PRESS
2610 West Baylor Circle #201
Anaheim, CA 92801
Phone: 714-995-4023
Fax: 714-474-7250

DONALD M. TURNBULL
3596 Jane Drive
Midland, MI 48642
Phone: 517-835-5076

DONALD W. MARQUARDT & ASSOCIATES
1415 Athens Road
Wilmington, DE 19803
Phone: 302-478-6695
Fax: 302-478-9329

DUPONT PROFESSIONAL DEVELOPMENT SEMINAR
Quality Management & Technology Center
Louviers
P.O. Box 6090
Newark, DE 19714-6090
Phone: 302-366-2100
Phone: 800-441-8040
Fax: 302-999-6677

EASTERN MICHIGAN UNIVERSITY
34 North Washington Street
Ypsilanti, MI 48197
Phone: 313-487-2259
Phone: 800-932-8689
Fax: 313-481-0509

EBB ASSOCIATES, INC.
Box 8249
Norfolk, VA 23503
Phone: 804-588-3939
Fax: 804-558-5824

ECCO GAGING SYSTEMS, INC.
1270-F Rankin Street
P.O. Box 307
Troy, MI 48099-0307
Phone: 313-588-8830
Fax: 313-588-3735

EDU-TECH INDUSTRIES
881 Dover Drive
Suite 14
Newport Beach, CA 92663
Phone: 714-540-7660
Fax: 714-540-8345

EDUCATIONAL DATA SYSTEMS, INC.
One Parklane Boulevard
Suite 701w
Dearborn, MI 48126
Phone: 313-271-2660
Fax: 313-271-2698

EISO PATRIOT GROUP
P.O. Box 12345
Burke, Virginia 22009
Phone: 800-397-9001
Phone: 703-250-6650
Fax: 703-250-4117

ENTELA, INC., QUALITY SYSTEM REGISTRATION DIVISION
3033 Madison Avenue, SW
Grand Rapids, MI 49548
Phone: 616-247-0515
Fax: 616-247-7527

ERIN & ASSOCIATES
723 Woodshire Way
Dayton, OH 45430
Phone: 513-429-3339

ERNST & YOUNG
55 Almaden Boulevard, 4th Floor
San Jose, CA 95115
Phone: 408-947-6574
Fax: 408-947-4971

ETI CORP.
5870 S 194th Street
Kent, WA 98032
Phone: 206-340-4343
Fax: 206-872-8269

EXCEL PARTNERSHIP, INC.
75 Glen Road
Sandy Hook, CT 06482
Phone: 203-426-3281
Phone: 800-374-3818
Fax: 203-426-7811

EXCELLENCE IN TRAINING CORPORATION
11358 Aurora Avenue
Des Moines, IA 50322-7907
Phone: 515-276-6569
Phone: 800-747-6569
Fax: 515-276-9476

F.X. MAHONEY & ASSOCIATES
2000 South Dairy Ashford Road
Suite 230
Houston, TX 77077
Phone: 713-496-0455
Fax: 713-496-6439

FACTORY MUTUAL ENGINEERING CORP.
P.O. Box 9102
1151 Boston-Providence Turnpike
Norwood, MA 02062-9957
Phone: 617-255-4606
Fax: 617-255-4184

FED-PRO, INC.
5615 Jensen Drive
Rockford, IL 61111
Phone: 815-282-4300
Fax: 815-282-4304

FEDERAL MARKETING SERVICES, INC.
4100 North Rockton Avenue
Rockford, IL 61103
Phone: 800-654-6161
Fax: 815-654-6198

G.R. TECHNOLOGIES (USA), INC.
P.O. Box 810638
Boca Raton, FL 33481-0638
Phone: 407-995-4881
Fax: 407-995-0613

G.R. TECHNOLOGIES LTD.
9011 Leslie Street
Suite 211
Richmond Hill, Ontario L4B 3B6
Canada
Phone: 416-886-1307
Fax: 416-886-6327

GEORGE R BREARLEY
1916 NW 42nd Place
Gainsville, FL 32605
Phone: 904-375-4830

GEORGE WASHINGTON UNIVERSITY
School of Business & Public Management
2020 K Street Northwest
Suite 230
Washington, DC 20052
Phone: 202-994-5219
Fax: 202-994-5225

GEORGE WASHINGTON UNIVERSITY (CEEP)
Continuing Engineering Education Program
801 22nd Street Northwest
Washington, DC 20052
Phone: 800-424-9773
Phone: 202-994-6106
Fax: 202-872-0645

GEORGIA INSTITUTE OF TECHNOLOGY
Atlanta, GA 30332-0800
Phone: 404-853-0968
Fax: 404-853-9172

GLOBAL ENGINEERING DOCUMENTS
2508 McGraw Avenue
Irvine, CA 92714
Phone: 800-854-7179
Fax: 714-261-7892

GOAL/QPC
13 Branch Street
Methuen, MA 01844
Phone: 508-685-3900
Fax: 508-685-6151

GRADY & ASSOCIATES
40C Lake Street
Wincester, MA 01890
Phone: 617-721-5770

GUNNESON GROUP INTERNATIONAL
112 Kings Highway
Landing, NJ 07850
Phone: 201-770-4700
Fax: 201-770-4786

H. SILVER & ASSOCIATES
1875 Century Park East
Suite 1030
Los Angeles, CA 90067
Phone: 310-785-0518
Phone: 310-284-8780
Fax: 310-284-8780

H.W. FAHRLANDER & ASSOCIATES
640 Downing Drive
Richardson, TX 75080-6117
Phone: 214-783-1216
Fax: 214-783-6043

HANDLEY-WALKER CO., INC.
17371 Irvine Boulevard
Suite 250
Tustin, CA 92680
Phone: 714-730-0122
Fax: 805-255-2178

HARRINGTON GROUP, INC.
3208-C East Colonial Drive
Suite 253
Orlando, FL 32803
Phone: 407-275-9841
Fax: 407-281-4941

HARRISON M. WADWORTH & ASSOCIATES
660 Valley Green Drive Northeast
Atlanta, GA 30342
Phone: 404-255-8662
Fax: 404-250-1493

HENNING QUALITY SERVICES
145 Highvue Drive
Venetia, PA 15367
Phone: 412-941-6512

HERBERT MONNICH & ASSOCIATES
8710 Summit Pines Drive
Humble, TX 77346
Phone: 713-852-2118

HERTZLER SYSTEMS, INC.
(formerly Paul Hertzler & Co., Inc.)
17482 Eisenhower Drive
P.O. Box 588
Goshen, IN 46526
Phone: 219-533-0571
Fax: 219-533-3885

HESTER ASSOCIATES, INC.
210 A Orleans Road
North Chatham, MA 02650
Phone: 508-945-4860
Fax: 508-945-4862

HOGAN QUALITY INSTITUTE
16479 Dallas Parkway
Suite 390
Dallas, TX 75248
Phone: 214-931-7597
Fax: 214-407-0796

IIT RESEARCH INSTITUTE
201 Mill Street
Rome, NY 13440
Phone: 315-339-7068
Fax: 315-339-7002

IMPAQ ORGANIZATIONAL IMPROVEMENT SYSTEMS
1744 West Katella
Suite 3
Orange, CA 92667
Phone: 714-744-8941
Fax: 714-744-1034

INDIANA UNIVERSITY AT SOUTH BEND
Division of Continuing Education
P.O. Box 7111
South Bend, IN 46634-7111
Phone: 219-237-4261
Fax: 219-237-4428

INFORMATION MAPPING, INC.
300 Third Avenue
Waltham, MA 02154
Phone: 617-890-7003
Phone: 800-627-4544
Fax: 617-890-1339

INFORMATION SYSTEMS INSTITUTE
P.O. Box 3627
Gaithersburg, MD 20885
Phone: 301-670-9020

INSTITUTE FOR INTERNATIONAL RESEARCH
437 Madison Avenue, 23rd Floor
New York, NY 10022-7001
Phone: 800-999-3123
Fax: 212-826-6411

INSTITUTE FOR INTERNATIONAL RESEARCH, INC. NEW YORK
708 Third Avenue 4th Floor
New York, NY 10017
Phone: 800-345-8016
Phone: 212-661-3500
Fax: 212-661-6677

INSTITUTE FOR PROFESSIONAL EDUCATION
2300 Clarendon Boullevard, Suite 403
P.O. Box 756
Arlington, VA 22201
Phone: 703-527-8700

INSTITUTE OF INDUSTRIAL ENGINEERS
25 Technology Park
P.O. Box 6150
Norcross, GA 30092-2988
Phone: 404-449-0460
Fax: 404-263-8532

INSTITUTE OF PACKAGING PROFESSIONALS
481 Carlisle Drive
Herndon, VA 22070
Phone: 703-318-8970
Fax: 703-318-0310

INSTRUMENT SOCIETY OF AMERICA
67 Alexander Drive
P.O. Box 12277
Research Triangle Pa, NC 27709
Phone: 919-549-8411

INTEGRATED TECHNOLOGIES, INC.
9855 Crosspoint Boulevard
Suite 126
Indianapolis, IN 46256
Phone: 317-577-8100

INTERNATIONAL QUALITY & PRODUCTIVITY CENTER
209 Cooper Avenue
Suite 7
Upper Montclair, NJ 07043-1850
Phone: 800-882-8684
Fax: 201-783-3851

INTERNATIONAL QUALITY TECHNOLOGIES
4010 Moorpark Avenue, Suite 102
San Jose, CA 95117
Phone: 408-249-1625

INTERTEK SERVICES CORPORATION
9900 Main Street
Suite 500
Fairfax, VA 22031-3969
Phone: 703-476-9000
Phone: 800-336-0151
Fax: 703-273-2885

IOWA STATE UNIVERSITY
Extended & Continuing Education
102 Sheman
Ames, IA 50011
Phone: 515-294-6229

IQS, INC.
20525 Center Ridge Road
Suite 400
Cleveland, OH 44116
Phone: 800-635-5901
Fax: 216-333-3752

ITC
13515 Dulles Technology Drive
Herndon, VA 22071-3416
Phone: 703-713-3335
Fax: 703-713-0065

JAMES P. O'BRIEN & ASSOCIATES
18730 Arcadia Place
Brookfield, WI 53045
Phone: 414-783-5218

JAMOHR U.S.A. ENTERPRISES, INC.
P.O. Box 144
Jefferson, NY 12093
Phone: 800-452-6657
Fax: 607-652-3382

JBL SYSTEMS, INC.
41570 Hayes Road
Clinton Twp., MI 48038
Phone: 313-286-3800
Fax: 313-286-5446

JCM ENTERPRISES
4900 Blazer Parkway
Dublin, OH 43017
Phone: 800-835-5526
Fax: 614-792-1607

JOHN A. KEANE & ASSOCIATES
575 Ewing Street
Princeton, NJ 08540
Phone: 609-924-7904
Fax: 609-924-1078

JOHN KIDWELL & ASSOCIATES
116 Skimmer Way
Dayton Beach, FL 32119
Phone: 904-756-2504
Fax: 904-788-1472

JOHNSON-LAYTON CO., THE
8811 Alden Drive
Suite 7
Los Angeles, CA 90048
Phone: 310-859-2321
Fax: 310-274-3044

JONATHON COPE ASSOCIATES, INC.
1930 Indian Trail
Lake Oswego, OR 97034
Phone: 503-636-3709
Fax: 503-636-1578

JP & ASSOCIATES
5010 Cherrywood Drive
Oceanside, CA 92056
Phone: 619-945-9714
Fax: 619-945-9714

KARRIE ALEN & ASSOCIATES
1085 Tasman Drive
Suite 726
Sunnyvale, CA 94087
Phone: 408-734-8733
Fax: 408-734-8733

KEMA REGISTERED QUALITY, INC.
4379 County Line Road
Chalfont, PA 18914
Phone: 215-822-4281
Fax: 215-822-4285

KEYE PRODUCTIVITY CENTER
P.O. Box 27-480
Kansas City, MO 64180
Phone: 800-821-3919
Phone: 913-345-2140

KINSEL & ASSOCIATES
602 West Avenue
Cartersville, GA 30120
Phone: 404-386-0368
Fax: 404-386-0615

KMR GROUP
420 North Wabash Avenue, 4th Floor
Chicago, IL 60611
Phone: 312-670-2200
Fax: 312-670-2215

L. MARVIN JOHNSON & ASSOCIATES, INC.
822 Montezuma Way
West Covina, CA 91791
Phone: 818-919-1728
Fax: 818-919-7128

LAKEWOOD PUBLICATIONS
50 South Ninth Street
Minneapolis, MN 55402-3165
Phone: 800-328-4329
Phone: 612-333-0471

LAWRENCE A. WILSON & ASSOCIATES
3727 Summitridge Drive
Atlanta, GA 30340
Phone: 404-723-1785
Fax: 404-457-9808

LIBERTY CONSULTING GROUP
6 Drumhill Lane
Randolph, NJ 07869
Phone: 201-361-5952
Fax: 201-361-5939

LLOYD'S REGISTER QUALITY ASSURANCE LTD.
33-41 Newark Street
Hoboken, NJ 07030
Phone: 201-963-1111
Fax: 201-963-3299

M.M. WURTZEL ASSOCIATES
4 Childs Circle
Framingham, MA 01701
Phone: 508-872-1407

MANAGEMENT SCIENCES INTERNATIONAL
2120 Lebanon Road
Lawrenceville, GA 30243-5131
Phone: 404-962-9915

MANAGEX INTERNATIONAL
6 Jenner
Suite 130
Irvine, CA 92718
Phone: 714-727-7001
Fax: 714-727-7002

MANUFACTURING ADVISORY SERVICE
P.O. Box 304
Newburgh, IN 47629-0304
Phone: 800-695-8394
Fax: 812-853-9522

MC INSTRUMENT REPAIR, INC.
2791 Universal Drive
Saginaw, MI 48603
Phone: 517-793-0377
Fax: 517-793-3997

MCDONALD & ASSOCIATES, INC.
2511 East 46th Street
Suite A-4
Indianapolis, IN 46205
Phone: 317-549-0055

MCELRATH & ASSOCIATES, INC.
6101 Cresent Drive
Edina, MN 55436
Phone: 612-927-4785

MCHALE QUALITY SYSTEMS
P.O. Box 681093
Indianapolis, IN 46268
Phone: 317-251-7563

MCWILLIAMS QUALITY CONSULTING
RR1, Box 541
Avinger, TX 75630
Phone: 903-755-3134
Fax: 903-755-2208

MENTOR GROUP
8663 Tyler Boulevard
Mentor, OH 44060
Phone: 216-255-1445
Fax: 216-255-5900

MESCON GROUP
90 Executive Parkway South
Suite 100
Atlanta, GA 30329
Phone: 404-728-0110
Fax: 404-728-9862

MET LABORATORIES, INC.
914 W Patapsco Avenue
Baltimore, MD 21230-3432
Phone: 410-354-3300
Fax: 410-354-3313

MIAMI UNIVERSITY CONTINUING EDUCATION
Hamilton Campus
1601 Peck Boulevard
Hamilton, OH 45011
Phone: 513-863-8833
Phone: 513-424-4444

MIS TRAINING INSTITUTE, INC.
498 Concord Street
Framingham, MA 01701-2357
Phone: 508-879-7999
Fax: 508-872-1153

MLI/CGI
31 Milk Street
Boston, MA 02109
Phone: 617-482-5545
Fax: 617-482-7037

MOODY INTERNATIONAL QUALITY ASSURANCE REGISTRAR, INC.
350 McKnight Plaza Building
105 Braunlich Drive
Pittsburgh, PA 15237
Phone: 412-366-5567
Fax: 412-366-5571

MRA INSTITUTE OF MANAGEMENT
235 North Executive Drive
Suite 100
Brookfield, WI 53005
Phone: 414-797-7580
Fax: 414-797-7591

MULTIFACE, INC.
6721 Merriman Avenue
Garden City, MI 48135
Phone: 313-421-6330
Fax: 313-421-1142

NATIONAL BUSINESS TECHNOLOGIES
1805 Cypress Drive
Irving, TX 75061
Phone: 214-579-9494
Fax: 214-438-9149

NATIONAL CONFERENCE OF STANDARDS LABORATORIES
1800 30th Street
Suite 305 B
Boulder, CO 80301
Phone: 303-440-3339
Fax: 303-440-3384

**NATIONAL ELECTRICAL
MANUFACTURERS ASSOCIATION
(NEMA**
2101 L Street, N.W.
Suite 300
Washington, DC 20037-1580
Phone: 202-457-8400
Phone: 202-457-1968
Fax: 202-457-8468

NATIONAL INSTRUMENTS
6504 Bridge Point Parkway
Austin, TX 78730-5039
Phone: 512-794-0100
Fax: 512-794-8411

**NATIONAL QUALITY ASSURANCE,
USA**
1146 Massachusetts Avenue
Boxborough, MA 01719
Phone: 508-635-9256
Fax: 508-266-1073

NATIONAL QUALITY INTEGRATORS
P.O. Box 20094
Washington, DC 20041
Phone: 703-689-0618
Fax: 703-689-0618

**NATIONAL STANDARDS AUTHORITY
OF IRELAND (NSAI)**
5 Medallion Center (Greeley Street)
Merrimack, NH 03054
Phone: 603-424-7070
Fax: 603-429-1427

**NATIONAL TECHNOLOGICAL
UNIVERSITY**
700 Centre Avenue
Fort Collins, CO 80526
Phone: 303-484-6050
Phone: 303-498-0501
Fax: 303-484-0668

NAVNEET ENTERPRISES
5151 Nishga Court
Mississauga, Ontario L5R 2M7
Canada
Phone: 416-890-7204

NEW-TECH CONSULTING, INC.
9 Burnham Street
Cincinnati, OH 45218
Phone: 513-851-6256
Fax: 513-851-0165

NK CONSULTANTS
P.O. Box 453
Hebron, KY 41048
Phone: 606-586-9788

**NORTHERN ESSEX COMMUNITY
COLLEGE**
Division of Continuing Education &
Community Services
Elliott Way
Haverhill, MA 01830
Phone: 617-374-3900
Phone: 617-374-3816

NSF INTERNATIONAL
3475 Plymouth Road
P.O. Box 130140
Ann Arbor, MI 48113-0140
Phone: 313-769-5112
Fax: 313-769-0109

**OIL & GAS CONSULTANTS
INTERNATIONAL**
P.O. Box 35548
Tulsa, OK 74153-0448
Phone: 918-742-7057
Fax: 918-742-2272

**OKLAHOMA STATE
UNIVERSITY/OKLAHOMA CITY**
Business/International Relations
900 North Portland Avenue
Oklahoma City, OK 73107
Phone: 405-945-3278
Fax: 405-945-3397

OLIVER WIGHT COMPANIES
P.O. Box 435
Newbury, NH 03255-0435
Phone: 800-258-3862
Phone: 603-763-5926
Fax: 603-763-4615

OLIVER WIGHT PUBLICATIONS
5 Oliver Wight Drive
Essex Junction, VY 05452-9985
Phone: 800-343-0625
Fax: 802-878-3384

OLYMPIC PERFORMANCE, INC.
7002 SW Nyberg Street
Tualatin, OR 97062-8205
Phone: 503-692-5573
Fax: 503-692-5254

ORGANIZATIONAL DYNAMICS, INC.
25 Mall Road
Burlington, MA 01803
Phone: 800-634-4636
Fax: 617-273-2558

OTS QUALITY REGISTRARS, INC.
10700 Northwest Freeway
Suite 455
Houston, TX 77092
Phone: 713-688-9494
Fax: 713-688-9590

PAPA & ASSOCIATES
50 Sheppard Avenue West
Suite 300
North York, Ontario M2N 1M2
Canada
Phone: 416-512-7272
Fax: 416-512-7272

PARTICIPATION ASSOCIATES
2555 North Clark Street
Chicago, IL 60614
Phone: 312-935-5858
Fax: 312-935-3588

PAUL HERTZ GROUP, INC.
7990 S.W. 117th Avenue
Suite 100
Miami, FL 33183
Phone: 305-598-2601
Fax: 305-270-0627

**PENNSYLVANIA STATE UNIVERSITY
BEAVER CAMPUS**
Brodhead Road
Monaca, PA 15061
Phone: 412-773-3700

**PENTON SOFTWARE/QUALITY
ALERT INSTITUTE**
257 Park Avenue South
12th Floor
New York, NY 10010-7304
Phone: 800-221-3414
Fax: 212-353-4527

PERRY JOHNSON, INC.
3000 Town Center
Suite 2960
Southfield, MI 48075
Phone: 313-356-4410
Fax: 313-356-4230

PHILIP CROSBY ASSOCIATES, INC.
3260 University Boulevard
P.O. Box 606
Winter Park, FL 32793-6006
Phone: 407-677-3000
Fax: 407-677-3055

PHILLIPS QUALITY CONSULTANTS, INC.
2105 Damascus Church Road
Chapel Hill, NC 27516
Phone: 919-933-9075

PISTER GROUP, INC.
P.O. Box 38042
550 Eglington Avenue W.
Toronto, Ontario M5N 3A8
Canada
Phone: 416-886-9470
Fax: 416-764-6405

POWERS CONSULTING, INC.
6107 Knox Avenue South
Minneapolis, MN 55419
Phone: 612-861-4794

PRECISION MEASUREMENT LABORATORIES
201 West Beach Avenue
Inglewood, CA 90302
Phone: 310-671-4345
Fax: 310-671-0858

PRIME PROCESS MANAGEMENT
5315 W. 74th Street
Edina, MN 55439
Phone: 612-835-1913
Fax: 612-835-2458

PROCESS INTEGRITY, INC.
P.O. Box 153066
Arlington, TX 76015
Phone: 817-472-6694
Fax: 817-468-0008

PROCESS MANAGEMENT INTERNATIONAL (PMI)
7801 E. Bush Lake Road
Suite 360
Minneapolis, Minnesota 55439-3115
Phone: 612-893-0313
Fax: 612-893-0502

PRODUCTIVITY & QUALITY CONSULTANTS INTERNATIONAL
11802 Fidelia Court
Houston, TX 77024
Phone: 713-781-6255
Fax: 713-973-2055

PRODUCTIVITY ENHANCEMENT
P.O. Box 295
Montvale, NJ 07645
Phone: 201-930-8717

PRODUCTIVITY IMPROVEMENT CENTER
Durham College
2000 Simcoe Street North
Oshawa, Ontario L1H 7L7
Canada
Phone: 416-576-2000
Fax: 416-728-2530

PRODUCTIVITY PRESS, INC.
P.O. Box 13390
Portland, OR 97213-0390
Phone: 800-394-6868
Fax: 800-394-6286

PRODUCTIVITY, INC.
101 Merritt 7
Norwalk, CT 06856
Phone: 800-966-5423

Q.A. SYSTEMS, INC.
441 Devon Street
P.O. Box 3090
Kearny, NJ 07032
Phone: 210-998-2627
Fax: 201-998-4292

QCI INTERNATIONAL
P.O. Box 1503
Red Bluff, CA 96080-1503
Phone: 800-527-6970
Fax: 916-527-6970

QMI, A DIVISION OF THE CANADIAN STANDARDS ASSOCIATION
Mississauga Executive Center
Two Robert Speck Parkway
Suite 800
Mississauga, Ontario L4Z 1H8
Canada
Phone: 416-272-3920
Fax: 416-272-3942

QMMT ASSOCIATES
P.O. Box 3471
Greenville, NC 27836
Phone: 919-757-0667

QNR ASSOCIATES
1052 Partridge Drive
Palatine, IL 60067
Phone: 708-776-7703
Fax: 708-776-7703

QUALICON AG
Industrie Neuhof 21
Kirchburg, 3422
Switzerland
Phone: 011-4134-455-845
Fax: 011-4134-455-581

QUALIFICATIONS CONSULTANTS, INC.
3212 Winding Way
Dayton, OH 45419
Phone: 513-293-3377
Fax: 513-293-0220

QUALITRAN PROFESSIONAL SERVICES, INC.
P.O. Box 295
Stroud, Ontario L0L 2M0
Canada
Phone: 800-461-9902
Fax: 705-722-0324

QUALITY ALERT INSTITUTE
257 Park Avenue South
12th Floor
New York, NY 10010-7304
Phone: 800-221-2114

QUALITY ASSURANCE INSTITUTE
7575 Dr Phillips Boulevard
Suite 350
Orlando, FL 32819
Phone: 407-363-1111
Fax: 407-363-1112

QUALITY BREAKTHROUGHS
1407 South 7th Street
Brainerd, MN 56401
Phone: 218-829-0661

QUALITY EDUCATION SERVICES, INC.
5200 Roundrock Trail
Plano, TX 75023
Phone: 214-596-6865
Fax: 214-985-0246

QUALITY INTERNATIONAL LIMITED
2716 Orthodox Street
Philadelphia, PA 19137-1604
Phone: 800-524-5877

QUALITY MANAGEMENT ALLIANCE
6400 Barrie Road, No. 1101
Minneapolis, MN 55435-2317
Phone: 612-927-6003

QUALITY MANAGEMENT ASSISTANCE GROUP
1528 North Ballard Road
Appleton, WI 54911
Phone: 800-236-7802
Fax: 414-738-7802

QUALITY MANAGEMENT ASSOCIATES, INC.
No. 5 Scottsdale
Salisbury, NC 28146
Phone: 704-637-2299
Fax: 704-637-6181

QUALITY MANAGEMENT INSTITUTE
Mississauga Executive Center
Two Robert Speck Parkway, Suite 800
Mississauga, Ontario L4Z 1H8
Canada
Phone: 416-272-3920
Fax: 416-272-3942

QUALITY MANAGEMENT INTERNATIONAL LIMITED
55 Morley Circle
Saint John, New Brunswick E2J 2X5
Canada
Phone: 506-633-2060
Fax: 506-633-2060

QUALITY MANAGEMENT SUPPORT, INC.
P.O. Box 9572
Metairie, LA 70055
Phone: 504-455-1602
Fax: 504-885-8502

QUALITY MANAGEMENT SYSTEMS, INC.
P.O. Box 781
Palm Harbor, FL 34682-0781
Phone: 813-785-1688
Fax: 813-786-7920

QUALITY NETWORK
TQN Publishing
110 Linden Oaks Drive
Rochester, NY 14625
Phone: 716-248-5712

QUALITY PLUS ENGINEERING
4052 N.E. Couch
Portland, OR 97232
Phone: 800-266-7383

QUALITY RESOURCES INTERNATIONAL
1521 Georgetoen Road
Suite 203
Hudson, OH 44236
Phone: 216-650-2767
Fax: 216-528-0029

QUALITY SCIENCES CONSULTANTS, INC.
22531 S.E. 42nd Court
Issaquah, WA 98027-7241
Phone: 206-392-4006
Fax: 206-392-2621

QUALITY SERVICES INTERNATIONAL
5550 W. Central Avenue
Suite G
Toledo, OH 43615
Phone: 419-535-9555
Fax: 419-535-1370

QUALITY SYSTEMS REGISTRARS, INC.
13873 Park Center Road
Suite 217
Herndon, VA 22071-3279
Phone: 703-478-0241
Fax: 703-478-0645

QUALITY TECHNIQUES, INC.
552 Washington Avenue
Pittsburgh, PA 15106
Phone: 412-279-0730
Fax: 412-279-3382

QUALITY TECHNOLOGIES, INC.
2512 Second Avenue #308
Seattle, WA 98121
Phone: 206-441-0707

QUALITY TECHNOLOGY CO.
1270 Lance Lane
Carol Stream, IL 60188
Phone: 708-231-3142

QUALITY VISIONS
7315 Duluth Avenue
Milwaukee, WI 53220
Phone: 414-321-3869

QUALTEC QUALITY SERVICES, INC.
11760 U.S. Highway 1
Suite 400
Palm Beach, FL 33408-3029
Phone: 407-775-8300
Phone: 800-247-9871
Fax: 407-775-8301

QUALTECH OF RACINE, INC.
2200 Clark Street
P.O. Box 1527
Racine, WI 53401
Phone: 414-637-1212
Fax: 414-637-5285

QUEBEC QUALITY CERTIFICATION GROUP
70, rue Dalhousie, Bureau 220
Quebec, Quebec G1K 4B2
Canada
Phone: 418-643-5813
Fax: 418-646-3315

QUEXX INTERNATIONAL LIMITED
3043 Aries Place
Burnaby, British Columbia V3J 7G1
Canada
Phone: 604-421-2491
Fax: 604-421-2491

QUONG & ASSOCIATES, INC.
54 Fortuna Avenue
San Francisco, CA 94115
Phone: 415-922-2957
Fax: 415-931-4699

R.D. GARWOOD, INC.
501 Village Trace
Building 9
Marietta, GA 30067
Phone: 800-241-6653
Fax: 404-952-2976

R.T. WESTCOTT & ASSOCIATES
263 Main Street
Old Saybrook, CT 06475
Phone: 203-388-6094
Fax: 203-388-6944

RALPH D. CALL Q CONSULTANT
226 Hope Road
Tinton Falls, NJ 07724
Phone: 908-542-3028
Fax: 908-542-3028

RAND E. WINTERS CONSULTING GROUP
3677 Portman Lane
Grand Rapids, MI 49508
Phone: 616-247-1232
Fax: 616-452-8374

RATH & STRONG, INC.
92 Hayden Avenue
Lexington, MA 02173
Phone: 617-861-1700
Fax: 617-861-1424

RAU & ASSOCIATES
25 Timberly Drive
Lake Charles, LA 70605
Phone: 318-477-0758
Fax: 318-478-9440

RBS CONSULTANT IN QUALITY
319 Friendship Street
Iowa City, IA 52245
Phone: 319-337-8283
Fax: 319-338-3320

RC ASSOCIATES
3746 Saratoga Drive
Downers Grove, IL 60515
Phone: 708-969-5541
Fax: 708-963-1558

RICHARD CHANG ASSOCIATES
41 Corporate Park
Suite 230
Irvine, CA 92714
Phone: 714-756-8096
Fax: 714-756-0853

RICHARD TYLER INTERNATIONAL, INC.
7202 Benwich Circle
Houston, TX 77095
Phone: 713-974-7214
Fax: 713-855-0503

ROCHESTER INSTITUTE OF TECHNOLOGY
Center for Quality & Applied Statistics
One Lomb Memorial Drive
P.O. Box 9887
Rochester, NY 14623-0887
Phone: 716-475-6990
Fax: 716-475-5959

RON CRISTOFONO CO. - SPC TRAINING & IMPLEMENTATION, INC.
131 Mack Hill Road
Amherst, NH 03031
Phone: 603-673-7262
Fax: 603-672-6428

RUSSELL TECHNOLOGIES, INC
4909 75th Street
Edmonton, Alberta T6B 2S3
Canada
Phone: 403-469-4461
Fax: 403-462-9378

SANDERS QUALITY ASSOCIATES, INC.
820 Gessner
Suite 940
Houston, TX 77024
Phone: 713-465-8772
Fax: 713-465-9742

SCOTT QUALITY SYSTEMS REGISTRARS
40 Washington Street
Wellesley Hills, MA 02181
Phone: 617-239-1110
Fax: 617-239-0433

SCOTT TECHNICAL SERVICES
34 Channing Street
Suite 400
Newton, MA 02158
Phone: 617-527-7032
Fax: 617-527-0618

SERENDIPITY CONSULTING SERVICES
9972 Marquan Circle
Molalla, OR 97038
Phone: 503-829-5921

SGS INDUSTRIAL SERVICE
400 North Sam Houston Parkway East
Suite 800
Houston, TX 77060
Phone: 713-591-5800
Fax: 713-591-5825

SGS INTERNATIONAL CERTIFICATION SERVICES CANADA, INC.
90 Gough Road, Unit 4
Markham, Ontario L3R 5V5
Canada
Phone: 416-479-1160
Fax: 416-479-9452

SGS INTERNATIONAL CERTIFICATION SERVICES, INC.
1415 Park Avenue
Hoboken, NJ 07030
Phone: 201-792-2400
Fax: 201-792-2558

SILTON-BOOKMAN SYSTEMS
20410 Town Center Lane
Suite 280
Cupertino, CA 95014
Phone: 800-932-6311
Fax: 408-446-0731

SOCIETY OF MANUFACTURING ENGINEERS
1 SME Drive
P.O. Box 930
Dearborn, MI 48121
Phone: 313-271-1500
Phone: 800-733-EXPO
Fax: 313-271-0777

SOLARIS SYSTEMS
1230 S. Lewis Street
Anaheim, CA 92805
Phone: 714-563-4300
Fax: 714-563-4355

SOLUTION SPECIALISTS
8460 Dygert Drive
Alto, MI 49302
Phone: 616-891-9114
Phone:
Fax: 616-891-9114

SOUTHEASTERN QUALITY CONSULTANTS
800 Laurel Avenue
Black Mountain, NC 28711
Phone: 704-669-4600

STANTON & HUCKO
540 Midtown Tower
Rochester, NY 14604
Phone: 716-546-6480

STAT-A-MATRIX
2124 Oak Tree Road
Edison, NJ 08820-1059
Phone: 908-548-0600
Fax: 201-548-0409

STATIMATE SYSTEMS, INC.
3216 West St. Joseph
Lansing, MI 48917
Phone: 517-484-1144
Fax: 517-482-1962

STEEL RELATED INDUSTRIES QUALITY SYSTEM REGISTRARS
2000 Corporate Drive
Suite 450
Wexford, PA 15090
Phone: 412-935-2844
Fax: 412-935-6825

STELTECH
1375 Kerns Road
Burlington, Ontario L7P 3H8
Canada
Phone: 416-528-2511
Fax: 416-332-9067

STOCHOS, INC.
14 North College Street
Schenectady, NY 12305
Phone: 800-426-4014
Fax: 518-372-4789

SUPPLIER RESEARCH GROUP
79 Boston Turnpike
Suite 316
Shrewsbury, MA 01545
Phone: 508-842-5223
Fax: 508-798-6606

T.M. HENNESSY & ASSOCIATES
Brandrum
Monaghan,
Ireland
Phone: 353-47-84572

TALICO INC
2320 South Third Street
Suite 5
Jacksonville Beach, FL 32250
Phone: 904-241-1721
Phone: 904-241-1722
Fax: 904-241-4388

TECHNOLOGY DEVELOPMENT CORP.
5760 S. Semoran Boulevard
Orlando, FL 32822
Phone: 407-381-4518
Fax: 407-381-4517

THIRD GENERATION, INC.
4439 Rolling Pine Drive
Orchard Lake, MI 48323
Phone: 313-363-1654
Fax: 313-363-3440

TIMEPLACE, INC.
460 Totten Pond Road
Waltham, MA 02154
Phone: 617-890-4636
Phone: 800-544-4636
Fax: 617-890-7274

TOTAL QUALITY ASSOCIATES, INC.
P.O. Box 47
Lincolnshire, IL 60069
Phone: 800-377-4660
Fax: 708-634-2322

TOTAL QUALITY MANAGEMENT
500 Oxford Road
Bala Cynwyd, PA 19004
Phone: 215-664-8816

TQM CONSULTING
2701 Revere Street
Suite 232
Houston, TX 77098
Phone: 713-523-2312
Fax: 713-520-0495

TQM GROUP LIMITED
222 Berkeley Street
Suite 1550
Boston, MA 02116
Phone: 617-236-8110
Fax: 617-236-8120

TQM SERVICES
98 Foster Road
Swampscott, MA 01907
Phone: 617-593-4598
Fax: 617-593-4598

TRI-TECH SERVICES, INC., AUDITORS/REGISTRARS DIVISION
4700 Clairton Boulevard
Pittsburgh, PA 15236
Phone: 412-884-2290
Fax: 412-884-2268

TUV AMERICA
5 Cherry Hill Drive
Danvers, MA 01923
Phone: 508-777-7999
Fax: 508-777-8441

TUV PRODUCT SERVICES, INC.
1416 N.W. 9th Street
Corvallis, OR 97330
Phone: 503-753-4438
Fax: 503-753-4510

TUV RHEINLAND OF NORTH AMERICA, INC.
12 Commerce Road
Newtown, CT 06470
Phone: 203-426-0888
Fax: 203-426-3156

UNDERWRITERS LABORATORIES OF CANADA
7 Course Road
Scarborough, Ontario M1R 3A9
Canada
Phone: 416-757-3611
Fax: 416-757-1781

UNDERWRITERS LABORATORIES, INC.
1285 Walt Whitman Road
Melville, NY 11747-3081
Phone: 516-271-6200
Fax: 516-271-8259

UNIFIED QUALITY SYSTEMS
715- Standish Avenue
Westfield, NJ 07092
Phone: 908-232-1654

UNIQUE SOLUTIONS, INC.
P.O. Box 1711
Royal Oak, MI 48068
Phone: 313-435-5307
Fax: 313-435-5307

UNITED STATES TESTING CO., INC.
291 Fairfield Avenue
Fairfield, NJ 07004
Phone: 201-575-5252
Fax: 201-575-8271

UNIVERSITY OF CALIFORNIA EXTENSION
Business & Management
3120 De La Cruz Boulevard
Santa Clara, CA 95054
Phone: 408-748-2951
Fax: 408-748-7388

UNIVERSITY OF DELAWARE
Division of Continuing Education
206 Clayton Hall
Newark, DE 19716
Phone: 302-451-1138

UNIVERSITY OF RICHMOND MANAGEMENT INSTITUTE
E. Claiborne Robins School of Business
Sarah Brunet Memorial Hall
Richmond, VA 23173
Phone: 804-289-8011
Fax: 804-289-8872

UNIVERSITY OF WISCONSIN MADISON
Engineering Professional Development
432 North Lake Street
Madison, WI 53706
Phone: 800-462-0876
Phone: 608-262-2061
Fax: 608-263-3160

VICTORIA GROUP
Management Consultants, Ltd.
P.O. Box 536
Fairfax, Virginia 22030
Phone: 800-845-0567
Fax: 800-845-0767

VIDEOLEARNING RESOURCE GROUP
354 West Lancaster Avenue
Haverford, PA 19041
Phone: 215-896-6600
Phone: 800-622-3610

VRAGEL & ASSOCIATES, INC.
8950 Gross Point Road
Skokie, IL 60077
Phone: 708-470-2531
Fax: 708-470-3507

W.A. GOLOMSKI & ASSOCIATES
20 East Jackson Boulevard
Suite 850
Chicago, IL 60604-2208
Phone: 312-922-5986
Fax: 312-922-4070

W.R. WAYMAN & ASSOCIATES
3722 Twin Oak Court
Flower Mound, TX 75028
Phone: 214-539-0335

WARNE C. STAUSS CONSULTANT, INC.
3240 North Manor Drive
Lansing, IL 60438
Phone: 708-474-5290

WARNOCK HERSEY PROFESSIONAL SERVICES, LTD.
128 Elmslie Street
LaSalle, Quebec H8R 1V8
Canada
Phone: 514-366-3100
Fax: 514-366-5350

WILLIAM J. HILL, PE
7 Kramer Lane
Weston, CT 06883
Phone: 203-544-9035

WILLIAM M. HAYDEN JR. CONSULTANTS
P.O. Box 56022
Jacksonville, FL 32241-6022
Phone: 904-260-7700
Fax: 904-260-7701

WORKING SMARTER, INC.
P.O. Box 56
Manchester, PA 17345
Phone: 717-266-7234
Fax: 717-266-7234

XAVIER UNIVERSITY CENTER FOR MANAGEMENT
3800 Victory Parkway
Cincinnati, OH 45207-3241
Phone: 513-745-3394
Phone: 800-982-2673
Fax: 513-745-4307

U.S. SOURCES OF HELP SECTION

U.S. Govermment Sources of Help

U.S. GOVERNMENT SOURCES FOR INFORMATION ON EC92 AND DOING BUSINESS IN EUROPE

The U.S. government is an absolutely huge compiler and publisher of information. Almost all of this information is free or nearly so. Even better, the government is people. People who, for the most part, answer the telephone themselves and are ready to help with their special knowledge, information and insight.

The trick is to know where to look and how to find these resources. This section is dedicated to helping the reader with that task.

DEPARTMENT OF COMMERCE

Almost all of the help and resources available from the U.S. government regarding ISO 9000, EC92 and doing business in the European Single Market, are located within the Department of Commerce.

INTERNATIONAL TRADE ADMIMSTRATION

Within the Department of Commerce, the International Trade Administration is the branch with the information resources to help with all aspects of EC92.

The International Trade Administration was established on January 2, 1980 by the Secretary of Commerce to promote world trade and to strengthen the international trade and investment position of the United States.

INTERNATIONAL ECONOMIC POLICY DIVISION

This division is responsible for the analysis, formulation and implementation of international economic policies of a bilateral, multilateral or regional nature.

There are separate branches for Europe, Africa, East Asia and the Pacific, the Near East and South Asia, Japan and the Western Hemisphere.

These branches are responsible for trade and investi-nent issues with these regions. The branches maintain in-depth conunercial and economic information on the countries and regions for which they are responsible.

Within the division, every country in the world has a country desk officer. These specialists can look at the needs of an individual U.S. firm wishing to sell in a particular country in the full context of that country's overall economy, trade policies, and political situation, and also in light of U.S. policies toward that country.

These desk officers keep up-to-date on the economic and commercial conditions in their assigned countries. Each collects information on the country's regulations, tariffs, business practices, economic and political developments, trade data and trends, market size and growth. Their job is to be informed and up-to-date on the country's potential as a market for U.S. products, services and investments.

The Office of European Community Affairs is the branch specifically responsible for all EC information. This branch operates a separate Single Internal Market Information Service office Known as the SIMIS office.

283

SIMIS

This is the Single Internal Market Information Service of the Department of Commerce. Located within the Office of European Affairs, this office is an outstanding source for information regarding the EC's Single Market Act and its potential on U.S. firms.

The SIMIS office was established in June of 1988 in response to the unexpectedly large number of inquireies received following the publication of a department article regarding Single Market in the Washington Post.

The office receives hundreds of calls for information and help every month and staff members typically are on the road 1 or 2 days a month speaking at conferences and symposia on EC92 and the impact of the Single Intemal Market.

The SIMIS of is probably the best place to start for getting information about EC92 and the Single Internal Market.

U.S. & FOREIGN COMMERCIAL SERVICE

The U.S. & Foreign Commercial Service (US&FCS) is a service-oriented agency at the Department of Commerce created in 1980 to promote and protect U.S. business interests in the intemational world.

US&FCS employs over 1300 connnercial specialists in over 200 cities around the world to assist U.S. companies in all phases of exporting and commercial business.

The agency operates in 66 countries and maintains 48 district offices in the U.S.

The US&FCS Commercial Officers are specialists in international marketing and investment services with an average of eight years practical experience in the private sector. All understand firsthand the problems encountered by U.S. firms in their efforts to trade abroad.

US&FCS Overseas Posts

There is a US&FCS officer in all the EC member states except Luxembourg. Also, there are 2 US&FCS officers assigned to the U.S. mission to the EC to monitor the EC92 process and help U.S. firms develop commercial opportunities.

The foreign officers seek trade/investment opportunities to benefit U.S. firms. They can provide background information on foreign companies, foreign agent and distributor search services, market research, business counseling, help in making appointments with key buyers and government officials and representations on behalf of companies adversely affected by trade barriers.

US&FCS Programs

COUNSELING

The US&FCS provides one-on-one counseling on the export process. They help U.S. firms identify trade and investment opportunities abroad, foreign markets for U.S. products and services, intemational trade exhibitions, aid available for export financing and insurance, tax advantages of exporting, export documentation, and licensing and import requirements.

TRADE DISPUTE ASSISTANCE

US&FCS staff advise host country officials of U.S. government and industry concems about 'trade barriers hindering U.S. access to the intemational market.

BUSINESS FACILITATION

The US&FCS can furnish business lists, language and secretarial support and assistance in making appointments.

AGENT/DISTRIBUTOR SERVICE (ADS)

The ADS is a customized search for interested and qualified foreign representatives for a client inn's product.

WORLD TRADERS DATA REPORT (WTDR)

US&FCS officers can prepare evaluations on U.S. firms' potential trading partners, agents, distributors and licensees.

COMPARISON SHOPPING SERVICE (CSS)

This is a custom market survey on a U.S. firm's specific product in a selected country.

TRADE OPPORTUNITY REPORTING

Potential foreign importers interests as trade opportunities advertised daily in the Journal of Coim-nerce.

MATCHMAKER EVENTS

Special trade delegations to introduce U.S. companies to new markets by matching each U.S. firm with a prospective joint venture/licensee partner sharing a common product or service interest.

COMMERCIAL NEWS USA (CNUSA)

A catalog/magazine published ten times a year to promote new and state-of-the-art products and technology. Distribution is over I 00,000 copies.

TRADE MISSIONS & EXHIBITIONS

Cooperative efforts between Commerce Department staff and other groups to promote, display or bring into direct contact U.S. businesses and potential foreign buyers, agents and distributors for selected product lines.

In the following pages, you will find many additional government sources of information to help you with EC92, ISO 9000 and the new European Single Market.

U.S. DEPARTMENT OF COMMERCE

The Department of Commerce is the primary U.S. government source for information on EC92, EC Standards and Directives and doing business in Europe.

Department of Commerce
Herbert Clark Hoover Building
14th Street and Constitution Avenue NW
Washington, DC 20230

Public Information:	(202) 482-3263
Personnel Localer:	(202) 482-2000
Publications Information	(202) 482-2108

Office of the Secretary
Barbara H. Franklin - Secretary of Commerce
(202) 482-2112
Room 5858

SINGLE INTERNAL MARKET INFORMATION SERVICE (SIMIS)

This is the place to start if you are looking for general information regarding EC92 and government sources of help.

SIMIS can provide U.S. companies with copies of EC 1992 directives affecting a particular industry. However, they do not have the resources available to make mass distributions or mass copies of directives.

SIMIS also has a summary list of European Community 1992 Directives and Proposals.

Single Internal Market Information Service

Room 3036
Office European Community Affairs
14th Street and Constitution Avenue
Washington, DC 20203

If you are visiting the SIMIS office, the U.S. Department of Commerce neaest METRO stop is Federal Triangle.

CONTACTS

Although names were accurate at the time of publication, it is always possible that a change has occurred. The room numbers and telephone numbers, however, do not often change and will most likely connect you with the appropriate contact. There may be other contacts at SIMIS who can provide additional help and assistance.

Office of European Community Affairs Director

Charles Ludolph
(202) 482-5276
Room 3034

EC 1992 Division Director

Mary Saunders
(202) 482-5276
Room   3036

Other SIMIS Contacts

Sara Hagigh	CatherineVial	Don Wright
(202) 482-5276	(202) 482-5823	(202) 482-5279
Room 3036	Room 3036	Room 3036

ITA COUNTRY DESK OFFICERS

Country Desk Officers are a source of information on the economic and commercial conditions in their assigned countries. They collect and keep up-to-date on their country's regulations, tariffs, business practices, economic and political developments, trade data and trends, market size and growth.

Although these names were accurate at the time of publication, it's always possible that a change has occurred The room numbers and telephone numbers, however, do not often change and will most likely connect you the appropriate officer.

Mail should be sent to the Desk Officer, by name, with his/her room number listed. The mailing address is:

U.S. Department of Commerce
Washington, DC 20230

**BELGIUM/
LUXEMBOURG**
Simon Bensimon
(202) 482-7373
Room 3046

DENMARK
Maryanne Lyons
(202) 482-3254
Room 3413

FRANCE
Kelly Jacobs
Elena Mikalis
(202) 482-8008
Room 3042

GERMANY
Velizer Stanoyevitch
(202) 482-2434
Brenda Fisher
(202) 482-2841
Joan Kloepfer
(202) 482-2841
All in Room 3409

GREECE
Ann Corro **(also Portugal)**
(202) 482-3945
Room 3044

IRELAND
Boyce Fitzpatrick
(also Netherlands)
(202) 482-5401
Room 3039

ITALY
Noel Negretti
(202) 482-2177
Room 3045

NETHERLANDS
Boyce Fitzpatrick (also Ireland)
(202) 482-5401
Room 2039

PORTUGAL
Ann Corro (also Greece)
(202) 377-3945
Room 3044

SPAIN
Mary Beth Double
(202) 482-4508
Room 3045

UNITED KINGDOM
Robert McLaughlin
(202) 482-3748
Room 3045

ITA INDUSTRY DESKS LISTING

INDUSTRY	CONTACT	PHONE
Abrasive Products	Presbury, Graylin	(202)482-5157
Accounting	Chittum, J Marc	(202)482-0345
Adhesives/Sealants	Prat, Raimundo	(202)482-0128
Advertising	Chittum, J Marc	(202)482-3050
Aerospace Financing Issues	Jackson, Jeff	(202)482-0222
Aerospace Industry Analysis	Walsh, Hugh	(202)482-0678
Aerospace Market Development	Bowie, David C	(202)482-4222
Aerospace-Space Programs	Pajor, Peter	(202)482-8228
Aerospace Trade Policy	Bath, Sally	(202)482-4222
Aerospace (Trade Promo)	White, John C	(202)482-2835
Agribusiness (Major Project)	Bell, Richard	(202)482-2460
Agricultural Chemicals	Maxey, Francis P	(202)482-0128
Agricultural Machinery	Wiening, Mary	(202)482-4708
Air Couriers	Elliott, Frederick	(202)482-3734
Air Conditioning Equipment	Holley, Tyrena	(202)482-3509
Air, Gas Compressors	McDonald, Edward	(202)482-0680
Air, Gas Compressors (Trade Promo)	Zanetakos, George	(202)482-0552
Air Pollution Control Equipment	Jonkers, Loretta	(202)482-0564
Aircraft & Aircraft Engines	Driscoll, George	(202)482-8228
Aircraft & Aircraft Engines (Trade Promo)	White, John C	(202)482-2835
Aircraft Auxiliary Equipment	Driscoll, George	(202)482-8228
Aircraft Parts (Market Support)	Driscoll, George	(202)482-8228
Aircraft Parts/Aux Equipment (Trade Promo)	White, John C	(202)482-2835
Airlines	Johnson, C William	(202)482-5071
Airport Equipment	Driscoll, George	(202)482-8228
Airport Equipment (Trade Promo)	White, John	(202)482-2835
Airports, Ports, Harbors (Major Project)	Piggot, Deboorne	(202)482-3352
Air Traffic Control Equipment	Driscoll, George	(202)482-8228
Alcoholic Beverages	Kenney, Cornelius	(202)482-2428
Alum Sheet, Plate/Foil	Cammarota, David	(202)482-0575
Alum Forgings, Electro.	Cammarota, David	(202)482-0575
Aluminum Extrud Alum Rolling	Cammarota, David	(202)482-0575
Analytical Instruments	Podolske, Lewis	(202)482-3360
Analytical Instruments (Trade Promo)	Manzolillo, Franc	(202)482-2991
Animal Feeds	Janis, William V	(202)482-2250
Apparel	Dulka, William	(202)482-4058
Apparel (Trade Promo)	Molnar, F	(202)482-2043
Asbestos/Cement Prod	Pitcher, Charles	(202)482-0132
Assembly Equipment	Abrahams, Edward	(202)482-0132
Audio Visual Equipment(Trade Promo)	Beckham, Reginald	(202)482-5478
Audio Visual Services	Siegmund, John	(202)482-4781
Auto Parts/Suppliers (Trade Promo)	Reck, Robert	(202)482-5479
Auto Industry Affairs	Keitz, Stuart	(202)482-0554
Air Transport Services	Johnson, C William	(202)482-5071
Avionics Marketng	Driscoll, George	(202)482-8228
Bakery Products	Janis, William V	(202)482-2250
Ball Bearings	Reise, Richard	(202)482-3489

Basic Paper and Board Mfg	Smith, Leonard S	(202)482-0375
Bauxite, Alumina, Prim Alum	Cammarota, David	(202)482-0575
Beer	Kenney, Neil	(202)482-2428
Belting & Hose	Prat, Raimundo	(202)482-0128
Beryllium	Duggan, Brian	(202)482-0575
Beverages	Kenney, Cornelius	(202)482-2428
Bicycles	Vanderwolf, John	(202)482-0348
Biotechnology	Arakaki, Emily	(202)482-3888
Biotechnology (Trade Promo)	Gwaltney, GP	(202)482-3090
Boat Building (Major Proj)	Piggot, Deboorne	(202)482-3352
Boats (pleasure)	Vanderwolf, John	(202)482-0348
Books	Lofquist, William S	(202)482-0379
Books (Trade Promo)	Kimmel, Ed	(202)482-3640
Brooms & Brushes	Harris, John	(202)482-1178
Breakfast Cereal	Janis, William V	(202)482-2250
Building Materials & Construction	Pitcher, Charles B	(202)482-0132
Business Forms	Bratland, Rose Marie	(202)482-0380
CAD/CAM	McGibbon, Patrick	(202)482-0314
Cable TV	Plock, Ernest	(202)482-4781
Canned Food Products	Higden, Donald	(202)482-3346
Capital Goods (Trade Promo)	Morse, Jerry	(202)482-5907
Carbon Black	Prat, Raimundo	(202)482-0128
Cellular Radio Telephone Equip	Gossack, Linda	(202)482-4466
Cement	Pitcher, Charles	(202)482-0132
Cement Plants (Major Proj)	White, Barbara	(202)482-4160
Ceramics (Advanced)	Shea, Moira	(202)482-0128
Ceramics Machinery	Shaw, Eugene	(202)482-3494
Cereals	Janis, William V	(202)482-2250
Chemicals (Liaison & Policy)	Kelly, Michael J	(202)482-0128
Chemical Plants (Major Proj)	Haraguchi, Wally	(202)482-4877
Chemicals & Allied Products	Kamenicky, Vincent	(202)482-0128
Chinaware	Corea, Judy	(202)482-0311
Civil Aircraft Agreement	Bath, Sally	(202)482-4222
Civil Aviation Policy	Johnson, C William	(202)482-5071
Coal Exports	Yancik, Joseph J	(202)482-1466
Cobalt	Cammarota, David	(202)482-0575
Cocoa Products	Petrucco-Littleton	(202)482-5124
Coffee Products	Petrucco-Littleton	(202)482-5124
Commercial Aircraft (Trade Policy)	Bath, Sally	(202)482-4222
Commercial Lighting Fixtures	Whitley, Richard A	(202)482-0682
Commercial/Indus Refrig Eqpmt	Holley, Tyrena	(202)482-3509
Commercial Printing	Lofquist, William S	(202)482-0379
Commercialization of Space (Market)	Bowie, David C	(202)482-8228
Commercialization of Space (Services)	Plock, Ernest	(202)482-4781
Composites, Advanced	Manion, James	(202)482-5157
Computer and DP Services	Atkins, Robert G	(202)482-4781
	Inoussa, Mary C	(202)482-5820
Computer Industry	Miles, Timothy O	(202)482-2990
Computers (personal)	Woods, R Clay	(202)482-3013
Computers (Trade Promo)	Fogg, Judy A	(202)482-4936
Computer Consulting	Atkins, Robert G	(202)482-4781
Confectionery Products	Kenney, Cornelius	(202)482-2428
Construction	MacAuley, Patrick	(202)482-0132

Construction Machinery	Heimowitz, Leonard	(202)482-0558
Consumer Electronics	Fleming, Howard	(202)482-5163
Consumer Goods	Boyd, Hayden	(202)482-0337
Containers & Packaging	Cooperthite, Kim	(202)482-5159
Cosmetics (Trade Promo)	Kimmel, Ed	(202)482-3640
Cutlery	Corea, Judy	(202)482-0311
Dairy Products	Janis, William V	(202)482-2250
Data Base Services	Inoussa, Mary C	(202)482-5820
Data Processing Services	Atkins, Robert G	(202)482-4781
Desalination/Water Reuse	Greer, Damon	(202)482-0564
Direct Marketing	Elliott, Frederick	(202)482-3734
Distilled Spirits	Kenney, Neil	(202)482-2428
Disk Drives	Kader, Victoria	(202)482-0571
Dolls	Corea, Judy	(202)482-0311
Drugs	McIntyre, Leo	(202)482-0128
Durable Consumer Goods	Ellis, Kevin	(202)482-1176
Earthenware	Corea, Judy	(202)482-0311
Education Facilities (Major Proj)	White, Barbara	(202)482-4160
Educational/Training	Francis, Simon	(202)482-0350
Electric Industrial Apparatus	Whitley, Richard A	(202)482-0682
Elec/Power Gen/Transmission	Brandes, Jay	(202)482-0560
Electric Plwer Plants (Major Proj)	Dollison, Robert	(202)482-2733
Electrical Test & Measuring	Hall, Sarah	(202)482-2846
Electricity	Sugg, William	(202)482-1466
ElectroOptical Instruments (Trade Promo)	Manzolillo, Franc	(202)482-2991
ElectroOptical Instruments	Podolske, Lewis	(202)482-3360
Electronic Components	Scott, Robert	(202)482-2795
Electronic Components/ Production & Test Equip (Trade Promo)	Burke, Joseph J	(202)482-5014
Electronic Database Services	Inoussa, Mary C	(202)482-5820
Elevators, Moving Stairways	Wiening, Mary	(202)482-4708
Employment Services	Francis, Simon	(202)482-0350
Energy (Commodities)	Yancik, Joseph J	(202)482-1466
Energy, Renewable	Rasmussen, John	(202)482-1466
Engineering/Construction Services (Trade Promo)	Ruan, Robert	(202)482-0359
Entertainment Industries	Siegmund, John	(202)482-4781
Entertainment Ind.	Plock, Ernest	(202)482-4781
Explosives	Maxey, Francis P	(202)482-0128
Export Trading Companies	Muller, George	(202)482-5131
Fabricated Metal Construction Materials	Williams, Franklin	(202)482-0132
Farm Machinery	Wiening, Mary	(202)482-4708
Fasteners (Industrial)	Reise, Richard	(202)482-3489
Fats and Oils	Janis, William V	(202)482-2250
Fencing (Metal)	Shaw, Robert	(202)482-0132
Ferroalloys Products	Presbury, Graylin	(202)482-5158
Ferrous Scrap	Sharkey, Robert	(202)482-0606
Fertilizers	Maxey, Francis P	(202)482-0128
Fiber Optics	McCarthy, James	(202)482-4466

Fitters/Purifying Eqmt	Jonkers, Loretta	(202)482-0564
Finance & Management Industries	Candilis, Wray O	(202)482-0339
Fisheries (Major Proj)	Bell, Richard	(202)482-2460
Flexible Mftg. Systems	McGibbon, Patrick	(202)482-0314
Flour	Janis, William V	(202)482-2250
Flowers	Janis, William V	(202)482-2250
Fluid Power	McDonald, Edward	(202)482-0680
Food Products Machinery	Shaw, Eugene	(202)482-3494
Food Retailing	Kenney, Cornelius	(202)482-2428
Footwear	Byron, James	(202)482-4034
Forest Products	Smith, Leonard S	(202)482-0375
Forest Products, Domestic Construction	Kristensen, Chris	(202)482-0384
Forest Products (Trade Policy)	Hicks, Michael	(202)482-0375
Forgings Semifinished Steel	Bell, Charles	(202)482-0609
Fossil Fuel Power Generation (Major Proj)	Dollison, Robert	(202)482-2733
Foundry Eqmt	Corner, Barbara	(202)482-0316
Foundry Industry	Bell, Charles	(202)482-0609
Fruits	Hogden, Donald	(202)482-3346
Frozen Foods Products	Hogden, Donald	(202)482-3346
Fur Goods	Bryon, James	(202)482-4034
Furniture	Enright, Joe	(202)482-3459
Gallium	Cammarota, David	(202)482-0575
Games & Children's Vehicle	Corea, Judy	(202)482-5479
Gaskets/Gasketing Materials	Reise, Richard	(202)482-3489
General Aviation Aircraft	Walsh, Hugh	(202)482-4222
Gen Indus Mach Nec.	Shaw, Eugene	(202)482-3494
General Industrial Machinery	Harrison, Joseph	(202)482-5455
Generator Sets/Turbines (Major Proj)	Dollison, Robert	(202)482-2733
Germanium	Cammarota, David	(202)482-0575
Glass, Flat	Williams, Franklin	(202)482-0132
Glassware	Corea, Judy	(202)482-0311
Gloves,Work	Byron, James	(202)482-4034
Giftware (Trade Promo)	Beckham, Reginald	(202)482-5478
Grain Mill Products	Janis, William V	(202)482-2250
Greeting Cards	Bratland, Rose Marie	(202)482-0380
Grocery Retailing	Kenney, Neil	(202)482-2428
Ground Water Exploration & Development	Greer, Damon	(202)482-0564
Hand Saws, Saw Blades	Shaw, Eugene	(202)482-3494
Hand Edge Tools Ex Mach TI/Saws	Shaw, Eugene	(202)482-3494
Handbags	Byron, James	(202)482-4034
Hard Surfaced Floor Coverings	Shaw, Robert	(202)482-0132
Hardware (Export Promo)	Johnson, Charles E	(202)482-3422
Health	Francis, Simon	(202)482-0350
Heat Treating Equipment	Comer, Barbara	(202)482-0316
Healing Eqmt Ex furnaces	Holley, Tyrena	(202)482-3509
Helicopters	Walsh, Hugh	(202)482-4222
Helicopters (Market Support)	Driscoll, George	(202)482-8228
High Tech Trade, U.S. Competitiveness	Hatter, Victoria L	(202)482-3913
Hoists, Overhead Cranes	Wiening, Mary	(202)482-4708
Home Video	Plock, Ernest	(202)482-4781
Hose & Belting	Prat, Raimundo	(202)482-0128
Hotel & Restaurants/Equip (Trade Promo)	Kimmel, Edward K	(202)482-3640

Hotels And Motels	Sousane, J Richard	(202)482-4582
Household Appliances	Harris, John M	(202)482-1178
Household Appliances (Trade Promo)	Johnson, Charles E	(202)482-3422
Household Furniture	Enright, Joe	(202)482-3459
Housewares (Export Promo)	Johnson, Charles E	(202)482-3422
Housing Construction	Cosslett, Patrick	(202)482-0132
Housing & Urban Development (Major Proj)	White, Barbara	(202)482-4160
Hydro Power, Plants (Major Proj)	Healey, Mary Alice	(202)482-4333
Industrial Controls	Whitley, Richard A	(202)482-0682
Industrial Drives/Gears	Reise, Richard	(202)482-3489
Industrial Gases	Kostalas, Antonios	(202)482-0128
Industrial Organic Chemicals	McIntyre, Leo	(202)482-0128
Industrial Process Controls	Podolske, Lewis	(202)482-3360
Industrial Robots	McGibbon, Patrick	(202)482-0314
Industrial Sewing Machines	Holley, Tyrena	(202)482-3509
Industrial Structure	Davis, Lester A	(202)482-4924
Industrial Trucks	Wiening, Mary	(202)482-4608
Information Services	Inoussa, Mary C	(202)482-5820
Information Industries	Crupe, Friedrich R	(202)482-4781
Inorganic Chemicals	Kamenicky, Vincent	(202)482-0128
Inorganic Pigments	Kamenicky, Vincent	(202)482-0128
Insulation	Shaw, Robert	(202)482-0132
Insurance	McAdam, Bruce	(202)482-0346
Intellectual Property Rights (Services)	Siegmund, John E	(202)482-4781
International Commodities	Siesseger, Fred	(202)482-5124
International Major Projects	Thibeault, Robert	(202)482-5225
Investment Management	Muir, S Cassin	(202)482-0349
Irrigation Equipment	Greer, Damon	(202)482-0564
Irrigation (Major Proj)	Bell, Richard	(202)482-2460
Jams & Jellies	Hogden, Donald A	(202)482-3361
Jewelry	Harris, John	(202)482-1178
Jewelry (Trade Promo)	Beckham, Reginald	(202)482-5478
Jute Products	Tasnadi, Diani	(202)482-5124
Kitchen Cabinets	Wise, Barbara	(202)482-0375
Laboratory Instruments	Prodolske, Lewis	(202)482-3360
Laboratory Instruments (Trade Promo)	Manzolillo, Franc	(202)482-2991
Lasers (Trade Promo)	Manzolillo, Franc	(202)482-2991
Lawn & Garden Equip	Vanderwolf, John	(202)482-0348
Lead Products	Larrabee, David	(202)482-0575
Leasing: Eqmt & Vehicles	Shuman, John	(202)482-3050
Leather Tanning	Byron, James E	(202)482-4034
Leather Products	Byron, James E	(202)482-4034
Legal Services	Chittum, J Marc	(202)482-0345
LNG Plants (Major Proj)	Thomas, Janet	(202)482-4146
Local Area Networks	Spathopoulos, Vivian	(202)482-0572
Logs, Wood	Hicks, Michael	(202)482-0375
Luggage	Byron, James	(202)482-4034
Lumber	Wise, Barbara	(202)482-0375

Machine Tool Accessories	McGibbon, Patrick	(202)482-0314
Magazines	Bratland, Rose Marie	(202)482-0380
Magnesium	Cammarota, David	(202)482-0575
Major Projects	Thibeault, Robert	(202)482-5225
Management Consulting	Chittum, J Marc	(202)482-0345
Manifold Business Forms	Bratland, Rose Marie	(202)482-0380
Manmade Fiber	Dulka, William	(202)482-4058
Margarine	Janis, William V	(202)482-2250
Marine Recreational Equipment (Trade Promo)	Beckham, Reginald	(202)482-5478
Marine Insurance	Johnson, C William	(202)482-5012
Maritime Shipping	Johnson, C William	(202)482-5012
Materials, Advanced	Cammarota, David	(202)482-0575
Mattresses & Bedding	Enright, Joe	(202)482-3459
Meat Products	Hogden, Donald A	(202)482-3346
Mech Power Transmission Eqmt	Reise, Richard	(202)482-3489
Medical Facilities (Major Proj)	White, Barbara	(202)482-4160
Medical Instruments	Fuchs, Michael	(202)482-0550
Medical Instruments & Equip (Trade Promo)	Keen, George B	(202)482-2010
Mercury, Fluorspar	Manion, James J	(202)482-5157
Metal Building Products	Williams, Franklin	(202)482-0132
Metal Cookware	Corea, Judy	(202)482-0311
Metal Cutting Machine Tools	McGibbon, Patrick	(202)482-0314
Metal Forming Machine Tools	McGibbon, Patrick	(202)482-0314
Metal Powders	Duggan, Brian	(202)482-0575
Metals, Secondary	Brueckmann, Al	(202)482-0606
Metalworking	Mearman, John	(202)482-0315
Metalworking Eqmt Nec.	McGibbon, Patrick	(202)482-0314
Millwork	Wise, Barbara	(202)482-0375
Mineral Based Construction Materials (Clay, Concrete, Gypsum, Asphalt, Stone)	Pitcher, Charles B	(202)482-0132
Mining Machinery	McDonald, Edward	(202)482-0680
Mining Machinery (Trade Promo)	Zanetakos, George	(202)482-0552
Mobile Homes	Cosslett, Patrick	(202)482-0132
Molybdenum	Cammarota, David	(202)482-0575
Monorails (Trade Promo)	Wiening, Mary	(202)482-4708
Motion Pictures	Siegmund, John	(202)482-4781
Motor Vehicles	Warner, Albert T	(202)482-0669
Motorcycles	Vanderwolf, John	(202)482-0348
Motors, Electric	Whitley, Richard A	(202)482-0682
Music	Siegmund, John	(202)482-4781
Musical Instruments	Corea, Judy	(202)482-0811
Mutual Funds	Muir, S Cassin	(202)482-0349
Natural Gas	Gillett, Tom	(202)482-1466
Natural, Synthetic Rubber	McIntyre, Leo	(202)482-0128
Newspapers	Bratland, Rose Marie	(202)482-0380
Nickel Products	Presbury, Graylin	(202)482-0575
Non-alcoholic Beverages	Kenney, Cornelius	(202)482-2428
Noncurrent Carrying Wiring Devices	Whitley, Richard A	(202)482-0682
Nondurable Goods	Simon, Les	(202)482-0341
Nonferrous Foundries	Duggan, Brian	(202)482-0610

Nonferrous Metals	Manion, James J	(202)482-0575
Nonmetallic Minerals Nec.	Manion, James J	(202)482-0575
Nonresidential Constr	MacAuley, Patrick	(202)482-0132
Nuclear Power Plants/Machinery	Greer, Damon	(202)482-0681
Nuclear Power Plants (Major Proj)	Dollison, Robert	(202)482-2733
Numerical Controls For Mach Tools	McGibbon, Patrick	(202)482-0314
Nuts, Edible	Janis, William V	(202)482-2250
Nuts, Bolts, Washers	Reise, Richard	(202)482-3489
Ocean Shipping	Johnson, C William	(202)482-5012
Office Furniture	Enright, Joe	(202)482-3459
Oil & Gas Development & Refining (Major Proj)	Thomas, Janet	(202)482-4146
Oil & Gas (Fuels Only)	Gillett, Tom	(202)482-1466
Oil Field Machinery	McDonald, Edward	(202)482-0680
Oil Field Machinery (Trade Promo)	Miles, Max	(202)482-0679
Oil Shale (Major Proj)	Thomas, Janet	(202)482-4146
Operations & Maintenance	Chittum, J Marc	(202)482-0345
Organic Chemicals	McIntyre, Leo	(202)482-0128
Outdoor Lighting Fixtures	Whitley, Richard A	(202)482-0682
Outdoor Power Equip (Trade Promo)	Johnson, Charles E	(202)482-3422
Packaging & Containers	Copperthite, Kim	(202)482-0575
Packaging Machinery	Shaw, Eugene	(202)482-2204
Paints/Coatings	Prat, Raimundo	(202)482-0128
Paper	Smith, Leonard S	(202)482-0375
Paper & Board Packaging	Smith, Leonard S	(202)482-0375
Paper Industries Machinery	Abrahams, Edward	(202)482-0312
Pasta	Janis, William V	(202)482-2250
Paving Materials (Asphalt & Concrete)	Pitcher, Charles	(202)482-0132
Pectin	Janis, William V	(202)482-2250
Pens, Pencils, etc.	Corea, Judy	(202)482-0311
Periodicals	Bratland, Rose Marie	(202)482-0380
Pet Food	Janis, William V	(202)482-2250
Pet Products (Trade Promo)	Kimmel, Ed	(202)482-3640
Petrochemicals	McIntyre, Leo	(202)482-0128
Petrochem, Cyclic Crudes	McIntyre, Leo	(202)482-0128
Petrochemicals Plants (Major Proj)	Haraguchi, Wally	(202)482-4877
Petroleum, Crude & Refined Products	Gillett, Tom	(202)482-1466
Pharmaceuticals	McIntyre, Leo	(202)482-0128
Pipelines (Major Proj)	Thomas, Janet	(202)482-4146
Photographic Eqmt & Supplies	Watson, Joyce	(202)482-0574
Plastic Construction Products (Most)	Williams, Franklin	(202)482-0132
Plastic Materials	Shea, Moira	(202)482-0128
Plastic Products	Prat, Raimundo	(202)482-0128
Plastics Products Machinery	Shaw, Eugene	(202)482-3494
Plumbing Fixtures & Fittings	Shaw, Robert	(202)482-0132
Plywood/Panel Products	Wise, Barbara	(202)482-0375
Point-of-Use Water Treatment	Greer, Damon	(202)482-0564
Pollution Control Equipment	Jonkers, Loretta	(202)482-0564
Porcelain Electrical Supplies	Whitley, Richard A	(202)482-0682
Potatos Chips	Janis, William	(202)482-2250
Pottery	Corea, Judy	(202)482-0311
Poultry Products	Hogden, Donald A	(202)482-3346
Power Hand Tools	Abrahams, Edward	(202)482-0312

Precious Metal Jewelry	Harris, John M	(202)482-1178
Prefabricated Buildings, wood	Cosslett, Patrick	(202)482-0132
Prefabricated Buildings, metal		
Williams, Franklin	(202)482-0132	
Prepared Meats	Hodgen, Donald A	(202)482-3346
Pretzels	Janis, William V	(202)482-2250
Primary Commodities	Siesseger, Fred	(202)482-5124
Printing & Publishing	Lofquit, William S	(202)482-0379
Printing Trade Services	Bratland, Rose Marie	(202)482-0380
Printing Trades Mach/Eqmt	Kemper, Alexis	(202)482-5956
Process Control Instruments	Podolske, Lon	(202)482-3360
Process Control Instruments (Trade Promo)	Marcolillo, Franc	(202)482-2991
Pulp And Paper Mills (Major Proj)	White, Barbara	(202)482-4160
Pulpmills	Stanley, Gary	(202)482-0375
Pumps, Pumping Eqmt	McDonald, Edward	(202)482-0680
Pumps, Valve, Compressors (Trade Promo)	Zanetakos, George	(202)482-0552
Radio & TV Broadcasting	Siegmund, John	(202)482-4781
Radio & TV Communications Eqmt	Gossack, Linda	(202)482-2872
Recorded Music	Siegmund, John	(202)482-4781
Recreational Eqmt (Trade Promo)	Beckham, Reginald	(202)482-5478
Refractory Products	Duggan, Brian	(202)482-0575
Renewable Energy Eqpmt	Garden, Les	(202)482-0556
Residential Lighting Fixtures	Whitley, Richard A	(202)482-0682
Retail Trade	Margulies, Marvin J	(202)482-5086
Rice Milling	Janis, William V	(202)482-2250
Roads, Railroads, Mass Trans (Major Proj)	Smith, Jay L	(202)482-4642
Robots	McGibbon, Patrick	(202)482-0314
Roofing, Asphalt	Pitcher, Charles	(202)482-0132
Roller Bearings	Reise, Richard	(202)482-3489
Rolling Mill Machinery	Comer, Barbara	(202)482-0316
Rubber	Prat, Raimundo	(202)482-0128
Rubber Products	Prat, Raimundo	(202)482-0128
Saddlery & Harness Products	Byron, James	(202)482-4034
Safety & Security Equip (Trade Promo)	Umstead, Dwight	(202)482-8410
Space Services	Plock, Ernest	(202)482-5620
Satellites & Space Vehicles (Marketing)	Bowie, David C	(202)482-8228
Satellites, Communications	Cooper, Patricia	(202)482-4466
Science & Electronic (Trade Promo)	Moose, Jake	(202)482-4125
Scientific Instruments (Trade Promo)	Manzolillo, Franc	(202)482-2991
Scientific Measurement/ Control Eqmt	Podolske, Lewis	(202)482-3360
Screw Machine Products	Reise, Richard	(202)482-3489
Screws, Washers	Reise, Richard	(202)482-3489
Security & Commodity Brokers	Fenwick, Thomas R	(202)482-0347
Security Management Svcs.	Chittum, J Marc	(202)482-0345
Semiconductors (except Japan)	Scott, Robert	(202)482-2795
Semiconductors, Japan	Nealon, Marguerite	(202)482-8411
Semiconductor Prod Eqmt & Materials	Hall, Sarah	(202)482-2846
Service Industries (Uruguay Round)	Dowling, Jay	(202)482-1134
Services Data Base Development	Atkins, Robert G	(202)482-4781
Services, Telecom	Shefrin, Ivan	(202)482-4466
Shingles (Wood)	Wise, Barbara	(202)482-0375
Silverware	Harris, John	(202)482-1178

Sisal Products	Manger, Jon	(202)482-5124
Small Arms, Ammunition	Vanderwolf, John	(202)482-0348
Snackfood	Janis, William V	(202)482-2250
Soaps, Detergents, Cleaners	McIntyre, Leo	(202)482-0128
Software	Hyikata, Heidi	(202)482-0572
Software (Trade Promo)	Fogg, Judy	(202)482-4936
Solar Cells/Photovoltaic Devices	Garden, Les	(202)482-0556
Solar Eqmt Ocean/Biomass/ Geothermal	Garden, Les	(202)482-0556
Soy Products	Janis, William V	(202)482-2250
Space Commercialization (Equipment)	Bowie, David C	(202)482-8228
Space Commercialization (Services)	Plock, Ernest	(202)482-5820
Space Policy Development	Pajor, Peter	(202)482-8228
Special Industry Machinery	Shaw, Eugene	(202)482-3494
Speed Changers	Reise, Richard	(202)482-3489
Sporting & Athletic Goods	Vanderwolf, John	(202)482-0348
Sporting Goods (Trade Promo)	Beckham, Reginald	(202)482-5478
Steel Industry Products	Bell, Charles	(202)482-0608
Steel Industry	Brueckmann, Al	(202)482-0606
Steel Markets	Bell, Charles	(202)482-0608
Storage Batteries	Larrabee, David	(202)482-5124
Sugar Products	Tasnadi, Diana	(202)482-5124
Supercomputers	Streeter, Jonathan	(202)482-0572
Superconductors	Chiarado, Roger	(202)482-0402
Switchgear & Switchboard Apparatus	Whitley, Richard A	(202)482-0682
Tea	Janis, William V	(202)482-2250
Technology Affairs	Shykind, Edwin B	(202)482-4694
Telecommunications	Stechschulte, Roger	(202)482-4466
Telecommunications (Major Proj)	Paddock, Richard	(202)482-4466
Telecommunications (Trade Promo)	Rettig, Theresa E	(202)482-2952
Telecommunications (Network Equip)	Henry, John	(202)482-4466
Telecommunications (Military Communications Equip)	Mocenigo, Anthony	(202)482-4466
Teletext Services	Inoussa, Mary C	(202)482-5820
Textile Machinery	McDonald, Edward	(202)482-0680
Textiles	Dulka, William S	(202)482-4058
Textiles (Trade Promo)	Molnar, Ferenc	(202)482-2043
Timber Products (Tropical)	Tasnadi, Diana	(202)482-5124
Tin Products	Manger, Jon	(202)482-5124
Tires	Prat, Raimundo	(202)482-0128
Tools/Dies/Jigs/Fixtures	McGibbon, Patrick	(202)482-0314
Tourism (Major Proj)	White, Barbara	(202)482-4160
Tourism Services	Sousane, J Richard	(202)482-4582
Toys	Corea, Judy	(202)482-0311
Toys & Games (Trade Promo)	Becham, Reginald	(202)482-5478
Trade Related Employment	Davis, Lester A	(202)482-4924
Transborder Data Flows	Inoussa, Mary C	(202)482-5820
Transformers	Whitley, Richard A	(202)482-0682
Transportation Industries	Alexander, Albert	(202)482-4581
Tropical Commodities	Tasnadi, Diana	(202)482-5124
Trucking Services	Sousane, J Richard	(202)482-4581
Tungsten Products	Manger, Jon	(202)482-5124
Turbines, Steam	Greer, Damon	(202)482-0681

Uranium	Sugg, William	(202)482-1466
Value Added Telecommunications Serv	Atkins, Robert G	(202)482-4781
Value, Pipe Fittings (Except Brass)	Reise, Richard	(202)482-3489
Vegetables	Hogden, Donald A	(202)482-3346
Video Services	Plock, Ernest	(202)482-5820
Videotex Services	Inoussa, Mary C/ Siegmund, John	(202)482-5820
Wallets, Billfolds, Flatgoods	Byron, James	(202)482-4034
Warm Air Heating Eqmt	Holley, Tyrena	(202)482-3509
Wastepaper	Stanley, Gary	(202)482-0375
Watches	Harris, John	(202)482-1178
Water and Sewerage Treatment Plants (Major Proj)	Hcaley, Mary Alice	(202)482-4643
Water Resource Eqmt	Greer, Damon	(202)482-0564
Water Supply & Distribution	Greer, Damon	(202)482-0564
Welding/Cutting Apparatus	Comer, Barbara	(202)482-0316
Wholesale Trade	Margulis, Marvin	(202)482-3050
Wine	Kenney, Cornelius	(202)482-2428
Windmill Components	Garden, Les	(202)482-0556
Wire & Wire Products	Breuckmann, Al	(202)482-0606
Wire Cloth, Industrial	Reise, Richard	(202)482-3489
Wire Cloth	Williams, Franklin	(202)482-0132
Wood Containers	Hicks, Michael	(202)482-0375
Wood Preserving	Hicks, Michael	(202)482-0375
Wood Products	Smith, Leonard S	(202)482-0375
Wood Working Machinery	McDonald, Edward	(202)482-0680
Writing Instruments	Corea, Judy	(202)482-0311
Yeast	Janis, William V	(202)482-2250

INTERNATIONAL TRADE ADMINISTRATION US&FCS DISTRICT OFFICES

ALABAMA

Rm. 302, Berry Bldg. *
2015 2nd Ave. North
Birmingham, AL 35203
(205) 731-1331

ALASKA

World Trade Center
4201 Tudor Centre Dr. Suite 319
Anchorage, AK 99508
(907) 271-6237

ARIZONA

Federal Bldg.
230 North 1st Ave.,Rm. 3412
Phoenix, AZ 85025
(602) 379-3285

ARKANSAS

Suite 811, Savers Fed. Bldg.,
320 W. Capitol Ave.
Little Rock, AR 72201
(501) 324-5794

CALIFORNIA

Rm. 9200, 11000 Wilshire Blvd.
Los Angeles, CA 90024
(213) 575-7104

116-A W. 4th St.
Suite # 1,
Santa Ana, CA 92701
(714) 836-2461

6363 Greenwich Dr., Suite 145,
San Diego, CA 92122
(619) 557-5395

250 Montgomery St.,14th Floor *
San Francisco, CA 94104
(415) 705-2300

COLORADO

Suite 680 *
1625 Broadway
Denver, CO 80202
(303) 844-3246

CONNECTICUT

Rm. 610-B, Fed. Office
Bldg.*
450 Main St.
Hartford, CT 06103
(203) 240-3530

DELAWARE

Serviced by Philadelphia District
Office

FLORIDA

Suite 224
Fed. Bldg.,
51 S.W. First Ave.
Miami, FL 33130
(305) 536-5267

128 North Osceola Ave. +
Clearwater, FL 34615
(813) 461-0011

College of Business
Administration +
University of Central Florida
CEBA 11, Rm. 346
Orlando, FL 32816
(407) 648-6235

Collins Bldg. +
Rm. 401
107 W. Gaines St.,
Tallahassee, FL 32304
(904) 488-6469

GEORGIA

Plaza Square North
4360 Chamblee Dunwoody Rd.
Atlanta, GA 30341
(404) 452-9101

120 Barnard St., A-107
Savannah, GA 31401
(912) 944-4204

HAWAII

P.O. Box 50026
300 Ala Moana Blvd.
Honolulu, HI 96850
(808) 541-1782

IDAHO

(Portland District) +
Joe R.Williams Bldg.
700 W. State St.-2nd Flr.
Boise, ID 83720
(208) 334-3857

ILLINOIS

Rm. 1406
55 East Monroe St.,
Chicago, IL 60603
(312) 353-4450

Illinois Institute of Technology +
201 East Loop Rd.
Wheaton, IL 60187
(312) 353-4332

515 North Court St. +
P.O. Box 1747
Rockford, IL 61110-0247
(815) 987-8123

INDIANA

One North Capitol Ave., Suite
520
Indianapolis, IN 46204
(317) 226-6214

IOWA

817 Fed. Bldg.
210 Walnut St.,
Des Moines, IA 50309
(515) 284-4222

424 First Ave. N.E. +
Cedar Rapids, IA 52401
(319) 362-8418

KANSAS

(Kansas City, Mo., District) +
151 N. Voltusia
Wichita, KS 67214-4695
(316) 269-6160

KENTUCKY

Rm.636B, Gene Snyder
Courthouse
and Customhouse Bldg.,
601 W. Broadway
Louisville, KY 40202
(502) 582-5066

LOUISIANA

432 World Trade Center,
No. 2 Canal St.
New Orleans, LA 70130
(504) 589-6546

MAINE

(Boston District)+
77 Sewall St.
Augusta, ME 04330
(207) 622-8249

MARYLAND

413 U.S. Customhouse
40 South Gay St.
Baltimore, MD 21202
(301) 962-3560

c/o National Institute
Standards & Technology
Bldg. 411
Gaithersburg, MD 20899
(301) 962-3560

MASSACHUSETTS

World Trade Center, Suite 307
Commonwealth Pier Area
Boston, MA 02210
(617) 565-8563

MICHIGAN

1140 McNamara Bldg.
477 Michigan Ave.
Detroit MI 48226
(313) 226-3650

300 Monroe N.W. +
Grand Rapids, MI 49503
(616) 456-2411

MINNESOTA

108 Federal Bldg.
110 S. 4th St.
Minneapolis, MN 55401
(612) 348-1638

MISSISSIPPI

328 Jackson Mall Office Ctr.
300 Woodrow Wilson Blvd.
Jackson, MS 39213
(601) 965-4388

MISSOURI

7911 Forsyth Blvd. *
Suite 610
St. Louis, MO 63105
(314) 425-3302

Rm. 635
601 East 12th St.
Kansas City, MO 64106
(816) 426-3141

MONTANA

Serviced by Portland District
Office

NEBRASKA

11133 "O" St.
Omaha, NE 68137
(402) 221-3664

NEVADA

1755 E. Plumb Ln.#152
Reno, NV 89502
(702) 784-5203

NEW HAMPSHIRE

Serviced by Boston District
Office

NEW JERSEY

3131 Princeton Pike Bldg.
#6. Suite 100
Trenton, NJ 08648
(609) 989-2100

NEW MEXICO

(Dallas District) +
625 Silver SW., 3rd Fl.
Albuquerque, NM 87102
(505) 766-2070

(Dallas District)+
c/o Economic Develop. and
Tourism Dept.
1100 St. Francis Drive
Santa Fe, NM 87503
(505) 988-6261

NEW YORK

1312 Federal Bldg.
111 West Huron St.
Buffalo, NY 14202
(716) 846-4191

111 East Ave. +
Suite 220
Rochester, NY 14604
(716) 263-6480

Federal Office Bldg.
26 Federal Plaza,
Rm. 3718, Foley Sq.
New York, NY 10278
(212) 264-0600

NORTH CAROLINA

324 W. Market St. *
Room 203, P.O. Box 1950
Greensboro, NC 27402
(919) 333-5345

NORTH DAKOTA

Serviced by Omaha District
Office

OHIO

9504 Federal Office Bldg. *
550 Main St.
Cincinnati, OH 45202
(513) 684-2944

Rm. 600
668 Euclid Ave.
Cleveland, OH 44114
(216) 522-4750

OKLAHOMA

6601 Broadway Ext.
Oklahoma City, OK 73116
(405) 231-5302

440 S. Houston St. +
Tulsa, OK 74127
(918) 581-7650

OREGON

Suite 242,
One World Trade Center
121 S.W. Salmon St.
Portland, OR 97204
(503) 326-3001

PENNSYLVANIA

475 Allendale Road
Suite 202,
King of Prussia, PA 19406
(215) 962-4980

2002 Fed. Bldg.
1000 Liberty Ave.
Pittsburgh, PA 15222
(412) 644-2850

PUERTO RICO

Hato Rey
Rm.G-55 Fed. Bldg.,
San Juan, PR 00918
(809) 766-5555

RHODE ISLAND

(Boston District)+
7 Jackson Walkway
Providence, RI 02903
(401) 528-5104, ext. 22

SOUTH CAROLINA

Strom Thurmond Federal Bldg.
Suite 172, 1835 Assembly St.
Columbia, SC 29201
(803) 765-5345

JC Long Bldg. +
Rm. 128, 9 Liberty St.
Charleston, SC 29424
(803) 724-4361

SOUTH DAKOTA

Serviced by Omaha District
Office

TENNESSEE

Suite 1114, Parkway Towers
404 James Robertson Parkway
Nashville, TN 37219-1505
(615) 736-5161

301 E. Church Ave. +
Knoxville, TN 37915,
(615) 549-9268

The Falls Building +
Suite 200
22 North Front St.
Memphis, TN 38103
(901) 544-4137

TEXAS

Rm. 7A5 1100 Commerce St. *
Dallas, TX 75242-0787
(214) 767-0542

P.O. Box 12728 +
816 Congress Ave.
Suite 1200,
Austin, TX 78711
(512) 482-5939

2625 Fed. Courthouse
515 Rusk St.
Houston, TX 77002
(713) 229-2578

UTAH

Suite 105
324 South State St.
Salt Lake City, UT 84111
(801) 524-5116

VERMONT

Serviced by Boston District
Office

VIRGINIA

8010 Federal Bldg.
400 North 8th St.
Richmond, VA 23240
(804) 771-2246

WASHINGTON

3131 Elliott Ave.
Suite 290
Seattle, WA 98121
(206) 553-5615

West 808 Spokane Falls Blvd. +
Suite 625
Spokane, WA 99201
(509) 353-2922

WEST VIRGINIA

405 Capitol St.
Suite 809
Charleston, WV 25301
(304) 347-5123

WISCONSIN

Federal. Bldg
U.S. Courthouse ,Rm. 606

517 E. Wisc. Ave.
Milwaukee, WI 53202
(414) 297-3473

WYOMING
Serviced by Denver District
Office

* DENOTES REGIONAL OFFICE WITH SUPERVISORY REGIONAL RESPONSIBILITIES
+ DENOTES TRADE SPECIALIST AT A BRANCH OFFICE

NATIONAL INSTITUTE OF STANDARDS AND TECHNOLOGY (NIST)

NIST operates a Center for Standards and Certification Information and a HOT LINE service that can provide information on draft EC laws, directives and standards developed by either the EC or its major standards development organizations.

National Institute of Standards and Technology
Quince Orchard and Clopper Roads
Gaithersburg, MD 20899

Public Information:	(301) 975-2758
Personnel Locater:	(301) 975-2000
Publications Information:	(301) 975-3058

CONTACTS

Although these names were accurate at time of publication, it's always possible that a change has occurred. The room numbers and telephone numbers, however, do not often change and most likely will connect you with an appropriate contact. There may also be other contacts at NIST who can provide additional help and assistance.

Office of Standards Services Director
Stanley Warshaw
(301) 975-4000
Room A602, Administration Building

Standards Code & Information Program Chief
John L. Donaldson
(301) 975-4029
Room A631, Administration Building

Joanne Overman
(301) 975-4040

Maureen Breitenberg
(301) 975-4031

HOT LINE
(301) 921-4164

The HOT LINE is a recorded message service for draft EC standards and directives information. Topics are listed by subject area and product. Information is provided on deadlines for comments. A contact is given to obtain a review copy of the text.

STATE OFFICES PROVIDING EXPORT ASSISTANCE

For some time, governors have guided and stimulated economic development and job creation in their states. In the past 10 years, this activism extended beyond state and national borders. Today, many governors lead overseas trade missions that are an important part of state economic development programs. President Bush told the National Governors' Association that governors "are becoming our economic envoys and ambassadors of democracy. You are a new force in restoring American international competitiveness and expanding world markets for American goods and services." Most states have trade programs that serve as catalysts and brokers in the international arena. States provide technical assistance - from seminars on the "how to's" of trade, to individual exporter counseling, to dissemination of specific trade leads. They promote joint ventures, seek foreign investment, and encourage international travel to the United States. Forty-one states maintain offices in 24 different countries. Seven states have export finance programs. Others provide information on non-state sources of financing. The top international trade officials in the 50 states, the District of Columbia, and Puerto Rico are listed below, with their addresses and telephone numbers.

ALABAMA

Alabama Development Office
Fred Denton, Dir., Int'l Mktg. Div.
State Capitol
Montgomery, AL 362130
(205)263-0048

ALASKA

State of Alaska
Governor's Office of Intl. Trade
Director
3601 C St., Ste. 798
Anchorage, AK 99503
(907)561-5585

ARIZONA

Arizona Dept. of Commerce
Peter Cunningham, Intl. Trade Dir.
3800 N. Central
Phoenix, AZ 85012
(602)280-1371

ARKANSAS

Ark. Industrial Dev. Commission
Charles Sloan, Mkting. Dir.
#1 State Capitol Mall
Little Rock, AR 72201
(501)682-1121

CALIFORNIA

Calif. State World Trade Commission
Robert DeMartini, Dir., Export Dev.
1121 L St., Ste. 310
Sacramento, CA 95814
(916)324-5511

COLORADO

Colo. Intl. Trade Office
Morgan Smith, Dir.
1625 Broadway, Ste. 680
Denver, CO 80202
(303)892-3850

CONNECTICUT

Conn. Dept. Econ. Devel. Intl. Division
Matthew J. Broder, Dir.
865 Brook St.
Rocky Hill, CT 06067-3405
(203)258-4256

DELAWARE

Delaware Dev. Office
Business Dev. Office
Donald Sullivan, Dir.
P.O. Box 1401
Dover, DE 19903
(302)739-4271

DISTRICT OF COLUMBIA

D.C. Office of Intl. Business
Rosa Whitaker, Dir.
1250 I St.
Ste. 1003
Washington, D.C. 20005
(202)727-1576

FLORIDA

Florida Dept. of Commerce
Bureau of Intl. Trade and Dev.
Tom Slattery, Dir.
331 Collins Building
Tallahassee, FL 32399-2000
(904)488-6124

GEORGIA

Georgia Dept. of Industry and Trade
Kevin Langston, Dir.
285 Peachtree Center Ave.
Stes. 1000 and 1100
P.O. Box 1776
Atlanta, GA 30301-1776
(404)656-3571

HAWAII

State of Hawaii
Dept. of Bus. and Econ. Dev.
Trade and Ind. Dev. Branch
Dennis Ling, Chief
P.O. Box 2359
Honolulu, HI 96804
(808)548-7719

IDAHO

Division of Intl. Business
David P. Christensen,
Administrator
Idaho Dept. of Commerce
700 W. State St.
Boise, ID 83720
(208)334-2470

ILLINOIS

Ill. Dept. of Commerce and
Community Affairs
Nan K. Hendrickson, Mgr.
Intl. Business Div.
310 S. Michigan Ave., Ste. 1000
Chicago, IL 60604
(312) 814-7164

INDIANA

Indiana Dept. of Commerce
Maria Mercedes Plant, Dir. of
Intl. Trade, Business Dev. Div.
One N. Capitol, Ste. 700
Indianapolis, IN 46204-2288
(317)232-8845

IOWA

Iowa Dept. of Econ. Dev.
Michael Doyle, Bureau Chief,
Intl. Mkting. Div.
200 E. Grand Ave.
Des Moines, IA 50309
(515)242-4743

KANSAS

Kansas Dept. of Commerce
Trade Development Div.
Jim Beckley, Dir.
400 SW 8th St., Ste. 500
Topeka , KS 66603
(913)296-4027

KENTUCKY

Ky. Cabinet for Econ. Dev.
Michael Hayes Dir.
Capital Plaza Tower
Frankfort, KY 40601
(502)564-2170

LOUISIANA

Office of Intl. Trade, Finance and
Devel.
William Jackson, Dir.
P.O. Box 94185
Baton Rouge, LA 70804-9185
(504)342-4320

MAINE

Maine State Dev. Office
Lynn Wachtel, Commissioner
State House, Station 59
Augusta, ME 04333
(207)289-2656

MARYLAND

Md. Office of Intl. Trade
(MOIT)
Eric Feldman, Exec. Dir.
7th Floor, World Trade Center
401 E. Pratt St.
Baltimore, MD 21202
(301)333-8180

MASSACHUSETTS

Mass. Office of Intl. Trade
Gwen Pritchard, Exec. Dir.
100 Cambridge St., Ste. 902
Boston, MA 02202
(617)367-1830

MICHIGAN

Mich. Dept. of Commerce
Gene Ruff, Actg. Dir.,
World Trade Services Div.
P.O. Box 30225
Lansing, MI 48909
(517) 373-1054

MINNESOTA

Minn. Trade Office
Director
1000 World Trade Center
30 E. 7th St.
St. Paul, MN 55101
(612) 297-4227

MISSISSIPPI

Miss. Dept. of Econ. &
Community Dev.
Elizabeth Cleveland, Dir.
P.O. Box 849
Jackson, MS 39205
(601)359-3618

MISSOURI

Missouri Dept. of Commerce
Intl. Business Office
Robert Black, Dir.
P.O. Box 118
Jefferson City, MO 65102
(314)751-4855

MONTANA

Mont. Dept. of Commerce
Business Dev. Div.
Matthew Cohn, Dir.
1429-9th Ave.
Helena, MT 59620
(406)444-4380

NEBRASKA

Nebraska Dept. of Econ. Devel.
Steve Buttress, Dir.
301 Centennial Mall S.
Lincoln, NE 68509
(402)471-4668

NEVADA

(State of) Nevada
Commission on Econ. Dev.
Julie Wilcox, Dir.
Las Vegas Mail Rooni Complex
Las Vegas, NV 89158
(702)486-7282

NEW HAMPSHIRE

(State of) New Hampshire
Dept. of Resources and Econ.
Dev.
William Pillsbury, Dir.
Office of Industrial Trade
P.O. Box 856
Concord, NH 03301
(603)271-2591

NEW JERSEY

(State of) N.J. Div. of Intl. Trade
Philip Ferzen, Dir.
P.O. Box 47024
153 Halsey St., 5th Floor
Newark, NJ 07102
(201)648-3518

NEW MEXICO

(State of) New Mexico
Economic Dev. and Tourism
Dept.
Trade Division
Roberto Castillo, Dir.
1100 St. Francis Dr.,
Joseph M. Montoya Bldg.
Santa Fe, NM 87503
(505)827-0307

NEW YORK

N.Y. State Dept. of Commerce
Dept. of Econ. Dev.
Intl. Trade Div.
Stephen Koller, Dir.
1515 Broadway
New York, NY 10036
(212)827-6200

NORTH CAROLINA

N.C. Dept. of Econ. and
Community Dev., Intl. Division
Richard (Dick) Quinlan, Dir.
430 N. Salisbury St.
Raleigh, NC 27611
(919)733-7193

NORTH DAKOTA

N.D. Econ. Devel. Commission
L.R. Minton, Dir.
Liberty Memorial Bldg.
State Capital Grounds
Bismarck, ND 58505
(701)224-2810

OHIO

Ohio Dept. of Dev.
Intl. Trade Division
Dan Waterman, Dep. Dir.
77 S. High St., 29th Floor
Columbus, OH 43215
(614)466-5017

OKLAHOMA

Oklahoma Dept. of Commerce
Gary H. Miller, Dir.
6601 Broadway Extension
Oklahoma City, OK 73116
(405)841-5217

OREGON

Oregon Econ. Devel. Dept.,
Intl. Trade Division
Glenn Ford, Dir.
One World Trade Center
121 SW Salmon, Ste. 300
Portland, OR 97204
(503)229-5625

PENNSYLVANIA

Pa. Dept. of Commerce
Office of Intl. Dev.
Paul Haugland, Dir.
433 Forum Bldg.
Harrisburg, PA 17120
(717)787-7190

PUERTO RICO

P.R. Department of Commerce
Jorge Santiago, Secy.
P.O. Box 4275
San Juan, PR 00905
(809)725-7254

RHODE ISLAND

R.I. Dept. of Econ. Dev.
Intl. Trade Div.
Christine Smith, Dir.
7 Jackson Walkway
Providence, RI 02903
(401)277-2601 x47

SOUTH CAROLINA

S.C. State Dev. Board
Frank Newman, Assoc. Dir., Intl.
Business Division
P.O. Box 927
Columbia, SC 29202
(803)737-0403

SOUTH DAKOTA

S.D. Governor's Office of Econ.
Dev., Export, Trade & Mktg.
Div.
David Brotzman, Dir.
Capitol Lake Plaza
Pierre, SD 57501
(605)773-5735

TENNESSEE

Tenn. Export Office
Ms. Leigh Wieland, Dir.
320 6th Ave. N.
7th Floor
Nashville, TN 37219-5308
(615)741-5870

TEXAS

Texas Dept. of Commerce
Office of Intl. Trade
Deborah Hernandez, Mgr.
P.O. Box 12728, Capitol Sta.
816 Conpress
Austin, TX 78711
(512)320-9439
*The Department maintains export
assistance centers in a number of
Texas cities.*

UTAH

Utah Dept. of community &
Econ. Devel.
Dan Mabey, Actg. Dir., Intl.
Dev.
Ste. 200
324 S. State St.
Salt Lake City, UT 84111
(801)538-8736

VERMONT

(State of) Vermont Agency of
Dev. and Community Affairs
Ron Mackinnon, Commissioner
Pavilion Office Bldg.
109 State St.
Montpelier, VT 05602
(802) 828-3221

VIRGINIA

Va. Dept. of Econ. Dev.
Stuart Perkins, Dir.,
Export Dev.
1021 East Cary St.
Richmond, VA 23206
(804)371-8242

WASHINGTON

Wash. State Dept. of Trade and
Econ. Dev.
Importing/Exporting Office
Paul Isaki, Dir.
2001 Sixth Ave.
26th Floor
Seattle, WA 98121
(206)464-7143

WEST VIRGINIA

Governor's Office of Community
and Ind. Dev.
Stephen Spence, Dir.,
Intl. Division
Room 517, Building #6
1900 Washington St. E.
Charleston, WV 25305
(304)348-2234

WISCONSIN

Wis. Dept. of Development
Bureau of Intl. Dev.
Ralph Graner, Dir.
P.O. Box 7970
123 W. Washington Ave.
Madison, WI 53707
(608)266-9487

WYOMING

(State of) Wyoming
Office of the Governor
Richard Lindsey, Dir.
Capitol Building
Cheyenne, WY 82002
(307)777-6412

PRIVATE SECTOR EXPORT ORGANIZATIONS

**American Association of
Exporters and Importers**
11 W. 42nd Street
New York, NY 10036
(212) 944-2230

**Federation of International
Trade Associations**
1851 Alexander Bell
Drive
Reston, VA 22091
(703) 391-6108

**Foreign Credit Interchange
Bureau**
520 Eighth Avenue
New York, NY 10018
(212) 947-5363

**National Council on
International Trade and
Documentation**
350 Broadway
Suite 205
New York, NY 10013
(212) 925-1400

**U.S. Council for International
Business**
1212 Avenue of the
Americas
New York, NY 10036
(212) 354-4480

EC INFORMATION SOURCES SECTION

EC INFORMATION SOURCES

INTRODUCTION

There are really only a few EC information sources easily accessible from within the U.S. However, these sources are quite complete and virtually anything published or produced by the EC for public consumption can be obtained through these sources.

Delegation of the Commission of the European Communities

The Delegation is located in Washington, DC

Delegation of the Commission
of the European Communities
2100 M Street NW 7th Floor
Washington, DC 20037
(202) 862-9500
Fax: (202) 429-1766

The Public Inquiries Section of the Delegation can usually direct an inquiry to the correct source for information. They can provide some materials of a general nature regaring EC92 but in most cases you will be directed to a more appropriate source.

The Public Inquires Section does not put U.S. businesses in direct contact with potential European customers, importers, suppliers, joint venture partners, or sources of investment capital. The US & Foreign Commercial Service of the Department of Conunerce's International Trade Administration is the best source for this type of assistance.

European Community Depository Libraries

Over 50 college libraries have been designed as Depository Libraries for ECpublicatrons.

These libraiks are located in 32 states plus Washington, DC and Puerto Rico. A complete list of these libraries is included in this section.

UNIPLIB

UNIPUB is the official U. S. agent for the European Communities publications.

UAUPLIB can provide books, yearbooks, periodicals, monographs and other document subscriptions in both paper and microfiche form.

UNIPUB can provide both current subscriptions and past collections - and also offers standing order procedures for corporate libraries and others who must have copies of all materials published in a particular series.

INFORMATION SERVICES OF THE EC MEMBER STATES

Belgian Consulate
Information Service
5 0 Rockefeller Plaza - 1104
New York, NY 10020
(212) 586-5110

British Information Service
845 Third Avenue
New York, NY 10022
(212) 745-0200

Danish Consulate
Information Office
825 Third Ave - 32nd Floor
New York, NY 10022
(212) 223-4545

Embassy of France
Information Service
4101 Reservoir Rd., N.W.
Washington, D.C. 20007
(202) 944-6000

German Information Center
950 Third Avenue - 24th Floor
New York, NY 10022
(212) 888-9840

Embassy of Portugal
2125 Kalorama Rd., N.W.
Washington, D.C. 20008
(202) 328-8610

Embassy of Greece
Office of Press and Information
2211 Massachusetts Ave, N.W.
Washington, D.C. 20008
(202) 332-2727

Embassy of Ireland
Information Service
2234 Massachusetts Ave, N.W.
Washington, D.C. 20008
(202) 462-3939

Italian Cultural Institute
686 Park Avenue
New York, NY 10021
(212) 879-4242

Embassy of Luxembourg*
2200 Massachusetts Ave, N.W.
Washington, D.C. 20008
(202) 265-4171

Embassy of the Netherlands
Information Service
4200 Linnean Ave, N.W.
Washington, D.C. 20008
(202) 244-5300

Spanish Information Department
950 National Press Building
Washington, D.C. 20045
(202) 347-2317

*The Embassy of Luxembourg does not have an Information Service.

EUROPEAN TRADE ASSOCIATIONS

Banking Federation of the EC
rue Montoyer 10
B-1040 Brussels, Belgium
(322) 511-7800
Fax: (322) 511-2328

Committee for European Construction Equipment
Carolyn House
22-26 Dingwall Road
Croydon, Surrey CRO 9XF, England
(4481) 688-2727
Fax: (4481) 681-2134

Confederation of Food and Drink Industries of the EEC
rue de la Loi 74, Bte 9
B-1040 Brussels, Belgium
(322) 230-8145
Fax: (322) 230-8569

Coordination Committee for the Textile Industries in the EEC
rue Montoyer 24
B-1040 Brussels, Belgium
(322) 230-9580
Fax: (322) 230-6054

Council of the Bars & Law Societies of the EC
rue Washington 40
B-1050 Brussels, Belgium
(322) 640-4274

Eurochambres (Association of European Chambers of Commerce and Industry)
rue Archimede 5, Bte 4
B-1040 Brussels, Belgium
(322) 231-0715
Fax: (322) 230-0038

European Association of Advertising Agencies
avenue du Barbeau 28
B-1160 Brussels, Belgium
(322) 672-4336
Fax: (322) 672-0014

European Association of Aerospace Manufacturers
88, boulevard Malesherbes
F-75008 Paris, France
(3314) 563-8285
Fax: (3314) 225-1548

European Association of Information Services
9/9A High St. - 1st Floor Offices
Calne, Wiltshirr, SN11 OBS, England
(44249) 814-584
Fax: (44249) 813-656

European Centre of Public Enterprises
rue de la Charite 15, Bte 12
B-1040 Brussels, Belgium
(322) 219-2798
Fax: (322) 218-1213

European Chemical Industry Council
avenue E. Van Nieuwenhuyse 4
Bte 2 B-1160 Brussels, Belgium
(322) 676-7211
Fax: (322) 676-7300

EC Committee of the American Chamber of Commerce
avenue des Arts 50, Bte 5
B-1040 Brussels, Belgium
(322) 513-6892
Fax: (322) 513-7928

European Computer Manufacturers' Association
nic du Rhone I 1 4
CH-1204 Geneva, Switzerland
(41-22) 735-3634
Fax: (41-22) 786-5231

European Confederation of Iron and Steel Industries
square de Meeus 5
Bte 9 B-1040 Brussels, Belgium
(322) 512-9830
Fax: (322) 512-0146

European Confederation of Medical Suppliers' Associations
551 Finchley Road, Hempstead
London NW3 7BJ, England
(4471) 431-2187
Fax: (4471) 794-5271

European Consumers Organization
aveinue de Tervueren 36, Bte. 4
B-1040 Brussels, Belgium
(322) 735-3110
Fax: (322) 735-7455

European Electronic Component Manufacturers' Association
rue d'Arlon 69-71, Bte 8
B-1040 Brussels, Belgium
(322) 230-9630
Fax: (322) 230-9605

European Environmental Bureau
rue du Luxembourg 20
B-1040 Brussels, Belgium
(322) 514-1250
Fax: (322) 514-0937

European Federation of Animal Health
rue Defacqz 1, Bte 8
B-1050 Brussels, Belgium
(322) 537-2125
Fax: (322) 537-0049

European Federation of Associations of Manufacturers of Frozen Food
avenue de Cortenbergh 172
B-1040 Brussels, Belgium
(322) 735-8170
Fax: (322) 736-8175

European Federation of Pharmaceutical Industries' Associations
avenue Louise 250, Bte 91
B-1050 Brussels, Belgium
(322) 640-6815
Fax: (322) 647-6049

European Food Law Association
boulevard de la Cainbre 3, Bte 34
B-1050 Brussels, Belgium
(322) 649-4363

European Franchising Federation
Ave de Broqueville 5
B-1150 Brussels, Belgium
(322) 736-6464
Fax: (322) 736-7226

European Telecommunications & Professional Electronics Industry
c/o Electronic Engineering Association
Leicester House
8 Leicester Street
London WC2H 7BN, England
(4471) 437-0678
Fax: (4471) 434-3477

European Trade Union Confederation
rue Montagne aux Herbes Potageres 37
B-I 000 Brussels, Belgium
(322) 218-3100
Fax: (322) 218-3566

European Trade Union Institute
boulevard de L'Imperatrice 66, Bte. 4
B-1000 Brussels, Belgium
(322) 512-3070
Fax: (322) 514-1731

European Union of Fruit and Vegetable Wholesale, Import and Export Trade
avenue de la Brabanconne 18, Bte 8
B-1040 Brussels, Belgium
(322) 736-1584
Fax: (322) 734-8771

European Union of Importers, Exporters and Dealers in Dairy Products
avenue Livingstone 26
B-1040 Brussels, Belgium
(322) 230-4448
FAX: (322) 230-4044

Federation of Stock Exchanges in the EEC
rue du Midi 2, 5th Floor
B-1000 Brussels, Belgium
(322) 513-0518
Fax: (322) 512-4905

General Committee for Agricultural Cooperation in the EEC (COCEGA)
rue de la Science 23-25, Bte 3
B-1040 Brussels, Belgium
(322) 230-3945
Fax: (322) 230-4046

Grain and Iced Trade Committee of the EEC
rue Belliard 197, Bte 6
B-1040 Brussels, Belgium
(322) 230-6170
Fax: (322) 230-3063

Liaison Group for the European Engineering Industries
rue de Stassart 99
B-1050 Brussels, Belgium
(322) 511-3484
Fax: (322) 511-9970

Pharmaceutical Group of the EC
square Ambiorix 13
B-1040 Brussels, Belgium
(322) 736-7281
Fax: (322) 736-0206

Sugar Traders Association ofthe EC
ave de la Brabanconne 18, Bte 8
B-1040 Brussels, Belgium
(322) 736-1584
Fax: (322) 734-8771

Union of Industrial and Employers' Confederations of Europe (UNICE)
rue Joseph H 40, Bte 4
B-1040 Brussels, Belgium
(322) 237-6511
Fax: (322) 231-1445

CRAMBERS OF COMMERCE OF THE EC MEMBERS IN THE U.S.

Belgian-American Chamber of Commerce
Empire State Building
350 Fifth Avenue - 703
New York, NY 10118
(212) 967-9898

Danish-American Chamber of Commerce
825 Third Ave - 32nd Floor
New York, NY 10022
(212) 980-6240

French-American Chamber of Commerce
509 Madison Ave - 1900
New York, NY 10022
(212) 371-4466

German-American Chamber of Commerce
666 Fifth Avenue
New York, NY 10 1 03
(212) 974-8830

Hellenic-American Chamber of Commerce
960 Avenue of the Americas - 1204
New York, NY 100047
(212) 629-6380

Ireland-U.S. Chamber of Commerce
551 Madison Ave. 11th Floor
New York, NY 10022
(212) 248-0008

Italian-American Chamber of Commerce
350 Fifth Avenue
New York, NY 10118
(212)   279-5520

Netherlands Chamber of Conunerce
One Rockefeller Plaza - 11th Floor
New York, NY 10022
(212) 265-6460

Portugese-U.S. Chamber of Commerce
690 Eighth Ave.
New York, NY 10036
(212) 354-4610

Spanish Chamber of Commerce
350 Fifth Ave - 3514
New York, NY 10016
(212) 967-2170

British-American Chamber of Commerce
275 Madison Ave. - 1714
New York, NY 10016
(212) 661-4060

EC GOVERNMENT INVESTMENT ADVISORIES

Belgium

Embassy of Belgium
Investment Section
3330 Garfield St. NW
Washington, DC 20008
(202) 333-6900

Denmark

Embassy of Denmark
Commercial Couselor
3200 Whitehaven St. NW
Washington. DC 20008
(202) 234-4300

F.R. Germany

Federation of German Industries
1 Farragut Square South - 6th Floor
Washington, DC 20006
(202) 347-0274

Greece

Embassy of Greece
Economic Counselor
1636 Connecticut Ave NW
Washington, DC 20009
(202) 745-7100

France

French Industrial Development Agency
610 Fifth Ave NW
New York, NY 10020
(212) 757-9340

Ireland

Irish Development Agency
140 East 45th St. 41st Floor
New York, NY 10017
(212) 972-1000

Italy

IMI - Capital Markets USA
375 Park Ave. - Suite 1501
New York, NY 10022

Luxembourg

Board of Economic Development
of Luxembourg
1 Sansome St. - Suite 830
San Francisco, CA 94104
(415) 788-0816

The Netherlands

Netherlands Foreign Investment
Agency
One Rockefeller Plaza - 11th
Floor
New York, NY 10020
(212) 246-1434

Netherlands Foreign Investment
Agency
11755 Wilshire Blvd.
Los Angeles, CA 90025
(213) 477-8288

Portugal

Portugese Trade Commission
1900 L St. NW - Suite 401
Washington, DC 20036
(202) 331-8222

Spain

Embassy of Spain
Commercial Office
2558 Massachusetts Ave NW
Washington, DC 20008
(202) 265-8600

United Kingdom

British Trade Development
Office
Inward Investment
845 Third Avenue
New York, NY 10022
(212) 745-0495

Embassy of Great Britain
Trade Section/Inward Investment
2221 Massachusetts Ave., N.W.
Washington, D.C. 20008
(202) 462-1340

EUROPEAN COMMUNITY DEPOSITORY LIBRARIES

Harvard University
Law School Library
Langdell Hall - Law 431
Cambridge MA 02138

University of Maine
Law Library
246 Deering Avenue
Portland ME 04102

Yale University
Government Documents Center
Seeley G. Mudd Library
38 Mansfield
New Haven CT 06520

Princeton University
Documents Division
Library
Princeton NJ 08544

New York University Law
Library
School of Law
40 Washington Square S.
New York NY 10012

New York Public Library
Research Library, Economic
& Public Affairs
Grand Central Station
P.O.Box 2221
New York NY 10017

Council on Foreign Relations
Library
58 East 68th Street
New York NY 10021

State University of New York
Government Publications Library
1400 Washington Ave
Albany NY 12222

State University of New York
Governments Documents
Lockwood Library Bldg.
Buffalo NY 14260

University of Pittsburgh
Gift and Exchange
Hilhnan Library G 72
Pittsburgh PA 15260

Pennsylvania State University
Documents Section University
Library
University Park PA 16802

University of Pennsylvania
Serials Department Van Pelt
Library
Philadelphia PA 19104

American University
Law Library
4400 Massachusetts N.W.
Washington D.C. 20016

Library of Congress
Serial Division Madison Bldg.
10 First St., S.E.
Washington D.C. 20540

George Mason University
Center for European Studies
4001 N. Fairfax Dr.
Suite 450
Arlington VA 22203

University of Virginia
Government Documents
Alderman Library
Charlottesville VA 22903

Duke University
Public Documents Department
University Library
Durham NC 27706

University of South Carolina
Documents/Microforms
Thomas Cooper Library
Columbia SC 29208

Emory University
Law Library
School of Law
Atlanta GA 30322

University of Georgia Law
Library
Law School
Athens GA 30602

University of Florida
Documents Department
Libraries West
Gainesville FL 32611

University of Kentucky
Government Publications
Margaret I King Library
Lexington KY 40506

Ohio State University
Documents Division
University Library
1858 Neil Avenue Mall
Columbus OH 43210

University of Notre Dame
Document Center
Memorial Library
Notre Dame IN 46556

Indiana University
Government Documents
University Library
Bloomington IN 47405

University of Michigan
Serials Department
Law Library
Ann Arbor Ml 48109-1210

Michigan State University
Documents Department
University Library
East Lansing MI 48824-1048

University of Iowa
Government Publications
Library
Iowa City IA 52242

University of Wisconsin
Documents Department
Memorial Library
728 State Street
Madison W] 53706

University of Minnesota
Government Publications
Wilson Library - 409
Minneapolis MN 55455

Northwestern University
Goverm-nent Publications
University Library
Evanston IL 60201

Illinois Institute of Technology
Law Library
77 South Wacker Dr.
Chicago IL 60606

University of Chicago
Government Documents
Regenstein Library
1 1 00 E. 5 7th Street
Chicago IL 60637

University of Illinois Law
Library
School of Law
504 E. Pennsylvania Ave.
Champaign IL 61820

Washington University
John M. Olin Library
Campub Box 1061
1 Brookings Dr.
St. Louis MO 63130

University of Kansas
Govt. Documents & Maps
University Library
6001 Malott Hall
Lawrence KS 66045

University of Nebraska
Acquisitions Division
University Libraries
Lincoln NE 68588-0410

University of New Orleans
Business Reference
Earl K. Long Library
New Orleans LA 70148

University of Arkansas
Documents Department
UALR Library
33rd & University
Little Rock AR 72204

University of Oklahoma
Government Documents
Bizzell Memorial Library
Room 440
401 West Brooks
Norman OK 73019

University of Texas
Law Library
School of Law
727 East 26th Street
Austin TX 78705

University of Colorado
Government Publications
University Library
Box 184
Boulder CO 80309-0184

University of Utah
International Documents
Marriott Library
Salt Lake City UT 84112

University of Arizona
International Documents
University Library
Tucson AZ 85721

University of New Mexico
Social Science Coll. Dev.
Zimmerman Library
Albuquerque NM 87131

University of California
International Documents
Public Affairs Service
Research Library
Los Angeles CA 90024

University of Southern California
International Documents
Von Kleinschmidt Library
Los Angeles CA 90089

University of California
Documents Department
Central Library
La Jolla CA 92093

Stanford University
Central Westem European Coll.
The Hoover Institution
Stanford CA 94305

University of Califomia
Documents Departrnent
General Library

Berkeley CA 94720
University of Hawaii
Government Documents
University Library
2550 The Mall
Honolulu HI 96822

University of Oregon
Documents Section
University Library
Eugene OR 97403

University of Washington
Government Publications
University Library FM-25
Seattle WA 98195

University of Puerto Rico
Law Library
Law School
Rio Piedras
Puerto Rico 00931

Other books of interest to you from Irwin Professional Publishing . . .

THE TQM ALMANAC

1994–95 Edition

Timeplace, Inc.

An all-encompassing guide to quality-related materials, resources, and information that quality managers need to start and maintain successful TQM programs. This time-saving guide to TQM books, videos, software, consultants, seminars, conferences, and more also provides an overview of the current trends in the quality improvement field.
ISBN: 0–7863–0242–9

WHY TQM FAILS AND WHAT TO DO ABOUT IT

Mark Graham Brown, Darcy E. Hitchcock, and Marsha L. Willard
Co-published with the Association for Quality and Participation

Discover the root causes for the collapse and failure of total quality and find practical advice for correcting and preventing them.
ISBN: 0–7863–0140–6

SYNCHROSERVICE!

The Innovative Way to Build a Dynasty of Customers

Richard J. Schonberger and Edward M. Knod, Jr.

From the best-selling author of *Building a Chain of Customers!* Schonberger and Knod give your their latest ground-breaking strategy—synchroservice—to help your company ensure an organizationwide commitment to seamless, consistent, customer-driven service for enhanced customer loyalty.
ISBN: 0–7863–0245–3

THE SERVICE/QUALITY SOLUTION

Using Service Management to Gain Competitive Advantage

David A. Collier
Co-published with ASQC Quality Press

Improve your service strategy and survive the pressures within today's marketplace with Collier's 16 tools for effective service/quality management.
ISBN: 1–55623–753–7

GLOBAL QUALITY

A Synthesis of the World's Best Management Methods

Richard Tabor Greene
Co-published with ASQC Quality Press

This comprehensive resource organizes the chaos of quality improvement techniques so you can identify the best approaches for your organization. Includes the 24 quality approaches used worldwide, the essentials of process reengineering, software techniques, and seven new quality improvement techniques being tested in Japan.
ISBN: 1–55623–915–7

Available at bookstores and libraries everywhere.